ASK & TELL

ASK & TELL

GAY AND LESBIAN
VETERANS SPEAK OUT

BY STEVE ESTES

The University of North Carolina Press

Chapel Hill

© 2007 The University of North Carolina Press
All rights reserved
Set in Scala, The Sans, and Campaign types by
Keystone Typesetting, Inc.
Manufactured in the United States of America

This book was published with the assistance of
the Thornton H. Brooks Fund of the University of
North Carolina Press.

The paper in this book meets the guidelines for permanence
and durability of the Committee on Production Guidelines for
Book Longevity of the Council on Library Resources.

Library of Congress Cataloging-in-Publication Data
Estes, Steve, 1972–
Ask and tell : gay and lesbian veterans speak out / by Steve Estes.
    p. cm. — (Introduction— 1. The greatest generation— 2. Korea
and the Cold War— 3. Vietnam— 4. The Academies— 5. The
women's war for inclusion— 6. The Gulf War— 7. The ban—
8. Out ranks— 9. Kosovo, Afghanistan, and Iraq— Appendix 1: A
note on oral history and editing interviews— Appendix 2:
interviewees.)
Includes bibliographical references and index.
ISBN-13: 978-0-8078-3115-1 (cloth: alk. paper)
1. Gays in the military—United States—History. 2. Gays in the
military—United States—Interviews. 3. Oral history. I. Title.
UB418.G38E77   2007
355.0086'640973—dc22   2006100948

Some of the introductory text in this book was originally published
as "Ask & Tell: Gay Veterans, Identity, and Oral History on a
Civil Rights Frontier," *Oral History Review* 32, no. 2 (September 2005):
21–47. © 2005 by the Oral History Association.

11 10 09 08 07   5 4 3 2 1

For the men and women

who have served our country—

and especially for those

who have served in silence

CONTENTS

ILLUSTRATIONS

ACKNOWLEDGMENTS

Originally, I did not want to write about gays in the military. I wanted to listen. I'd read and heard so much about what pundits and politicians thought when "Don't Ask, Don't Tell" was being debated, but I hadn't heard from the people for whom the policy mattered most. Luckily, when I began to seek out what they thought, I found that there were a whole lot of gay and lesbian veterans who wanted to tell their stories. It is to these veterans, of course, that I owe the greatest thanks for this oral history project and this book. They deserve thanks first of all for serving their country—for facing enemies without and prejudice within. Beyond that, I need to thank them personally for taking the time to talk about their service—for recounting stories that ranged from the harrowing to the humorous, from the courageous to the commonplace. It was not always easy for me to ask or for them to tell, but the conversations ultimately yielded amazing insights into life, love, and war.

These conversations often began with introductions or tips from activist organizations and veterans groups. The Human Rights Campaign, American Veterans for Equal Rights, the Servicemembers Legal Defense Network, and the Military Equality Alliance were instrumental in putting me in touch with veterans. Especially helpful in this regard were Lara Ballard and Jim Maloney. A veteran herself, Lara did many of her own oral history interviews, while also serving as my Washington, D.C., liaison to the Library of Congress. Jim served as my introduction to countless veterans in the Bay Area and as a stalwart supporter throughout this project. Gay veterans groups were also helpful in getting out the word about my project. Thanks to the Alexander Hamilton American Legion Post 448 in San Francisco, USNA Out, and Service Academy Gay and Lesbian Alumni.

In the academic world, scholars interested in this issue owe a debt of gratitude to Aaron Belkin and the Center for the Study of Sexual Minorities in the Military (CSSMM). From a home base at the University of California, Santa Barbara, Aaron is an untiring researcher, networker, speaker, and leader of scholarly efforts to understand the relationship between sexuality and service. In addition to a small fellowship from CSSMM, I was fortunate enough to win continuing financial support from Sonoma State University, where I also teach. Though they could not offer financial support, the staff of the Regional Oral History Office at the University of California, Berkeley, gave me the chance to share my ideas for this project in their speaker series. At the Berkeley talk, Martin Meeker, Richard Cándida Smith, and Bill Benemann gave me excellent feedback and words of wisdom. For commenting on various aspects of the book and/or sharing their own work with me, I need to thank Nan Alamilla Boyd, Gary Gates, John D'Emilio, Andrew Dunar, Melissa Embser-Herbert, Beth Hillman, Terence Kissack, Ian Lekus, and Leisa Meyer. At the University of North Carolina Press, Chuck Grench, Katy O'Brien, Kathy Ketterman, and Paul Betz patiently shepherded this work from a proposal to a book.

As any oral historian knows, help with transcription is perhaps the most vital part of a successful project. Loren Basham, Danielle Bruns, Todd Cereghino, Joanne Gifford, Tamara Green, Amanda Kreklau, Ryan Partika, Kerrie Russell, Bethany Sevold, Derek Steffen, David Stolowitz, and Mary Wilson, generously lent their blood, sweat, and tears in the transcription process. I shared in their pain.

Friends and family deserve the final thanks for helping this project see the light of day. At long last, Mike Meyers gets the recognition he deserves for coming up with the title for chapter 8. Randy Dodgen convinced me that catching Pacific swells was just as important as transcribing another interview. At home, Carol and Zinnia reminded me that between love and war there is no contest.

ASK & TELL

INTRODUCTION

Robert Stout peered through his night vision goggles at the road ahead. He was manning the m-2 Browning machine gun atop a u.s. Army Humvee. The Tigris River was not far off, and neither was the safety of his base. It had been a long night already. Stout's platoon of army engineers had been sent to investigate an abandoned truck by the side of the road. They were checking for IEDs—Improvised Explosive Devices—which have caused many of the casualties in the Iraq War. But this time, it was just an abandoned truck. On the way back to base, as they passed the high walls lining the narrow road, Stout's unit was ambushed. "The only thing I really remember is a loud flash off to my left side, pretty much the loudest noise I've ever heard in my life," Stout recalls. "After that, I was blinded by the explosion, which in the night vision goggles was insane." Wounded in the ambush, Stout received a Purple Heart and eventually a promotion to sergeant. After he returned to Iraq, Stout had a new set of priorities. First, he wanted to make sure that "his guys"—the young men he now led—made it home safe and sound. Second, he was no longer going to hide the fact that he was gay.

When "Don't Ask, Don't Tell" was implemented as a political compromise in 1993 and 1994, it legislated the silence of gay and lesbian soldiers like Robert Stout who served on active duty and in the reserves.[1] Though gays and lesbians have long served this country in the military, their official exclusion mandated silence and secrecy about their sexuality. In one sense, the debates about "Don't Ask, Don't Tell" shattered this silence, making public discussions about sexuality central to considerations of military policy in the 1990s. Gay rights advocates welcomed such public debates, but the focus on sexuality in the service created frustrating and frightening situations for many gays and lesbians in uniform. Because military policies before and after the implementation of "Don't Ask, Don't Tell" necessitated silence, the men and women most directly affected by these policies were unable to testify openly about their impact. Yet this was more than political silence; it was personal. In day-to-day interactions with friends, superiors, and even family members, "Don't Ask, Don't Tell" required a skillful navigation of silence (and often deception) to hide homosexuality. "What did you do last weekend?" or "Are you seeing anyone?" might seem like innocent questions, but for gay and lesbian military personnel, they took on the weight of interrogation even in friendly conversation. Obviously, such conversations called for more than silence. They often required the creation of fake heterosexual identities—the picture of the "boyfriend" on an office desk or the female "companion" to attend base dances and dinners. Given the political and personal consequences of the policy, the legal scholar Tobias Wolff believes that the silence imposed by the law should raise questions about the First Amendment right to free speech. "Indeed," Wolff argues, "the striking bluntness of the policy in restricting the speech of gay servicemembers renders the principles associated with the First Amendment exceptionally visible."[2]

I argue that, historically, the silence concerning gays in the military has led to a collective amnesia about the patriotic service and courageous sacrifices of homosexual troops. In this case, the politics of military service are also the politics of memory. If we forget that gay and lesbian Americans have served their country, then we as a nation are much less likely to view them as full citizens, deserving of civil rights and equal protection of the law. Oral history provides one way to break this silence, to "ask and tell" about the military careers of gay and lesbian soldiers and to allow these veterans to speak for themselves about the current military policy.

In 2000 the American Folklife Center of the Library of Congress launched the Veterans History Project (VHP), one of the most ambitious volunteer oral history projects this country has ever seen, rivaling even the massive interview project with ex-slaves undertaken by the Works Progress Administration during the Great Depression. To date, the VHP has collected more than 25,000 personal narratives of veterans who served from World War I to the Iraq War. Interviews for the project have led to a book titled *Voices of War*, a Library of Congress exhibit called From the Home Front to the Front Lines, and even a play at the American Place Theater in New York.[3]

Gay veterans groups have partnered with the Library of Congress to document the stories of veterans who have long been denied recognition in other forums, but interviews with gay and lesbian veterans have not yet been placed in a historical context.[4] Interviewers working with American Veterans for Equal Rights (AVER) have recorded the stories of dozens of gay and lesbian veterans, but this only scratches the surface of the estimated 1 million homosexual veterans in this country. Of course, the estimated 65,000 gay and lesbian personnel serving on active duty and in the reserves are unable to share their stories and their identities as a result of "Don't Ask, Don't Tell."[5]

As one of the volunteer interviewers for the Veterans History Project, I spoke with more than fifty veterans, and about half of them tell their stories in this book. These interviewees—among whom are white, Latino, African

American, and Native American veterans—offer a wide spectrum of perspectives on gay and lesbian experiences in the military. Some of these individuals were drafted and served only during wartime. Others were volunteers who made the military their career. There are privates and petty officers, generals and admirals. There are combat heroes recognized with Bronze Stars and Purple Hearts, and there are soldiers who faced dishonorable discharges simply because of their sexuality. After leaving the military, these men and women became teachers, doctors, computer technicians, lawyers, preachers, and construction workers. The range and diversity of these stories reveals that the experiences of gay and lesbian soldiers are as varied and valorous as those of their straight comrades.

In the research for *Ask and Tell*, I found that I was standing on the shoulders of some passionate scholars, journalists, and activists who did pioneering work in this field. Most instructive and inspirational for my own research was the work of Allan Bérubé, whose *Coming Out under Fire* was the seminal book on gays in the military during World War II, and of Randy Shilts, who covered gays in the military from the 1950s to the early 1990s in *Conduct Unbecoming*. Mary Ann Humphrey, Steve Zeeland, and Zsa Zsa Gershick compiled powerful earlier volumes of interviews. Sociologists, political scientists, and legal theorists have produced most of the remaining scholarship on gays in the military. The best of this recent academic work has come from Aaron Belkin and other fellows at the Center for the Study of Sexual Minorities in the Military at the University of California, Santa Barbara. Their writing and research has laid an excellent foundation for the interviews in this book.[6]

Although this book has benefited greatly from earlier works on gays in the military, it aims to fill several gaps in the existing literature. First, this is the only oral history project to include the stories of veterans from World War II to the wars in Afghanistan and Iraq. Second, with so many combat veterans involved in this project, it will be difficult for critics to disparage these veterans by saying that they were not battle-tested or that they are somehow atypical American soldiers. Third, this book is the first to include interviews with both service academy alumni and flag officers. These gay officers rose to the highest ranks of the u.s. armed forces by keeping their identities secret (sometimes for decades). They have finally broken their long silence to talk about their service, their sexuality, and the evolution of military policy. Because of who these men and women are it was important that every single one of the interviews in this book be on the record. Anonymity in previous studies and oral history collections has undercut the credibility of the sources and, ironically, reinforced the hidden nature of gay service and sacrifice. Finally, and most important, this book provides a forum for the interviewees to give their own testimony about the "Don't Ask, Don't Tell" policy and its legacies for the u.s. military.

Though it may not have been the original intention of Congress in establishing this undertaking, the Veterans History Project is allowing gay veterans to speak out. In their interviews, these veterans talk about the sacrifices that they made to defend this country and about the discrimination they faced in uniform and out. As an oral historian, I feel an obligation to "ask and tell," to uncover the hidden transcripts that are left out of recorded history. In this case, the stories are not simply left out; they are silenced by official federal policy. How wonderful then that an oral history project supported by the federal government has provided the impetus to collect these personal narratives.

It is my hope that this book provides evidence that may someday help lift the ban on the military service of openly gay and lesbian Americans. At the very least, this volume documents courage that should not be forgotten. These interviews are extraordinary stories, but I hope that readers will come to realize that they are stories told by ordinary Americans, men and women who simply did their duty and served their country.

THE GREATEST GENERATION

The men and women who served in the military during World War II have become known as "the greatest generation." Although there are exceptions, the majority of these veterans have been exceedingly humble about the sacrifices that they made in service to the United States. When asked why they served, almost every one of them answers: "I was just doing my duty." This is true of gay as well as heterosexual veterans. Patriotism runs strong among them all.[1]

Just talk to Charles Rowland, a gay draftee from Phoenix, Arizona. Rowland knew "an awful lot of gay people but nobody, with one exception, ever considered not serving. We were not about to be deprived the privilege of serving our country in a time of great national emergency by virtue of some stupid regulation about being gay."[2]

Antisodomy laws and military regulations had limited gay service since World War I, leading to courts-martial for men found having sex with other men. Still, gay men were in uniform from the very start of World War II. There were gay sailors at Pearl Harbor when the Japanese attacked on December 7, 1941, and gay sergeants training the massive influx of recruits and draftees immediately afterward. In the early 1940s, draft boards examined 18 million American men for possible service in World War II. Military psychiatrists sought to screen out gay men as "sexual psychopaths," but fewer than 5,000 of the 18 million draftees were initially rejected because of homosexual tendencies. A conservative estimate of the number of gay men who served during World War II is 650,000 out of 16 million American servicemen.[3]

Paul Jordan had already been in the army for years when the vast majority of volunteers and draftees joined him to fight in World War II. He had enlisted in 1933, the year that Adolf Hitler came to power in Germany, but Paul's enlistment had more to do with the Great Depression than with international politics. With few jobs in his rural Maine community, the military was one of the very few alternatives to unemployment and poverty. After helping to train the new wave of recruits brought into the army at the start of World War II, Paul volunteered to fight in Europe. His memories of the war echo the stories of hundreds of thousands of other young infantrymen who fought in the European theater. Paul was just one of the boys . . . one of the boys with a secret.

Another young man who shared a similar secret was Bill Taylor. Short in stature, Taylor was tapped as a tail gunner for a B-24 bomber based in England. Like Paul Jordan's, Bill's story varies only slightly from the ones that his straight crewmates would tell about service during the war. Like them and like his two brothers who served, Bill was just doing his duty: trying to win the war for the Allies and most of all, trying to survive.

On the home front, World War II accelerated the social changes that the Great Depression had begun, inspiring millions of people to migrate in search of jobs in the war industries or to relocate because of enlistment and deployment. As the historian Allan Bérubé argues in his book *Coming Out under Fire*, "The massive mobilization for World War II relaxed the social constraints of peacetime that kept many gay men and women unaware of themselves and each other." Away from the small town authorities and conservative mores, young gay men found new identities and new communities. Bud Robbins and Burt Gerrits saw these changes first hand. Stationed in New York City and the San Francisco Bay Area, respectively, these young men found kindred spirits in the nightclubs and bars that became the nuclei of urban gay communities after the war.[4]

The war also inspired revolutionary changes for American women, both gay and straight. The formation of the Women's Army Auxiliary Corps in 1942, renamed the Women's Army Corps (WACs) in 1943, was just one small part of this seismic shift in gender roles. Along with the WAVEs in the navy, the WACs replaced servicemen in clerical and other noncombat occupational specialties. By the end of the war, more than 150,000 women served on posts across the United States and overseas.

Worried that servicewomen would be seen as "amazons" or "camp followers," WAC officers emphasized the virtues of femininity and chastity in their recruits. There was clearly a fear that more masculine women—code for lesbians—would take over the WACs, but the military did not officially screen for lesbians until 1944. In fact, many lesbian recruits found a certain sisterhood in the organization. Iowa recruit Pat Bond was one of those women. "I came with my suitcase, staggering down the mess hall," Bond explained in the documentary film *Word Is Out*, "and I heard a voice from one of the barracks say, 'Good God, Elizabeth, look! Here comes another one!' "[5]

As the historian Leisa Meyer argues, the visibility of lesbians in the WACs sometimes made them targets of harassment, but their presence also "served as both an anchor and a rallying point for the formations of lesbian communities within the corps." This community would be especially important at the war's end, when lesbian purges were part of a general pattern of downsizing the number and the role of women in the military. Despite the purges and harassment at the end of World War II and the beginning of the Cold War, Pat Bond and other lesbian veterans left the service with a better sense of themselves and a strong support network.[6]

The final interviewee in this chapter, Charlotte Coleman, served in the women's auxiliary service with the Coast Guard. Called the SPARs—after the U.S. Coast Guard motto: *Semper Paratus* (Always Ready)—women in the coast guard during World War II had much the same experiences as women in the WACs and WAVEs, though there were far fewer SPARs. By the summer of 1944, around the time that Charlotte joined, there were 771 women officers and 7,600 female enlisted personnel in the coast guard. Unlike the women on the SPARs softball teams, Charlotte's sexuality was not so obvious to most people, but still she enjoyed the sisterhood of the women's auxiliary service. Most important, the service provided her a ticket out of the small New England town where she was raised. Though she heard about purges of lesbians from the SPARs before the group was disbanded at the close of the war, Charlotte was lucky and left the service with an honorable discharge.[7]

The purges of lesbians at the conclusion of the war and the less-than-honorable psychiatric discharges of gay men and women throughout the conflict exemplify the confusing evolution of military policies regarding homosexuality. Working on the psych ward of a Bay Area naval hospital, Burt Gerrits met many young men whose only psychosis was homosexuality. These men were being drummed out of the Navy with less-than-honorable discharges, while others, like Burt himself, were retained either because they successfully hid their sexuality or because the military needed their skills. A third and much smaller category of gay service personnel were court-martialed under prewar antisodomy regulations, but such criminal punishment of homosexuality was deemed costly and inefficient given wartime manpower demands. This three-tiered military policy toward homosexuals—court-martial, discharge, or retention—was the reality that underlay the stricter public prohibition of gay military service from World War II to the passage of "Don't Ask, Don't Tell."[8]

Despite their humility, the members of the Greatest Generation have finally gotten their due, with a surge of popular histories and movies and the creation of a monument on the National Mall in Washington, D.C. It is about time. In the first decade of the twenty-first century, as many as 1,100 World War II veterans are passing away every day, their memories lost to history forever.[9] Unfortunately, mainstream histories of the war and eulogies to the Greatest Generation are often silent about the sacrifices and contributions of gay servicemen and servicewomen. If we are to "ask and tell" about the history of gays in the military, we should begin by giving those in the Greatest Generation their due.

ONE OF THE BOYS

An Interview with Paul Jordan

The oldest veteran in this collection, Paul Jordan joined the U.S. Army in the early 1930s. He knew from an early age that he was gay, but otherwise, he was just "one of the boys." The secret of his sexuality was much less important than the survival skills that he imparted to the new recruits and draftees entering the army at the beginning of World War II. As Paul recalled in this interview, these skills allowed him to survive some of the most harrowing battles of the European theater.[10]

I was born in Orono, Maine, on September the twenty-seventh, 1911. Bangor, Maine, has been my hometown since my family moved from Orono a year right after I was born. I went to St. Mary's and from there to Bangor High School. A couple of months before graduation, the Great Depression came on, and my father took me in the back room and said, "I've lost my job. I don't know if I'll be able to keep up the payments on the house." He said, "The best place for you, since you've had three years training at Bangor High School on ROTC [Reserve Officers' Training Corps], is the army. There, you'll get food, shelter, and clothing, and I won't have you to worry about. I'll just have the three girls." And with that, I lost all interest in doing pre-med at the University of Maine. My original intent was to have become a physician.

I went to the recruiting sergeant in Portland, and I told him, quite honestly, "I'm not wearing this monkey suit in the United States." He says, "Why do you take that attitude?" I says, "Look in any bar window and you'll see a sign, says, 'No soldiers or dogs allowed.' That is offensive to me, and if you don't have something for me in foreign service, then I prefer to go to the Civilian Conservation Corps and do road work."

He said, "We've got a place for you," and he shipped me off to the Thirty-third u.s. Infantry at Fort Clayton in Panama, where I was assigned to Headquarters Company, and there I began my career as a soldier.

They recognized right away that I'd had military training, and in no time at all I was teaching the other men how to do a snappier manual of arms, how to do a right face without looking sloppy, how to do an about-face and make it real sharp. Before that enlistment was over, I had progressed to corporal. That was unheard of in a first enlistment in those days. This was 1933.

I've been gay since I knew what gayness was. That came upon me in my teens. I was seventeen, and I had several experiences of rather pleasurable excitement in the presence of certain types of other men that disturbed me because I knew, or felt deeply, this wasn't natural. I'd have to leave the scene because I was getting excited. I began to look through the literature to see what I could find out about these things. I found a book on abnormal psychology in the Bangor Public Library, and there it was, black and white: I was homosexual. I had to learn how to conceal that, live with it, accept it, and try to get others to accept it. It has not been an easy task.

No one in the army knew, because I took great pains to emulate the more masculine types in my different organizations, and I was a good mimic. I guess I'm a little bit of an actor anyway. But in doing this, I found myself being accepted as "one of the boys." One of the boys, with a secret.

Homosexuality has been a part of every army since the ancient Egyptian army, the Greek army, and the Roman army. Some of these gay men, called "camp followers," were prostitutes, and they followed these armies when they moved. This is all historical, and I don't know why today so many people think they're just discovering something.

All the time I was in the army . . . you've heard the expression, "It takes one to know one"? Well, I ran into some gay guys that had a certain appeal. Gay people are not attracted to all their own gender. It's just certain people with something in their personality that's very attractive. Anyway, our method was: "This weekend, we'll get a hotel room, share the expenses of a hotel room." Raleigh was one of my favorites, Raleigh, North Carolina, which is quite close to Camp Buckner, where I was division artillery sergeant major. We'd go over there and we'd party.

Unlike the millions of citizen soldiers drafted only after World War II began, Paul witnessed the inexorable march to war from within the ranks of the infantry.

I was at Fort Slocum, I believe, in New York. I had just been sent down there from Fort Ethan Allen in Vermont, and I saw the handwriting on the wall when I heard things on the radio. It became very clear to me that the United States was not going to be able to stay out of this conflict, and it wasn't too long before we got to Pearl Harbor, and that confirmed my suspicions.

At Fort Ethan Allen in Vermont, they were receiving a lot of recruits. They were drafting young men off the streets of every city and state in the Union. And that was one of the collecting areas where the basic training—thirteen weeks of basic—was given, and I was participating in that. And it wasn't long before they needed somebody that knew enough about army methods, so I was transferred from an active unit to another headquarters company. Became a staff sergeant then, I believe.

It was my decision to go overseas, and it was difficult for me to convince my immediate commander, Colonel Nelson. I had the job of division artillery sergeant major supervisor, a job I didn't like. I was merely a supervisor for eight clerks. They were punching out social orders and making copies and delivering them to all the other units in the organization after I'd proofread them, and it was dull for me. I had been trained as an infantryman. I was never without a rifle in my hands. In Maine, as a boy, my daddy gave me a rifle—a little .22 rifle—when I was seven years old, and no squirrel was safe. I understood cover and concealment, and sneaking through the woods and getting close to your victim to make your shot a good shot.

So I went to the colonel when I found out from classified documents that I was cleared to handle that the invasion of Europe was to take place in the spring of 1944. This rang bells in my head, because here was what I was trained for. Here was an invasion of historical proportions, and I wanted to be a part of that history-making invasion. I could picture in my mind the coast of France and what this all meant to the military leaders and planners. And I went to the colonel and asked him, "If I surrender my rank and pay, will you transfer me to an organization that's headed for Europe as a replacement in the invasion?" He said, "Only if you can find me a suitable replacement."

And I did. I found a man who, with a little urging and the inducement of higher pay, volunteered for the job, and I introduced him to the colonel. They had an interview, and I was out of there in no time as a private.

It got me placed in a spot in Southampton in England. I knew from the position of Southampton that we were at the jumping-off spot. The casualties were bound to be heavy. The Nazis were not playing around. They were stubborn, and they were foolhardy. There's a difference between courage and foolhardiness. They were foolhardy, because they believed everything that the Führer had told them. They were going to run the world. And they all wanted to be a part of it, just as I wanted to be part of the invasion of Europe to put an end to their dream.

D-plus-3 landed me on Normandy.[11] We were just ordered down to the water, the water's edge in the dark, and we got aboard the transports, the troop transporters. They had bulletproof sides on them. The gunnels were thick steel, so that told me something.

The officer in charge who drove that particular vehicle gave us all a terrible shock. When we got to the shore of Normandy, small-arms fire was coming from the heights above us, and these 9 millimeters were banging off the side of the gunnels, and he panicked and he dropped the ramp too soon. He dropped it in fifteen feet of water, and we were crowded in there so tight that the guys in front were pushed off. We had personal floatation devices. But you had to activate them by releasing a carbon dioxide cylinder to inflate them, and these boys were so excited, they hadn't done it. And a lot of those that had gone off the ramp into fifteen feet of water drowned, and there wasn't a damn thing the rest of us could do about it. With the rifle, two bandoliers of ammunition, and two grenades, you weren't able to help anybody but yourself to scramble ashore.

We made it to shore, most of us, and it was every man for himself. Here, at last, we're on the loose—no one controlling us. It started as confusion. The plans had already been made, and we were well trained, but things started going wrong, one thing after another. There was yelling and screaming and small-arms fire, and you were just lost in a crazy nightmare.

There was a real steep slope, and the observation planes had told our command that they had artillery up there. So the Rangers were given that job. The Rangers did their best, and there was a lot of falling and a lot of crumbling of earth, and nothing stable, everything coming apart. When they got up there, there were no guns. The Germans had taken their guns and left.

We chased them all across France, Belgium, Luxembourg—Luxembourg cost us a lot of casualties, too; the 28th Division, 112th Infantry got zapped in Luxembourg—but we drove 'em out of there, too. And right across the Rhine River into Germany. We had them on the run then, and it was encouraging. But then they had some tricks left: land mines, antipersonnel mines, and booby traps. They were taking a toll on our men.

It never stopped for fifteen months. I began to realize that my twelve years of infantry training was going to be, along with my rifle, my best asset. And I began to see some of the men doing foolhardy things. When you're being attacked with mortar shells, they fragment nose down, 'cause the trajectory is so high, and if you're not on your belly, one of those fragments is going to tear your guts out. And they're silent. When you hear the first one, be sure you're on your belly from then on until they stop firing them. Otherwise, you're going to get chopped up, and an awful lot of the guys got chopped up. You could tell by the way they weren't taking advantage of cover and concealment that they were improperly trained, and your heart went out, but there was no time for compassion. "Get with it, kid. This is for real. The chips are down."

No soldier ever went into a firefight without being filled with fear. But there's something magic that happens. When the shooting starts, and the bodies start dropping, that fear turns to something close to rage, and you forget about all your fear, and there's one object then: "Kill those sons of bitches. Make 'em pay." I was amazed at myself. Because I'm thinking, "Where the hell is this coming from?"

When we drove 'em across the Rhine River, the eastern bank of the Rhine River has a rise, and there's a road along there. When they got to that road on the other side of the Rhine, just stacked up with equipment and supplies and troops, our own artillery—and we had beaucoup artillery—they were all set up. They'd all been given their coordinates. They all had topographical maps, and they were ready. When that road over there was just full, they let go. We decimated them. We had to send bulldozers over there to clear that road so we could use it. And we just pushed everything off the road, down into the water. Just peeled them off.

Oh, God! Every time we had a success like that, it was sickening, and it gets you right in the pit of the stomach. "I should be happy. We're winning. This is a great victory." And all the time, I'm ready to puke. I suppose that had something to do with being gay, but I couldn't appreciate what I was seeing as a victory. It was mutilation. But that's war.

We went all the way to the Oder River, and there we met the Russians, and our commander said, "Hold it right here. Let the Russians have Berlin, because they've earned it. Their casualties were ten times ours." And they were so happy that we opened a second front to take the pressure off them, and they were hugging and kissing us. Of course, I loved that.

The worst thing was, I came back to the United States with this feeling of "Glory be to God! We have finally destroyed something that was threatening the world." But you know what? It's happening all over again. Every time I pick up a newspaper or turn on the news, somebody over there, some megalomaniac has got himself into a situation where he's rabble-roused a whole bunch of people to go kill off some other people. "Ethnic cleansing," what a dirty word that is. Then I think, "What was I doing over there?" All that effort was just to destroy one predator. There are more predators, and they keep coming.

After Paul came back to the States, he left the army, went to school on the GI Bill, and worked as a lab technician for DuPont for many years. He didn't come out publicly until he was eighty-five years old. At the time of this interview, Paul was ninety-one, living in Bangor, Maine.

TAIL GUNNERS TOO
An Interview with Bill Taylor

Bill Taylor worried that he wouldn't remember much about his short stint in the military nearly fifty years before we sat down together. But as I soon learned, Bill had no shortage of memories or opinions. One of the feistiest veterans in this book, at one point in the interview, Bill talked about his interest in Civil War history, waxing poetic about his belief in states' rights. At another point, when I asked him about "Don't Ask, Don't Tell," he said, "I think it stinks! We're the only modern country that has that stupid policy. Canada, you can go in as gay. All the European countries, you can go in as gay. It's terrible. And George Bush is not going to allow it to happen as long as he's president. The quicker we get rid of him, the better off we'll be." Then, he stood up suddenly, flipped the bird at my tape recorder, and said, "Fuck you, George!"

I was born in Madison, Wisconsin, April the twenty-third, 1925. We only spent a little time there. Basically, I'm a Kentuckian, as you can tell from my accent. We were very much southerners and proud of it. We moved back to Kentucky when I was a baby. My father was in charge of some school farms in Kentucky. He was very much into agriculture. I used to try to follow him around, tagging along as a kid.

Bowling Green was a town of 30,000 at the time. It was one hour's drive north of Nashville, Tennessee. It was great—very calm, very pleasant. Back in those days, back in the thirties, there was a recession or worse than that, a depression. But we didn't feel it very much, because we didn't live very highly. We didn't go hungry. We had men who it looked like had been working somewhere and they came to the back door and just asked for a slice of bread, because they were hungry. So we always gave it to them. In Kentucky, there was never any problems with thievery or anything like that, even in the Depression.

My joining the military had nothing to do with my being a southerner. I was an American. And I was the one that convinced my two older brothers to go into the air force, because that was a better place to be. There were no dirty, muddy foxholes or anything like that. I had the idea that if you ever got it, you got it all the way or else you came back in one piece. So that's about the way it happened.

My oldest brother was roughly seven years older than me, so he went in right when he was twenty-one. They needed everybody and everything then, and he wanted to be a flyer, which I feel like I had a certain amount of influence on. He became a B-17 pilot, and on his way to Europe with his bomber, he buzzed us in Bowling Green in a B-17, four-engine plane. [He laughs.] We'd never even seen a four-engine plane before. It really enthused the whole city. They dropped boxes out with notes on them and everything. Of course, we never saw him again. That was the first part of the war. He didn't last very long.

My other brother was only eighteen months older than me. He got in under the wire, which I did not. He became a fighter pilot, which was his nature more than my oldest brother actually. He flew with the Fifteenth Air Force out of Italy. I don't remember how many flights he made, but he made a lot in P51s. He stayed in for thirty years. I know he flew in Vietnam. I suppose he flew in Korea too, but I'm not sure about that.

Anyhow, my basic training was in Biloxi, Mississippi, and we all got heat rash. We were sweaty. It was very thorough. It seemed like it lasted a long time, but it probably didn't. It was good training—whipped us up into being heavier. I took my first pilot training in Clemson, South Carolina. But I didn't do any more, because they decided that the war was going to be over by the time I got through with my year-and-a-half of training, so I was washed out at the government's request, which made me very unhappy. After that, I volunteered for gunnery school, and they sent us to Tyndall Field in Panama City, Florida. I think that lasted a few months. I still wanted to fly. I still wanted to be in that airplane. I thought that was a lot better than anywhere else. I did not want to be a desk combatant or whatever they call them. I was gung ho at the age of eighteen, put it that way.

It was 1943, and we flew over to England. We flew up to Bangor, Maine, in the wintertime. And then I believe we flew directly to Wales or England. It was a long flight. I also flew back after the war. So I didn't make the trip on a ship either way, which I was very thankful for, because I understand that it was very slow and tedious. I liked flying in the B-24s. That was the four-engine plane with the big elephant ear tails on it, and I had a nice tail turret, which was comfortable.

I don't remember where exactly I met my crew. It might have been in Massachusetts. But we did train as a crew for quite a while. After we had trained for a while, we went to Long Island. There, we picked up the plane that we were going to fly across the Atlantic Ocean. They also issued us .45 caliber handguns, and we were just playing around with them. It turned out that they were loaded. [He laughs.] We didn't realize it at the time. While I was training as a gunner, I fired everything that there was to be fired: machine guns, shotguns, pistols, rifles, everything. So I pretty well knew about gunnery. I ended up as a tail gunner, firing two .50 caliber machine guns. So we had a tail gunner—me. We had two waist gunners. We had the belly gunner. We had the top turret gunner, who was usually also the engineer. And the nose gunner was usually the one who directed us over the target.

The first pilot, Andy, was very serious minded. He was more mature than his age I guess. He couldn't have been more than twenty-three or twenty-four. The copilot was only twenty-one. Cal was his name. He was tall and lanky. They were both pretty smart. The ball-turret gunner was Mormon. All three of them were married. There was Andrew W. Jestinkowski. He was one of the waist gunners. He was a Polack, and he always claimed that Polacks had the biggest dicks of anybody. He'd take that thing out, and he'd wind it up like a propeller. But we didn't get real horny about that. It was just a funny occurrence. He turned out to be a detective in New York City, or no, it was Chicago. Let's see, another gunner, I used to go to his hometown and visit his family in Providence, Rhode Island. His father was a motorcycle cop, and they were the cussin'ist family I ever heard in my life. Gee! He'd cuss in front of the little girl, and she'd cuss right back at him. I was kind-of embarrassed. I had a southern upbringing, and I didn't believe in cussin' in front of the women. I was brought up a Baptist. I got teased mercilessly about being a southerner, even though I was from a border state. But I didn't take it seriously. They just called me "rebel."

When we got to England, I liked it. We were paid a lot. The English military men didn't like us, because we were getting too much money. They would all say: "You are over here, over-sexed, and over-paid." When I got over there, everything in England was totally blacked out. We had our weekends in London, totally blacked out. So you just sort of felt your way around. Piccadilly Circus, I never saw it; I felt it because you just didn't have any light at all. The Germans had the V-bombs. In London, we'd be sitting around in the bars having a drink, and all of a sudden, we'd hear, "Nnnnngggh!" Here comes a V-bomb. And that's all right as long as we heard that engine going. But if it shut off, we knew it was going to drop near us. So we'd all jump under a table. But we didn't get really excited about it. You either got it or you didn't.

My base was up in the Norwich Peninsula, which is ninety miles northeast of London, and it was just blanketed with mostly American bombers. That was the closest place to Europe that they put us. There were so many, many, many planes. When we went on a mission, we spent, oh, at least half of our time getting into formation. By the time we headed over to Europe, you could look out and see the whole horizon full of other bombers at your same altitude—hundreds of them.

The fighters would meet us over the enemy territory because they didn't have the distance that we did. We bombed not only Germany, but we bombed Denmark, because the Germans were in Denmark. We bombed France, because the Germans were in the Bordeaux Peninsula. They had dive-bombers there. One time we bombed Switzerland, because they were making ball bearings for the Germans. We let them know that we were coming, so that there was nobody in the plant, but we obliterated the plant. We bombed the Netherlands and maybe Belgium, because the Nazis were already in all of those areas.

We could see a lot, because you don't go when you can't see the ground. The time we bombed France, and the Stuka Bombers were in the Bordeaux Peninsula that was very near the English Channel. We were very low there. We could see the dive-bombers up above us, and they would try to dive-bomb through us. That was a pretty short flight, because we didn't have to go so far. When we went to the main part of Germany, why we'd get up to 30,000 feet, and some of those flights were scrubbed. I never got credit for them. So I went up a lot more times than I get credit for as official missions, which was routine.

It was pretty spooky when we met German fighters. I fired at some of 'em. I don't think I got any hits, and they didn't get me. We didn't lose anyone in our plane, but we saw a lot of planes go down around us. In those days, by the time I got there, it was more flak from the ground than it was fighter pilots, because we'd already obliterated a lot of their fighter planes, and so they didn't have as many as they did in the beginning. But there was an awful lot of flak. We spent a lot of time throwing out what we called chaff, which was little silver strips, to throw off their radar sites. But as I recall, our plane never got hit. I know I didn't get hit, so I didn't get a Purple Heart.

After talking about his bombing missions, I asked Bill to talk about how sexuality affected his time in the service. He didn't have much to say.

The only time that I ever had any association with any other gay people was that we would find out, and we'd get together. There was never any sex, as far as I was concerned. I'm sure that there was a lot going on. I had approaches. In those days, I was considered cute. [He laughs.] Tail gunners were small and cute.

I had sex outside of the service, like when I went home to Bowling Green. I've been gay all my life, and there's an awful lot of gay life going on in the South, but you do it and you don't talk about it. I've been away from Bowling Green for several years, but there was an awful lot of it going on. You could have had as much or as little as you wanted. I had dates and went to all the cotillion parties and all of that sort of thing, and still had my sex later on. I took the girls home, and then we had some fun. The girls all thought that we were being very proper, because we didn't put the make on them. I had a lot of people tell me I was cute. I hated it. I didn't like it. Now nobody says it anymore.

Bill Taylor worked in Florida and West Virginia before moving to California in the 1980s. At the time of our interview he was retired and living in San Francisco, but he continued to travel the world, even at the age of seventy-eight.

HOSPITALS AND THE HOME FRONT

Interviews with Burt Gerrits and Bud Robbins

During World War II, a generation of young men and women were swept up by military mobilization. Even if these men and women were not shipped overseas, their exposure to big city life and to the range of people in the military broadened their horizons immeasurably. Elwood Burton "Burt" Gerrits and Joseph "Bud" Robbins were stationed on opposite coasts, working in hospitals to treat wounded soldiers from battlefields across the globe. In their late seventies and eighties, these two men talked proudly of their service and enthusiastically about the opportunities that the war offered to learn more about themselves and the gay worlds that were emerging in San Francisco and New York during the 1940s.[12]

BURT GERRITS: I was born in Lake County, South Dakota, in 1923. My father was a mail carrier and a farmer. After I was eight years old, we lived on the farm. My mother was an elementary school teacher as well as a housewife. In that time, we didn't have electricity. We had no plumbing. Essentially, we were living in conditions that people had been living in for hundreds of years. You used horse power rather than machines. When I left there at age eighteen to come here, all of a sudden, there were all of these bright lights, and the magic of a city like San Francisco. [He laughs.]

My mother's sister lived in San Francisco. She would come back to visit us from time to time and would bring us trinkets from Chinatown. It seemed to be an absolutely magic place. I came to California with an uncle of mine, who was moving from South Dakota to Napa to work in the shipyards at Mare Island. He charged me the standard price that people paid from the Midwest to California in those days. It was $10. That was in 1941. It was just a little while before the Pearl Harbor attack. I remember coming across the Golden Gate Bridge and all the newsboys were on the Toll Plaza yelling, "War!" And they had the newspapers with only a one word headline about six inches high that was "WAR!" all the way across the top of the page.

BUD ROBBINS: I was born on December 2, 1926, in Binghamton, New York. That's close to the Pennsylvania border. My father was a merchant with clothing stores. My mother was pretty much a homemaker. When they started their own clothing business, they would take merchandise out on the road. This was in the deep Depression, and my father's plan was if you could get a thousand customers each paying you a dollar a week on credit, you'd make a thousand dollars a week. So we went out to all the little farms around Elmira, New York, and Towanda, Pennsylvania, and such places as that. My mother was a very affable sales lady and she was able to make friends with all these people, who, pretty much, tried to give her a dollar a week as she showed up. But it was a rough time and many of them couldn't, so we'd be offered chickens, and one time even a pig. [He laughs.] But, people were basically honest, and it was an interesting way of meeting farmers and people that I wouldn't have met ordinarily.

After the war started, many of the local factories were making great money creating the Norton Bomb Sight and other ammunitions. My father's business got a boost because the town was suddenly having money when it hadn't before. By that time, he had a store, and we were well known in the community. It was a great place to grow up. I had a happy time from that point on up through high school.

It was the expectation that almost all the boys in the graduating class would go into the navy. This was June of '44. My dad had served in the navy in World War I. He didn't talk much about the navy. I think he was in France during part of the war, and he referred to that occasionally. He wanted me very, very early on to read *All Quiet on the Western Front*, because he thought I'd get a picture of the horror of war.

Okay, boot camp was about an hour and a half north of Elmira, New York, on Seneca Lake—the same exact spot I had to go to as a Boy Scout at one point. It had now been taken over and made into a navy boot camp. I was amused because people from . . . guys from the New York City metropolitan area would look across the lake and say, "That's Canada over there." And I would say, "That's not Canada [laughter], the other side of Seneca Lake, its New York State." I remember I was in Company G, and we had the reputation of being the strictest company. [He laughs.] I was sort of proud when we finally got out of boot camp. As I looked back on it, it was fun. I went into the navy after having seen *Anchor's Aweigh*. And I really thought I was going to sing and dance my way through the service [laughter] as Gene Kelly and Frank Sinatra had done. I had that in the back of my head.

BURT GERRITS: I enlisted, because I was in danger of being drafted. My father had been in the navy during World War I. He liked it, and he thought I would be wise to choose as much as I could. Otherwise, I would certainly be put in the infantry. I finished hospital corps school right after boot camp in Idaho, and then I was sent back to the Bay Area on a train. I went to Oak Knoll to work on a psychiatric ward where the patients mostly were hysterical or shell-shocked. A lot of them had come back from Guadalcanal. Sometimes we'd work shifts at night; sometimes we'd work during the day. It was uneventful. It was just a matter of making beds, and if the patients were bedridden, serving them meals, which were delivered to the ward.

Eventually, I was transferred to Treasure Island. I worked on the same sort of ward. It was a psychiatric ward, but this one was different because most of the men on the ward were homosexual and were being thrown out of the navy. They were being "surveyed" from the service. That was the term used. When the Navy throws away something, they "survey" it. Most of these men were getting dishonorable or bad conduct discharges. They weren't sick. They were just sitting around playing cards and chatting and so on, while we were trying to do work. [He laughs.] And we had a lesbian nurse on that ward. And the psychiatrist was named Dr. Wonder. [He laughs.] The thing that he particularly wondered about was "How do these guys know that a patient is gay or not? They seem to know instantly."

Most of these guys were urban people. They weren't going back to a little farm village, as I would have if I had been in that position. They were going back to cities. I think some of them were delighted to be leaving the navy, because they were sick of the war, sick of all the explosions, and the routine, the regimentation. They probably had found it unpleasant. It might even be possible that some had declared themselves as homosexual in order to get out. But I think some of them were caught in the act and were being thrown out for that reason. I remember one of those guys was a singer, and I think he had lived in San Francisco before the war. He did after the war, anyhow. He told me of some place that was kind of a gay meeting place down there in the area of the Federal Reserve Bank in San Francisco. He said it was the Artist's Club. This was '43.

*During World War II, Burt Gerrits served in the navy as a medical corpsman
assigned to a psychiatry ward where gay sailors were sent before being kicked out.
Photo courtesy of Burt Gerrits.*

BUD ROBBINS: Well, there was one guy that I worked with at the Chelsea Naval Hospital who made out with all the WAVES. My feeling was you don't fraternize with officers. But there was a navy nurse, a lieutenant, who became quite obviously fond of me, and this guy said, "Listen, she likes you, man. You're missing the opportunity of your life." And I said, "We're not supposed to fraternize with our officers." [He laughs.] He says, "Tell ya what, we're gonna go out to Revere Beach on Sunday, and she'll be waiting in bathing suit, and she won't have any little insignia on, so you won't know that she's a lieutenant, and you can just make out with her." [He laughs.] Well, I remember going to Revere Beach scared stiff. What am I supposed to do with that woman? And finding that they had fried clams, which I had never tasted in my life, and I just fell in love with those fried clams—and forgot all about her. [He laughs.]

We could go out at midnight, and some of us would go together. I hated beer, so if I'd go into a bar, I'd order a Coca-Cola. This one chief, he said to me, "Why do you keep ordering Cokes? You know, you're a navy man, you're supposed to order beer." I said, "Oh, well I hate beer." And he said, "Well, I'll tell you what, we're going out and we're going to learn to drink beer." So we went out one evening. He got off at midnight too, I guess. Anyhow, we ended up at a little bar in the Chelsea area, and we sat at a little round table and he ordered two beers, and I thought, "Oh God, Chief, this is really like medicine, I don't want this." And he said, "Well, I'll tell ya what, Robbins, we're gonna sit here until you drink it, so you just try it." I tried to hold my nose, and I couldn't do it. Pretty soon it got flat and he ordered another beer, and he poured salt in mine. I said, "I don't like salt either, Chief." [He laughs.] Well, at the end of the evening he said, "We're not going till you drink that damn thing." So I finally got it down like medicine, and when I did everyone in the bar applauded.

BURT GERRITS: My very first experience, I was picked up in some bar on Market Street. In those days, grain was not available for making whiskey, because the grains had to go off in the war effort to feed people. So the bars pushed a drink made of tequila and rum, grenadine, and several other things. It was called a zombie. It was a big tall glass with ice in it, very pretty colors. I heard people talking about it, so I ordered a zombie in this bar called McCarthy's. Before I finished drinking it, the bartender brought me another one, and told me that the merchant marine officer, sitting on the other side of this old bar had sent me the drink. So I smiled at him. Before I finished it, he was sitting beside me. [He laughs.] I got very drunk on those two zombies, and I guess he sort of rolled me into a taxi and took me to the Palace Hotel. That was my first homosexual experience.

After that, I made up for lost time. [He laughs.] I went on liberty from the psychiatric ward, and I had hotel rooms. Well, I didn't have the hotel rooms myself, but some of the patients did. They invited me to stay with them, and I did. We just had wonderful times. There were signs in various places in the city, saying, "Out of bounds." The navy shore patrol and the army MPs patrolled, the two of them together, around these places. But I didn't have any concern if I wasn't in one of those places. If I was just going to a hotel, I didn't see any need to worry about that. So I was just having a great time.

I did go to gay bars quite a lot. One in particular that I remember was on Maiden Lane just off of Union Square. The Claridge. There were female impersonator places like Finocchio's and the Beige Room. I went to Finocchio's right after I came out in 1943. It's the only time I've ever been there. I went there with another fellow who was in the navy. I thought it was rather entertaining, and yet I felt a little embarrassed, I suppose. I'd never seen drag before, and it was really impressive to me that men could impersonate women so successfully and at the same time make a criticism of what they were doing by overdoing it a little bit. I thought their costumes were gorgeous, and I just thought it was good entertainment.

Oh, I forgot to tell you about Top of the Mark! *That* was a gay meeting place too! It had this big, circular oval bar, and it was kind of nice for cruising because you could look at people across the bar. It was always crowded. They had a velvet rope across the entrance and they would let in only so many people. But there was a nice, old elevator man, elevator operator. I guess he liked sailors. There were some of us who made his acquaintance, and he would take us up in the service elevator and let us out in a room where they stored cartons of beer and things like that. We could get in through the back door that way and avoid the velvet rope.

In those days, there were very few places that were purely gay. There were a lot of these kind of mixtures like the Top of the Mark. I think there was just a gay undercurrent in a lot of these places—very respectable bars. There were just people sitting around at a bar, and noticing whoever came in. There wasn't any really overt activity except with the eyes, as I remember. There was a very high standard for behavior, I guess.

BUD ROBBINS: Once I got stationed at Chelsea and would go out at midnight, it was so easy to get picked up. I would do that, and let men blow me and all, but there was no affection. It was sort of an adventure, but it wasn't pleasant. In the meantime I would see all these hunky, Boston, Irish navy men, and would somehow find myself thinking, "Oh my god, if I could just get with someone like that." But what would happen, we'd start out, and as I say I was drinking Coke most of the time, I didn't get drunk, and these guys would get drunker and drunker, and then they'd go pick up some slut. [Laughter.] And I'd go home to the barracks alone.

In New York in those days, the Astor Hotel bar was a notorious place for men to meet. Somehow, I found that out and wandered in there. It was very easy to be picked up by officers, and taken to nice places. So that became a pattern for a while.

I don't think I was blatant. I was so naive, you know. I didn't think I was cute; I didn't think I was good looking. I had pimples, and I was skinny. I was not the kind person that I would find attractive. I was sort of surprised when people did come on to me. Here's another incident that I'm not terribly proud of. In the Times Square area, in the theater area, it was so easy to get picked up. This warrant officer saw me standing on the steps of that hotel, the Astor. He came up and talked to me, and wanted to know if we could go to his room. I thought, "Well sure, why not?" He was sort of butch looking. Anyhow, I fell asleep, and in the morning he was gone, and there was a twenty dollar bill on the dresser [He laughs.] I took it down, holding it like this [between two fingers, as if it were dirty], and there were these bell-ringing Santa Clauses on the street. I dropped the twenty in one of their buckets, and I thought, "Oh my god, I'm a whore." [He laughs.]

But you know, I think I was looking more for affection than sex. I never found that while I was in the service. I never did.

After the war, the GI Bill enabled Burt and Bud to earn college degrees. Burt became a teacher and lived with his partner for nineteen years. At the time of this interview, he had retired and was living in a beautiful house in the hills above Oakland, California. After working as an advertising copyeditor and later as a teacher in New York and Texas, Bud also moved to the Bay Area, where he lived with his partner, Joe Maloney, for thirty-three years. He was one of the founding members of the Alexander Hamilton American Legion Post. At the time of the interview, he remained active in the fight to lift the ban on gays serving in the military.

ROSIE THE REBEL
An Interview with Charlotte Coleman

Charlotte Coleman was one of the thousands of women who went to work in war industries like Rosie the Riveter. When the managers of the torpedo factory where she worked refused to pay Charlotte the same wages as the men she was training, this "Rosie" turned in her rivet gun and overalls for a coast guard uniform. During this era, women in the services were much less likely to be stationed overseas than men, and Charlotte was no exception to the rule. Yet the coast guard was her means of broadening her horizons. Ultimately, it was her ticket to San Francisco where we met for this interview.[13]

I'm Charlotte Coleman. I was born in Cranston, Rhode Island, September 5, 1923. My mother came from Sweden at age seventeen, with fifty American dollars and not one word of English. [She laughs.] She was a Swedish maid. They were very popular in those days. My father was Irish, but he was born in Rhode Island. He was a rumrunner during Prohibition. He didn't have a heck of a lot of education, but he was genius on motors and boats. The law was chasin' him all the time, but they never caught him. Of course, he didn't do that forever; he went into business.

Because of the rumrunner thing we were in a little town called Somerset, Massachusetts. There were only a few houses there, and there was a big dock. We were out in the middle of the bay practically. I lived on a beach, grew up there. It was a nice little town, but there was nothing to do. I worked as a bookkeeper for a gas station for a little while.

Then I worked making torpedoes down at Newport, Rhode Island. I worked there for a couple of years. I had to cut the hole where the piston fits into the tube. Yes, we made the whole thing there. We made them both for planes and the submarines. They knew who made the torpedoes, because they were numbered, and if a torpedo that you made sunk a ship or made a hit, your name would go up on a board in the factory. It was to cheer us up, I guess.

When we got hired at the torpedo factory, they said women would get paid the very same amount as men. I was pretty good at this job I was doing. So these high school guys would come in, and I taught them how to do the work. Pretty soon, they would be in another shop supervising, so I went down and talked to the admiral, the head of the whole thing, and I said, "You promised that women would get the same as men. Here I am training these guys. They go on and get a better job, but you keep me on this job." I knew I was doing a good job because it was so hard to cut the part, and it had to fit perfectly, so it didn't leak. He had no excuse for why women weren't getting paid the same, so I quit. He pulled my Social Security number for six months. They blacklisted me. It was completely unfair.

When World War II came, I thought, "Oh good! I can get away from Somerset. My mother opposed me signing up, because I was an only child and she and my father had separated. But I was going. As soon as I got to be twenty-one, I went. A friend of mine had joined the coast guard up in Boston, so I went up to Boston to see what was going on. The coast guard had done something really clever. From all the bus stations and train stations, there were women's footprints all the way to coast guard headquarters where you joined. [She laughs.]

It turned out that I was too short. They sent me home and said, "Every time you go through a doorway, reach up and try to touch it." I did that for a few months, and then I went back. It was still: "No, you're still too short. Go home and do it again." I don't think I ever got any taller, but I guess by the third time they needed me.

Boot camp was really nice. We were in the Palm Beach Biltmore Hotel. It was a very elegant hotel. We had six bunks in a room. Boot camp was not hard at all. We learned how to march, salute, and shake hands. One of the officers said that shaking hands with women was like shaking hands with a bunch of fish, and believe me, when we graduated he had to have the sorest hand in the world. Because we were like, "Grrrrr, grrrr!" [She shows me how hard they shook his hand and laughs.] And we got to go to the beach a couple times a week. We marched over to the beach. I don't remember any kind of hard work, you know, I was assigned part of the time to food detail. We served the officers first and the other people then after. Then, after lunch was over, I had to mop the floor. We were not learning to fight or anything. We were mostly going to be office workers. The Coast Guard didn't put any women on their ships.

When I was in boot camp, I met a woman who was a lesbian. Well, I didn't know she was. She picked up on me, I guess, 'cause she told me what gay meant. I had never heard of the word "gay" before, and she was older than me.

After boot camp, Charlotte and her friend went to the coast guard's "storekeeper" school in Sheepshead Bay, New York.

We went to class every day, and they were teaching us how to be book-keepers and typewrite, you know, just what you would learn in high school classes. It wasn't anything new for me, but it was for some people. I have to say that I was rotten at typewriting in high school, and we had an instructor in the coast guard from somewhere in the South. He had an accent that we could not understand and he had a stick and he would hit on the table as we typed. In two weeks I learned how to type with a typewriter better than I had in three years of high school. [She laughs.]

Once you finish school, you ask for this or that assignment. Then they say, "This is where you're going," and they send you there. That's it. We all wanted to get stationed in California, and my friend Shirley was lucky. She got stationed in Long Beach. But most of us had to go to Washington, D.C.

Washington was a beautiful city, but it was rotten for service people. There were millions of us. Waiting to get on a bus or something like that was just awful. I got paid eighty dollars a month, and I sent twenty home to my mother. We were all pretty poor, unless it was somebody who had a lot of money beforehand, which I didn't have. We'd be waiting in line to go to a restaurant or something and they'd take everybody ahead of us. They knew we didn't have any money. Things were really rotten.

But we got along. I had friends in the coast guard. The one who told me what gay meant, her name was Shirley Davis and she was from Chicago. My roommate in Washington was from South Carolina, and her name was Sarah. Oh, another one was from Boston. We called her Jonesy. I forget what her first name was. That's all I remember right now, but I was friendly with some of them for years. Only Shirley was gay. None of the others were.

The only lesbians that we recognized were cooks and bakers. They were also our softball team. They were obvious to me, and they were, I think, to most people. We loved them. They played good softball, cooked good food, and nobody ever mentioned anything about what they were or anything. You just knew it. Certainly the officers knew it, but they behaved themselves, so they never got into trouble. They were all pretty obvious. I never played softball. I drank beer. [She laughs.] Ten cents a glass, it was. Right near our barracks. I went sightseeing too.

Every weekend we could go to New York City—stay in the Waldorf Astoria for three dollars a night. And we got free passes for restaurants, I mean, good ones too, and plays and everything. New York City was absolutely wonderful to service people. Right down in Times Square, I think it was Pepsi-Cola gave you all the Pepsi you wanted to drink and free hotdogs. We had to wear our uniforms. We didn't have anything else. On Easter Sunday, down Fifth Avenue, we were voted the best-dressed people on the street. We looked pretty good, I guess.

My first job in the coast guard was to disburse pension checks to all the men that manned the lighthouses all over the United States. They were coast guard people too. They had to send in a postcard when they got their check saying they were still alive. They were old! God, they were old, and you could hardly read their names, the way they wrote their names on the thing. It was my job to match up the postcards with the guy so he'd get another check. It was hard to do.

When you're in the service you have an insurance policy—NSLI, National Service Life Insurance. Everybody had it. They almost made you buy it. The policy payments came in from all the coast guard people, all over the place, and my next job was to take this information from the checks and run a tape on an adding machine. It went on for three or four days, and it all went into a big box. Nobody was to come near it or touch it. Just me. Nobody knew if I made a mistake or not, but whatever the total said, they gave me a check for it, and I delivered it. They didn't want anybody to know about it. The check was for millions of dollars, but they gave it to me 'cause no one expected me to bring this million dollar check over to the insurance company.

All of my superior officers were women, and I had a very enjoyable time with everybody in the SPARs. I enjoyed what I was doing. I would have liked to stay on if they hadn't disbanded the SPARs after the war. The coast guard did offer me a job, because all of these women were leaving, and I was working at the coast guard headquarters. They offered me a grade-7 job. Well, I was not about to stay in Washington, D.C., no matter what they paid me. [She laughs.] I'd been there long enough, and I wanted to come to California.

After the war, Charlotte and the other women in the SPARs were offered cheap train tickets to anywhere in the United States. Charlotte took a long cross-country trip to see her friend Shirley in Long Beach, California. I asked Charlotte if, thinking back over her time in the service, she or any of her friends experienced discrimination because they were lesbians.

The coast guard didn't know it. Nobody knew it. I heard that down in Long Beach, where my friend had been, they *did* kick women out for being lesbians. They did the black drum thing, beat them out, cut the buttons off their uniforms.[14] The SPARs were disbanded by the time I got down there, but Shirley told me about that. It happened a couple of times. They just beat on the drums, stood them up, and cut all the buttons off their uniforms.

After the war, I got fired from the Internal Revenue Service for being gay. I had a very good job at Internal Revenue, and I liked it. But there came a point where they were cutting down on employees and weren't hiring anybody. Internal Revenue had an investigation staff, and they investigated you very good before you were hired. The investigation staff had nothing to do when nobody was being hired, so they investigated anybody that was going up for a grade raise. Boy, they spent a lot of time with me! They read my mail, tapped my telephone, and followed me every weekend. They fired me for "association with persons of ill repute." They could never say I was gay. They just couldn't. They couldn't prove that.

Ultimately, Charlotte opened up a bar called the Front in San Francisco. The Front hosted fund-raisers and parties for the Daughters of Bilitis, one of the first lesbian rights organizations in the United States.

KOREA AND THE COLD WAR

It seemed as if Americans were just cleaning up the ticker tape from World War II victory parades when the Cold War began in the late 1940s. Communism eclipsed fascism as the greatest apparent threat to democracy and capitalism. Formerly allies, the Soviet Union and the United States soon faced off across an ideological abyss. Since direct military conflict between the superpowers risked atomic war and later, nuclear holocaust, the Cold War was fought primarily through proxy wars in the developing world and espionage in the developed world.

Korea, divided after World War II between a communist regime in the north and a capitalist one in the south, became the site of one of the first proxy wars. When the North Koreans launched an invasion to reunify the country in the summer of 1950, the United States quickly intervened. Because of the communist revolution in China only one year earlier, American policymakers feared that if they did not intervene in Korea, all of Asia might fall to communism. A u.s.-led multinational force fought alongside the South Koreans and under the auspices of a United Nations resolution to bring peace to the region. General Douglas MacArthur orchestrated a surprise landing of the UN forces at Inchon in the fall of 1950 that turned the tide against the North Korean army; but when the UN forces launched a counteroffensive into North Korea, Chinese troops intervened, and the war bogged down into a bloody stalemate. The signing of an armistice in 1953 ended overt military conflict, but it did not bring peace.

Two of the interviewees in this chapter saw action in Korea. Ric Mendoza-Gleason served ten years in the army, a few of them on the ground in Korea. He landed at Inchon after the initial invasion, and though he "felt relatively safe" as a supply clerk, he was close enough to the front lines to pull dangerous guard duty and to console a mortally wounded marine comrade. According to Ric, there was very little homophobia in the army ranks during the war.

Ric's experiences stand in stark contrast to those of William Winn, a navy doctor who had begun his service as a medic on the home front in World War II before graduating from medical school and serving as a ship's doctor during the Korean conflict. William saw a rise in homophobia both on the home front and in the wartime navy. Still, the numbers of undesirable discharges for gay sailors during the years of the Korean conflict (483 in 1950 and 533 in 1951) were less than half the number in the year that the armistice was signed (1,353 in 1953). In fact, the number of gay-related discharges in the navy would not fall below 500 again until 1970 when the u.s. was involved in another Cold War conflict in Asia.[1]

The relatively small number of undesirable discharges in the navy during the Korean War era should not be misconstrued as an indication that the government was going easy on gays and lesbians. Ric Mendoza-Gleason remembers that for gay people "it was a nightmare here in the States." In the early 1950s, the military, Federal Bureau of Investigation, and even the u.s. Postal Service conducted surveillance of suspected homosexuals. Such federal initiatives against homosexuality mirrored antigay policies at the state and local levels and increasingly conservative community mores that led to action against gays and lesbians in both the public and private sectors.[2]

It began with a Senate subcommittee hearing in early 1950 when a State Department official admitted that several dozen employees recently fired by the department had been homosexuals. In an atmosphere marked by the hysteria of Joseph McCarthy's earlier warning that communists had infiltrated the State Department, fear of a "homosexual menace" gripped the Senate, inspiring a formal investigation of "sexual perverts" in the federal government. This investigation led to the dismissal of hundreds of gay and lesbian federal employees in the second half of 1950 alone. The historian David K. Johnson has called this the "lavender scare," a paranoia that reinforced the Red Scare rhetoric about invisible threats to America's national security.[3]

The lavender scare was based on the assumption that gay military personnel and other federal employees were susceptible to blackmail by enemy agents who could threaten to reveal the gay Americans' secret sexual identities. The only hard evidence of such a threat was the blackmail of a gay *Austrian* intelligence officer in 1912. On the other hand, if United States military officials could force admissions of homosexuality from their own troops after hours of interrogation what might the enemy do? According to David

Johnson, "no gay was ever blackmailed into revealing state secrets" during the Cold War, but thousands of American military personnel and federal employees were forced from their positions because they were gay.[4]

The creation of the Uniform Code of Military Justice (UCMJ) in 1951 was a legal reform intended to rationalize military law and make it consistent across the armed forces, but it also codified the antihomosexual ban in the military just as state laws were placing the same restrictions on gay civilians. Article 125 of the UCMJ defined "unnatural carnal copulation with another person of the same or opposite sex" as an offense worthy of court-martial.[5] Though it theoretically prohibited the "unnatural" sex acts of both homosexual and heterosexual service personnel, Article 125 was enforced almost exclusively against gays and lesbians in the armed forces.

The air force called it "housecleaning" when it investigated and dismissed lesbian service personnel from Lackland, Kessler, and Wright-Patterson Air Force Bases during the early 1950s.[6] Maurine McFerrin DeLeo called it a witch hunt. DeLeo served in the air force during the Korean War and saw similar investigations lead to dishonorable discharges for her friends. Despite the fact that air force officials often targeted women who played softball for investigations, she risked playing on the base team, because she loved it. Like many women in the armed forces during this era, Maurine struggled with the stereotyping of women in the military as either "whores" or "lesbians." These stereotypes left all women, gay and straight, vulnerable to investigations and harassment. In the end, it was not an investigation of her homosexuality that drove Maurine from the air force, but rather the unwanted sexual advances of male superior officers.

As oppressive as the lavender scare was for gay and lesbian service personnel during the early years of the Cold War, such state-sponsored oppression may have actually strengthened the bonds of gay and lesbian communities created during World War II. Mainstream America began to reckon with homosexuality and a gay subculture with the 1948 publication of the Kinsey Report, which suggested that nearly a third of American men had had at least one adult homosexual encounter and that 4 percent of American men were exclusively homosexual. Though Kinsey's findings were attacked and also utilized by conservative commentators worried about the homosexual menace, they were heartening to gay writers and activists.[7]

The 1950s saw the growth of gay American literature and the stirrings of a gay rights movement. "In the millions who are silent and submerged, I see a potential, a reservoir of protest," wrote Donald Webster Cory in 1951. Cory's book *The Homosexual in America* proclaimed that gays "are human beings, entitled to breathe the fresh air and enjoy, with all humanity, the pleasures of life and love."[8] Though he wrote under a pseudonym and was never as famous as his literary contemporaries—Tennessee Williams, Gore Vidal, and James Baldwin—Cory's idealistic call to arms did not go unheard. It was an early inspiration for the gay rights movement beginning to take shape with the formation of the Mattachine Society in Los Angeles in 1950 and the organizing of the Daughters of Bilitis in San Francisco in 1955. Focusing primarily on gay rights and lesbian rights respectively, the Mattachine Society and the Daughters of Bilitis carried the torch for a gay, activist identity through the culturally conservative years of the early Cold War.[9]

Veterans swelled the ranks of gay rights organizations, but they rarely tackled the military's antihomosexual policies during the 1950s and early 1960s. One exception was Frank Kameny, a World War II combat veteran and activist with the Mattachine Society in Washington, D.C. After graduating from Harvard University, Kameny had taught briefly at Georgetown University and then worked as a civil servant for the army. In the late 1950s, he was fired because he was gay. When a lawsuit against the federal government went nowhere, Kameny took his case to the streets, urging more militant activism by the Mattachine Society. "I am not a belligerent person, nor do I seek wars," Kameny wrote in 1960, "but having been forced into a battle, I am determined that this thing will be fought thru. . . . I will not be deprived of my proper rights, freedoms, and liberties." Under Kameny's leadership, the Washington Mattachine Society focused on discrimination in the military and in the U.S. Civil Service Commission.[10]

Their efforts were not enough to save the careers of men like Jim Estep. A classmate of Arizona senator John McCain at the U.S. Naval Academy, Estep was flying missions off the coast of Southeast Asia as a naval aviator when an investigation into his sexuality led to a less than honorable discharge. Jim was one of thousands of military personnel who became casualties not of the combat for which they were trained but of a policy about which they could do nothing.

While the military seemed publicly unmoved by the activism of organizations like the Mattachine Society and the plight of men like Jim Estep, there were signs of change even during the height of the Cold War. An internal review of the navy's policy regarding homosexuals in the mid-1950s revealed dissent within the ranks. Captain S. H. Crittenden Jr. chaired the committee, which completed its study in 1957. The Crittenden Report, as it became known, recommended few concrete policy changes, warning that the military should not "liberalize standards ahead of society," but its conclusions suggested a new, progressive mindset. The report challenged several "fallacies concerning homosexuality," arguing, for example, that "the idea that homosexuals necessarily pose a security risk" had persisted "without any basis in fact." The report also repudiated the claim that homosexuals "cannot acceptably serve in the military," by stating unequivocally, "There have been many known instances of [homosexual] individuals who have served honorably and well."[11]

The veterans who share their stories in this chapter underline this point.

KOREA

An Interview with Ric Mendoza-Gleason

Today, Ric Mendoza-Gleason is a self-described peacenik. Yet when he looks back on his service in Korea, he wishes that he had volunteered rather than waiting to be drafted. His memories of the war are powerful ones, and they seem to override his criticism of subsequent American military actions in Vietnam and the Middle East. His major regret is that he has lost touch with many of the men, gay and straight, with whom he served. In some sense, this interview may be an open letter to these men—forgotten comrades from a forgotten war.[12]

I was born on October 13, 1930. At the time I was drafted, I was living in Chicago, Illinois. I was in college, and my grades were, you know, not the greatest, so Uncle Sam said: [he curls a finger, making the gesture for "Come here"].

I went into the army. During that time it was supposed to be eight weeks of basic training, but it turned out to be sixteen. At the end of the sixteen weeks, they asked us if we wanted to join the airborne, and I thought, "Wow, that sounds exciting!" So I went and joined the 101st Airborne. That was another eight weeks of training—jump school.

My first days in the service were not too happy because it was so regimented and I was used to college and being able to, you know, go here, go there, do this, and do that. And then, of course, you're just low man on the totem pole as you first go in. You're just a private E-1, and you go to an E-2 after you finish basic, before you get any rank at all.

In boot camp, we had exercises every day, we had hikes, we had ten-mile hikes, twenty-mile hikes, we had bivouac. Bivouac means you go out in the field and you live out in the field. At that time, they did the thing where you go with gas masks, you go through this long hut and it's full of gas. They had a thing called infiltration, which means there's barbed wire and you—you keep low. There's machine-gun fire, and you keep your behind down to get under the wire, so that you crawl like this with your M1 rifle. I assumed that they were using live ammunition, but I have a feeling they weren't. But you were still scared. They don't tell you whether they're using it or not, 'cause they say, "Keep down, keep down," you know. So that was infiltration.

At first I did training at Camp Breckenridge, Kentucky. That's the home of the 101st. And then I went on to Fort Benning for eight weeks of jump school. I hated every one of the instructors. You're supposed to, you know, because they are the enemy. It's grueling. I mean, it's inspections, and it's "Fall out for this. Fall out for that." You have all kinds of KP [kitchen patrol] duty, and latrine duty, and all kinds of things like policing the area. I was glad when my basic training was over. Jump school was probably harder, but in some ways it wasn't quite as Mickey Mouse as basic training was.

I was fourteen years old when World War II ended, so I served in the Korean War. First of all, I remember the trip over. I forget which ship I was on, but it was just awful. We went by way of Adak, which is in the Aleutians, the last island in the Aleutians. The sea was rough. People were getting sick. It was horrible. And I didn't! I didn't until the last part of the journey, and I was so proud of myself. There was only five of us to go into the mess hall. One of the guys at the other end of my table got sick in his tray, and the sea was so rough that his tray landed underneath me. Then, I got sick.

I arrived at Inchon, and it was shortly after the last push through Inchon. Well, after Japan. Remember that Japan was just out of the war, and I was surprised about how poor it was and how cheap things were. But the war ended in '45 and this was already '51. So not many years had passed that they were able to get back on their feet. So, I was amazed at Japan, and at the poverty that I saw there. When I got to Korea, it was another thing; it's a culture shock. Every country you go to is a culture shock. Japan was a culture shock, and then Korea was another one, a different kind.

My first duty was just outside of Seoul. It was a converted girls' school that was turned into a quartermaster's depot. At that point they were going to assign us to ordnance, ammo ordnance. And we were doing some training there. I loved it there. We had a cook who was a chef at one of the hotels. And we ate like you would not believe. I hadn't eaten this well since I'd been in the service. I stayed there for a while, as a company clerk, but with the war going back and forth, they moved us. I was company clerk at the beginning, and then I was a secretary to the company commander, and they needed another clerk further up, and I kept moving further north. So I moved up to Seung-ni. "Ni" in Korean means village, and "Do" means island.

I had been in combat areas, 'cause it was still during the war, but I guess I felt relatively safe. You know, you're with your friends. There were no casualties in my unit. I was handing out ammunition and different things to the front—you know, artillery, rifle ammo, anything connected with ammo. My back went out, lifting the heavy cases of ammo and stacking them. We worked around the clock. We would work twelve hours on and twelve hours off, loading ammo. So you see, there was still a war going on, and I had gone up to the front in trucks. Oh, the guys who drove the trucks were marvelous. The road was mined, and how they knew to get around it was unbelievable.

It was a wonderful experience, and it was a horrible experience. At one point, I was at Munsan-ni, stacking ammo for the First Marine Division. There were five of us in charge of that. One night, prisoners of war, the North Koreans, had escaped from the island of Koji-do and they had come toward Munsan-ni. I was on guard duty, and I hollered, "Halt!" in Korean and in Japanese and I hollered in English. He didn't halt, so I had to shoot. That's the only time I ever killed.

There were so many things that I did for good luck at the time, you know. I was Catholic, so I used to pray, and I would go to Mass. I'll never forget that we couldn't get to a priest when we were at the front. I had this idea that "Oh, you miss Sunday Mass, and it's a sin." As it happened, my chaplain was a rabbi— one of the nicest, one of the most wonderful chaplains ever. I used to go to him when I had a problem. I told him what my problem was, and he said, "Ric, do not worry about that." He says, "Any Catholic chaplain will tell you, I'm empowered to take care of anything you have a problem with, like a confession." All of them—the Protestants, the Catholics, and the rabbis—had to know something to make the troops feel at ease. The Catholic chaplains had to know all about the Jewish religion too. The rabbi was wonderful, and when I finally told a Catholic priest about it, he says, "You did the right thing. Your rabbi was your chaplain, and you should go to him." And I did.

During the time before I got to Munsan-ni I was a courier for a while, which I found extremely interesting. I had a case chained to my arm, you know, just like handcuffs, and I never knew what was in it. I didn't want to know, didn't care, wasn't curious, but I always had it handcuffed from one end of the trip to the other. I happened to be on this train one time and there was a USO troupe on there, and it was Mickey Rooney and Audrey Totter, and they had come there and they were up in Seoul, and they were going to entertain in Taegu and Taejon and Pusan.

At that point, we had less of a problem with the North Koreans than we did with the southern guerrillas. They would come in out of the hills and attack the trains and the convoys and the trucks. Korean trains at that point had louvered windows, so you couldn't see out. Well, you could see out, but you had to turn the louver. It was at night, and we could see the tracer bullets coming onto the train, so we fired our weapons through the louvered windows. And of course, the USO troupe is all on the floor, and one of the sweet little chorus girls said, "Oh my God! This is just like a movie!" Apparently, she thought it was like a western movie, with us firing from the train.

And then, we had a bar, just like there was in *M*A*S*H*. And we'd go there every night, and you could wear civilian clothes if you wanted to. They were not strict about, about uniform after hours. So you could go there, you'd drink with your buddies. A lot of times you'd invite the Aussies over, and the New Zealanders, and all the rest.

Oh, the allies really bonded. My friends, the Turks and the Aussies, were short of paint and certain things. I would make sure that they got them. I mean, they were fighting on our side, too. One time, I got them some, some paint that they desperately needed and they gave me one of those Aussie hats that go up on the side with the little medal and everything. I always went to get tea and biscuits. The Greeks always invited you in. The Turks always invited you in. Everybody was extremely generous. I have nothing but kudos for our allies. They were there, and they suffered along with us.

I went on two R&Rs. I went to Yokohama, Japan, and I went to Bangkok. In Yokohama and in Bangkok, they treated the servicemen really fantastic, really. I have no complaints. We heard a lot of horror stories, about how you had to worry about this and that, but I had a wonderful time. I met a couple of Russian sailors in Yokohama. And all I knew was "da" and "nyet" and all they knew was, you know, "yes" and "no." We didn't have to know the language. They were fun. You're all young. The Cold War didn't affect us, you know, we didn't hate. There wasn't this feeling that because they were Russians we hated them, and they didn't seem to hate us.

Though Ric had gotten married young, while he was still in college, he was already aware of gay life both in the United States and in Korea. He compared attitudes toward homosexuality on the home front and the battlefront.

I want to be really crystal clear. It was a nightmare here in the States. It was a nightmare. 'Cause this is just before the McCarthy hearings, and I mean it was just awful. I mean, if you were gay here it was over, Grover—anywhere in the United States—unless of course you were out of uniform and went to Chicago or Milwaukee or Louisville. If you went out to the gay bars, then it was different. The tenor of the country was very bad, but once you got overseas, the commanders looked the other way. You'd be leaving somebody's tent, and they didn't say anything. They didn't care. We had a couple of guys who used to do drag at the bar, and the company commander thought they were wonderful. He used to cheer them on. He was a really great guy. He was Polish, and he was very, very straight.

I don't think I was really openly gay at that point, because you were so used to dragging your closet door around in those days. It's way before Stonewall and you were so used to doing that, and I certainly didn't do it when I was stateside—not at all. That's too frightening. But you were able to be as open as you wanted to be in a war zone. And most of the gay guys that were there, it was wonderful for them. They did their job; it didn't interfere with their work. It was an after-hours thing.

One of the things was, all the straight guys would come up to you, and if they knew you were gay, they'd say, "I'm going back in a month, I'm going back in two weeks, and I can't go to the village to see my woman, 'cause I can't come back with a disease, so could you come by my tent tonight?" That's one of the things I thought was funny, because today, with AIDS and everything like that, it's a reversal, but then, you couldn't get a disease from another GI.

When asked about some of the sadder experiences that he had in Korea, Ric recalled two stories that had a powerful effect on him.

I was at Panmunjom when the prisoner of war exchange was made across the bridge, and it was done over a week's time. We sent over our prisoners first, and they were all fat and happy and sassy and all had gained weight and they looked good. They didn't want to go back, because they were really eating well and living well, 'cause we treated our prisoners really great. So this, this is the first time I ever cried in Korea. After all of the North Korean, Chinese, and southern guerrilla prisoners were taken across the bridge at Panmunjom, our prisoners came across. They were in stretchers. They were helping each other. They, they, they were limping. Some of them were carrying their friends in their arms. Some of them just couldn't, couldn't make it across. They were all emaciated. It was a long bridge and it was a very slow process. It looked like what I must imagine the opening of Dachau must have looked like. It, it, it, it was horrible. They were all sickly and emaciated and obviously not well treated. It was a very sad thing.

But the saddest experience I ever had was, we had gone down to pick up supplies down at Inchon, and my driver said, "Look why don't you walk around?" He says, "I've got the manifest, I'll make sure we pick up the supplies." At that point, the hospital ship *Benevolence* was in port, and they were loading it full of wounded, mainly marines from the First Marine Division. I was talking to one of the doctors, and I couldn't believe it, it looked almost like the scene out of *Gone with the Wind*—just before the intermission—where there are nothing but wounded all around.

It was sad, and this voice said, "Ric? Ric, is that you?" I'm looking around and there's nobody around me except for the doctor and some nurses. They're kneeling down and they're busy, and somebody's pulling on my fatigue pants. It was one of the wounded guys. I went to high school with him! We weren't buddies. We weren't friends. I mean, I liked him, and he liked me, but we didn't hang around in the same group at the high school. This guy, pulling on my pant leg, and he says, "Is that you? We went to high school together!" And I said, "Yeah! I know who you are!"

We started talking and everything. He had some bandages over his eyes. So the nurse had come by and was kneeling down, I guess just checking, taking his pulse and everything like that, so I was telling him, "Oh, you're gonna be fine. You'll be chasing the women, you're gonna be, you're just gonna be. . . . I remember you, and you're going to be great." I said, "As soon as you get to Japan, the bandages are going to come off."

And I remember, the nurse went like [he shakes his head, "no"]. It's the most difficult thing in the world not to have your voice show what your eyes are doing. He wouldn't have seen it, you know, but I'm sure that there was a quaver in my voice. I, I, I continued to joke. I continued to kid him. That was, that was the saddest thing that ever happened to me in Korea.

It's so hard to explain the difference between stateside and service overseas. When I was in the service stateside, I thought, "I don't like the guys that I'm with," 'cause we were all trying to make it. We were all trying to do one-upmanship. I definitely hated the NCOs [noncommissioned officers], the sergeants, the corporals, and the officers. But when we got overseas, I saw how human they were and how you relied on your buddies for this and you relied on your buddies for that—the camaraderie and the closeness. Overseas, I found the officers to be understanding and friendly. You could go to them about anything. You would think with the gayness and everything that that would be a problem. I never had an officer that found it to be a problem. And the guys, well, overseas the guys just thought it was another thing like, you know, like your religion, your politics, whatever. 'Cause overseas is an entirely different ball of wax.

When I found out that I had enough points to go home, I wanted to stay a little longer, I wanted to extend it, but you know how anxious you are to get home. So I chose home, but—this is very strange—I really cried when I left Korea. I missed the Koreans. I missed my friends. I missed the service. I missed everything—not the war, but I missed that whole experience.

Not long after Ric got home, his wife died when a drunk driver smashed into her car. His young son survived the crash. Ric's parents took care of the boy for a couple of years, until Ric could pull his life back together and attend college on the GI Bill. At the time of the interview, fifty years after he left the service, he was retired and living in Washington, D.C.

THE LAVENDER SCARE

An Interview with William Winn

The delicate cadence of William Winn's speech and his crystal-clear articulation betray his well-to-do upbringing in Dallas, Texas, and his education at Southern Methodist University and Harvard Medical School. His beautiful home overlooks San Francisco Bay from high up on a hill, and we conducted the interview in his piano room. It seemed a far cry from his time in the service as a hospital corpsman during World War II and a naval doctor in the Korean War, but as William gazed out the window, the memories flooded back over him.

I was born in Beaumont, Texas, November 25, 1925. My father, when I was born, was a young engineer working for the Sun Petroleum Company in the Spindletop oil fields in East Texas. My mother was his high school sweetheart. Because they were high school sweethearts, they felt that I—being a black sheep type who went around and dated all and sundry—was somehow un-American. I'm quite sure that the only man that my mother ever knew in her whole life was my father, and the only girl he had ever known was my mother. They were devoted to each other in a way that I gather seldom occurs anymore.

You know, I have one brother and one sister, both younger than I. They both had the misfortune in my eyes of being divorced. I'm the only person in my whole extended family who is not divorced because I never legally got married —which is a kind of sad, sweet sadness kind of thing. I did have some very intense girlfriends, but finally at the end of a tumultuous exposure to heterosexuality, I found out some time after my thirtieth birthday, as I had suspected during my Korean War experience, that my ability to tolerate society was much more in the masculine vein. I had a very masculine upbringing, a very masculine adolescence, and I copulated with—I don't know if it would be fair to say hundreds, but—quite a number of females over the years, and then I discovered that intense affection for males was the most satisfactory to me.

I was raised in what is called Highland Park Methodist Church, which is *the* place to go to church in Dallas on the campus of Southern Methodist University. There is an almost inbred upper-middle class society in Dallas, full of independent oil people with, at that time, large cars and expensive lifestyles.

So in the summer of 1942, when I was sixteen, Highland Park Methodist Church sponsored a church camp. We were there for a whole week starting Sunday through the following Sunday, and you would have a church service with prayer meetings and singing and God knows what else. We went swimming, and had a totally outdoor life in a beautiful idealized setting. As it turned out, starting the very first night, I discovered that the other sixteen-year-old boy who slept next to me had somewhat more advanced concepts about sexual behavior than I had ever even dreamt of. The lights had hardly gone down. I felt his hand approaching me, and one thing led to another. I was so shocked and amazed, and I must admit it seemed all very pleasant.

I joined a navy training college program as a student with more or less straight A's at Highland Park High School. After January 1943, we went on active duty as students at Southern Methodist University. We had not yet even graduated from high school, but the navy made it possible for us to go to school one semester early. It was a national program. And colleges throughout the United States took this on. They enriched the country enormously by educating many hundreds of students who were primarily engineers or medical students in exchange for their commitment to the United States and its military service.

All the males in my family had been in the military in World War I. The military is very highly regarded in Texas. I never knew anyone or ever heard anybody who refused to be in the military. Conscientious objection was not part of our psyche—you couldn't be a good, straight American if you were against the war. Heavens to Betsy, you couldn't possibly do anything like that.

I was primarily in school for the first two-and-a-half to three years of World War II, and then, toward the end of the war, just before the Normandy invasion in 1944, I completed the navy college program. Then I was transferred to the u.s. Naval Hospital in Norman, Oklahoma. I had to wait until the following September before I could go to medical school, and that meant that December through August of 1945 I was on active military duty as a hospital corpsman at the naval hospital.

Then, of course, the end of the war came on in August of '45, and we had already received our orders to go to Boston, where we would enter medical school. Because I was a good student, I was admitted to Harvard Medical School. In Boston, I dated Wellesley girls, very high-flown society types, and occasionally nurses. I remember my first full-blown heterosexual experience was with a young nurse. I feel ashamed now because I really took advantage of that poor girl. She was so hot to trot, and one did not have to woo her.

But I also remember walking to Fenway Park, which is just about a thirty-minute walk from the church all the way up to Harvard Medical School. On these beautiful, romantic summer evenings, people, I learned later, could cruise along there—both gay and straights—particularly gay people. And that's where I had my first homosexual experience in my life—a real full-fledged one. There was a certain red light on Boyleston Avenue, as I recall, right as you cross into the park. You would have to wait there while the light changed, and one balmy summer evening, I was waiting there and this very attractive youngster, about my age, came up, and he muttered, "Do you have a light?" I said, "I beg your pardon, a light? No. I don't smoke." And he said, "Do you want a blowjob?" I said, "What's that again?" Apparently, my naïveté in asking what a blowjob was so freaked him that he immediately left and nothing happened. Well, I didn't know what a blowjob was myself, so I dropped a few remarks amongst my peers in the medical school. They thought it was terribly funny.

Some months later, someone made a similar proposal to me as I sat on a park bench. I was young, and I suppose not without my points. I would never sit for more than five minutes before someone would sit down along side and the conversation would start up and we'd become acquainted. I permitted that to happen four or five times, no more. I was very fearful of discovery or of admitting it to any of my peers. We were naive to the point of amusement.

At that time, the war had been over for three or four years, and I went to an internship at a big city hospital in Philadelphia, after I graduated from Harvard in the summer of '49. I was in Philadelphia for the better part of two years, and then the Korean War came along and I left Philadelphia in February of 1951. In Philadelphia I also had a few park experiences. I had never been in a gay bar, didn't know what they were. Unlike gay people today, I knew no other gay person. At the hospital, I went out with girls; I slept with girls. But alongside that, for several years, from 1949 all the way into the Korean War, I had an occasional two-or-three-times-a-year homosexual experience in which I would be more the active person because I was usually the one solicited.

Then the navy wanted us to go on active duty again, so I went on active duty and went into New York in February of 1951, and I stayed there until August of 1951 at the Office of Naval Officer Procurement. I was a young medical officer doing induction physicals for men joining the u.s. Navy. By coincidence, I was assigned to do the physicals on all the Ivy League schoolboys. And, my dear fellow, you have never seen a more gorgeous assembly. By this time, I'm a lieutenant. Certain opportunities would crop up, which I resolutely turned down, because "I'm not that way."

But I stumbled one day on a beautiful summer afternoon into a gay bar, which was right down near the southern end of Manhattan, down near the bohemian section. I was in my officer's whites, and I didn't even get to the bar, before someone bought me a beer. After that, another person bought me a beer, an extraordinarily handsome guy, blond hair, blue eyes, Teutonic complexion, and friendly. Well, I allowed myself to be cajoled and exchanged names and telephone numbers. Later on, I went to a movie with him, and did such active things as holding hands and simple kinds of affection. We had dinner together, and he invited me up to his apartment. He had a very nice little apartment somewhere in Manhattan. One thing led to another. I allowed myself to be seduced, and it was just delightful. This guy turned out to be a minor French movie star. Later, I walked by this place that showed French movies and there he was, big as life, a black and white poster of him as the male lead in Grade-B French movies. Anyway, I became rather impressed by him—you might even say enamored of him. He was the first person that I really slept with overnight. I really found a place in my heart for him.

After that, I was assigned to ship overseas as a medical officer and I went out to San Diego. San Diego, as anyone knows, is just teeming with sexual opportunities if you have your radar on. I didn't, but I eventually got it turned on. I remember going aboard ship, and I think this is highly significant, in the September of 1951. I walked right up in my civilian clothes, and I introduced myself, "I'm Lieutenant Winn." The officer of the deck was as cute as a bug's ear, and he said, "Well, I'm Lieutenant So-and-So." He practically did everything but throw his arms around me and kiss me, but he was very proper. I brought my baggage aboard ship. He showed me my room and all that, and he said, "Say, we're all going out for a beer later. Why don't you come join us?" I did, and it turned out that it was just the two of us. He had designs upon me. He was a very, very nice guy, as gay as pink ink.

He took me into San Diego that same evening and he dropped a few hairpins, which I didn't pick up because I was too stupid. He said, "Let's go to a bar. I know a really special beer bar, a navy bar." Well, it turned out that the navy bar was just off base maybe a mile, and we walked there, and there were these two or three hundred navy men, it being seven or eight o'clock on a summer evening, all in this big room. It was a piano bar, and they were singing and dancing with each other. It was a navy bar, as gay as it could be. They were in the United States Naval uniform, my dear. There was no overt groping. People were very polite. But if it wasn't a gay bar, it certainly fit the definition. And I felt slightly uncomfortable there.

Curiously enough, while I was a medical officer the following year, the Shore Patrol brought in a very handsome young man to me. The accusation was that he had been seen kissing the ear of another man at one of these navy bars by a Shore Patrol police officer, who had run him in for homosexual behavior. That was a real arrest. I couldn't believe it. Kissing the guy's ear? This is homosexual behavior? Now wait a minute, what am I missing? Well, it turned out that the Shore Patrol guy, who was just a plain, corn-fed guy from Iowa, thought that when somebody kisses another man's ear that's gay talk. I tried not to act shocked. Here I am, twenty-six years old at the time, I'm being asked to make a person acknowledge his sexuality, and to decide if it's OK to be in the navy if a guy kisses somebody's ear.

Remember, McCarthy is beginning to rattle the cages in Washington about gay life. I mean, this was a crisis all of the sudden. Here, I have to go deal with somebody's accusation of a gay man who's done nothing more than be caught kissing the ear of a friend in a bar. And that was really silly—I think most people would agree. So I tried to act calm and knowledgeable, and I said, "Well, sir, do you think that this did any harm? What do you think makes this homosexual behavior?" He said, "No, but guys don't go around kissing each other's ear." We went on like that for a few minutes, and I said, "Well, I really think that your desire to see a certain code of behavior is admirable, but I really don't find any problem here. What I will do is I will take it to my superior officers. Meanwhile, I don't think there's anything here that really is dangerous. The man has a perfect record, he's a good man, he's never done anything wrong."

Then I insisted on closing the door so I'd have some privacy, and I talked to this boy. I said, "I'm really very sympathetic; you can talk to me in complete confidence. As a doctor, I will not repeat anything you say. Do you think there was anything that you were doing that was overtly sexual?" He said, "No." It turned out that he was gay. He obviously was gay, but he wasn't doing anything. It was nothing that anyone would ever dream about prosecuting. I thought this has to be the very acme of absurdity that because he got ardent and put his arm around his friend, kissing his ear rather than the cheek that he's going to be run in. Well, this is the kind of absurdities that were commonplace then.

I went all the way through the Korean War for two full years aboard ship. I had four destroyers in my command, and I rotated around. Each ship had a complement of around 320 to 350 men, including the officers. My military experience was about as benign as it gets. When we were overseas, we went around Wonsan Harbor a great deal. Periodically our guns would shoot at the Chinese, but they would never shoot back at us. We had been lulled by our own gunnery officers into a kind of smug security.

Then, one afternoon, I was out on the deck, and they had been firing at the

Chinese awhile. All of the sudden, right out of the blue, comes this whole bunch of shells right at our ship! Everyone was alert to it, and they skedaddled out of there very quickly. But one of the shells landed in the water about twenty feet away, and I was standing right there. Yo-Ho! This is real stuff! So we got our ass out of there. And that's as close as I ever came to being shot. I'm very glad that's all that happened. One of our four ships, it was the *Laws*, had hit a mine—a Chinese mine—and it blew the bow or the tail end off. There was serious damage. It killed ten or twelve personnel aboard the ship, and it almost sank. Due to good management, they closed the bow, and they saved the ship. They had to take it backwards all the way around Wonsan Harbor, down around the Korean Peninsula, and back up into Japan, which is a total distance of several hundreds of miles of open sea. Can you imagine?

This is also the time when McCarthy's beginning to really accuse everybody of having gay relations and the whole thing played out in 1951 and 1952. Practically every morning for weeks, there would be some kind of written notice presented to the officers: "Seaman So-and-So says, 'The McCarthy people are on my tail. I can't stand it any more. I'm gay. I've got to leave.'" They would resign.

So each ship would lose in a period of six months overseas as many as twenty or thirty men, just because they said or someone said they were gay. It was a real police state. And these poor guys were put in the brig. They were accused of all kinds of behavior, which may or may not have been true. No one will ever know. Then they were given a dishonorable discharge. The officers of the ship were very disturbed because they said, "All our best men are being discharged. These are our best people, we're discharging them." They discharged a lot of good men who had good reputations, who were model seamen, and yet they were being discharged. Terrible.

I myself had been so proper and had never given the slightest hint about my biological inclinations. So I never felt as if I was under any kind of observation. But during the second year of my active duty in 1952, before I was discharged, I spent the summer down around San Diego, enjoying beach life. And in beach life, if you have your gay-dar turned on, you cannot ignore the gay overtones. You would have to be deaf, dumb, and blind. I ran into other people who had been doing nothing but standing on a gay beach and had been accused falsely by the police undercover agents. Of course, in order to keep from going to jail, most of them would cop a plea to some kind of secondary thing, and they would pay a $1,000 fine to San Diego. That kind of extortion was commonplace in the early '50s.

I remember one evening, I was walking along the upper hills just above the beach where those fancy restaurants were, and a very attractive young man came and sort of walked along beside me. This had never happened to me before, although I immediately got the drift of what he was after. He wanted an acquaintance. He assumed I was gay, and he was right, but not for the right reasons. I knew what I was doing by that time, but I was very careful. It was already 10:30 or 11:00 at night. I paid him no attention except to talk with him in a civilized way. We went and stood out on a promontory and we were about six feet apart.

Then, all of a sudden, somebody stepped out of the shadows. It was a policeman. "What are you guys doing? What are you doing here?" He was a real smart-ass and he said, "Let's see your identification." I said, "I'm Dr. Winn. I'm Lieutenant Winn." He grumbled: "Well, you shouldn't be out here walking along this way. You know this is not tourist behavior." I said, "Well, it's perfectly legal and I intend to continue." I didn't take any bullshit from him, and I demanded to know his name. "I want to see *your* identification, too. Here's mine. Now, I want to see your badge number and so on." Finally, I said, "Officer, do you want me to report this?" Well, he obviously didn't know what to do. I was on active duty at that time, and I knew that you just don't submit to that kind of nonsense. I was an officer. I was very respected.

William Winn was honorably discharged from the Navy in 1953. At the time of our interview, he was a retired physician, living in San Francisco, California.

WHORES AND LESBIANS

An Interview with Maurine McFerrin DeLeo

When Maurine McFerrin DeLeo tells a story, it pulses with energy and enthusiasm. Her voice is a unique blend of cadences from rural Louisiana, where she was raised, and the New England town where she has lived for many years. We laughed a lot in this interview, much more than could be notated here. But there were also tears. It has taken many years for Maurine to come to terms with her experiences as an air force nurse during the Korean War. Though she never saw combat or even service overseas, Maurine fought a very different kind of war from her gay male comrades.

I'm Maurine McFerrin DeLeo. I was born February 18, 1931, in Marthaville, Louisiana. Marthaville was a very, very small town—a lot of farmers and people who did logging or worked in a small sawmill. It was a very rural community. We had a big farm that we worked very hard on, and everything that we raised we ate. That's about all I knew. I kind of thought the world ended at the tree line when the sun went down, because there were no televisions, and we didn't have a telephone. But, growing up, I was really very happy. I had two brothers and two sisters. We'd go fishing and all kinds of things like that.

In high school, I played clarinet, and I had a female music teacher for the last couple of years. I had a very mad crush on this woman. I would get physically sick, and I had no idea what it was. I liked her very much. Gosh, I guess that was where it started for me. I didn't know what it was, but I knew whatever it was that people in my family and my church, they just wouldn't go for it—we'd say: "cotton to it." It's a southern expression.

I went to Central Christian College in McPherson, Kansas. I got a small scholarship there. It was a religious college, Free Methodist Church school. Before I went there, there was a woman minister that I had a crush on. But still I didn't know what it was. Being a southern person, I just said, "Look, God, this ain't right. Take this away from me." But he didn't, and he hasn't yet. [She laughs.]

In college, I was studying theology and nursing. When I was a young girl, I used to read *Ann Bertlett: Navy Nurse*, and I thought that was some life. I mean, I like excitement in my life, and to me that was exciting. Here is this young woman out on this boat being blown up and taking care of the sailors and everything. Also, that was a profession in those days that people went into. You got married, or you was a secretary, or you went into nursing. But I wanted to be a nurse, 'cause I wanted to help take care of people.

Well, I went to Central Christian College for two years, but me and my mother and father were farmers. We had plenty of food to eat, but we were poor. So I felt that financially I couldn't go on with college. I was living in Dallas, Texas, and one day I went to the recruiting office and I says, "I want to join the air force." The lady captain that was the recruiter looked at my school records, and she said, "Are you sure that's what you want to do?" And I said, "Yes." So I joined the air force. My mother had to sign for me because I wasn't twenty-one. Because my brother was in the navy, he didn't want her to sign, but I made her sign anyway.

Basic training for me was good. One of the instructors was from Michigan, and I know she was a lesbian. Gaydar, I guess—the way she acted, the way she walked. She was very friendly toward me, you know, never made any advances. She was a good drill sergeant. I didn't have a man, thank God.

I forget the platoon. I have a picture upstairs of all the people that I went through basic with. We were getting up at all hours. They would wake you up at two, three o'clock in the morning. Get dressed and stumble outside in your sleep for fire drill. We had to pull KP and march and go out in the field with gas masks and things like that just in case the atomic bomb was ever used. But we'd also go to classes, learn etiquette. We had to keep our place real, real clean. There was a special way you did your socks and your shirts, and I still do that to this day even though I have been out all this time. I remember you had to bounce a quarter or a dime on your bed, and one day, it didn't bounce! We had two flight chiefs, and one of them just walked over and took her hand and grabbed my bedding right in the middle, and I had to make it up again. But next time I made it, it was proper.

When I left Lackland Air Force Base, they sent me to Westover Air Force Base. It was November 1950. I can tell you what it's like in November in New England. Miserable. Rainy! Misty! It was the most miserable weather in the world! I said, "Oh my God, this is where I'm gonna be for the next four years!" But I learned to love New England.

I worked in medical supply. We didn't have computers or anything. Then, everything was done by hand. Any medications or anything that went out to the hospital, we had to keep a track of that. I also used to have to do psych duty, mostly for the service personnel wives. I despised psych duty. I hated it, and I usually had to take a couple of shots of whiskey before I went. It was very depressing. Plus, it was a military transport base and they would bring wounded personnel back from over in Germany, Korea, or wherever they were and then ship them to hospitals closer to their homes.

But also, we had to take body bags to the morgue. We did a lot of things. I had to work in family care, give shots to service personnel, or take their blood pressure and things. I was not a registered nurse, and I never wanted to be one really after that. I hate needles, but I enjoyed giving shots to the guys with syphilis. [She laughs.] Oh yeah, that was fun. [She laughs.] I worked mostly with guys, and they treated me like a sister. If anybody had done anything, they would've really. . . . They treated me like a sister.

I played on the base softball team. I was catcher, pitcher, and right field. I enjoyed that, and we used to play civilian teams up around Westover and Holy Oak, Diamond Match Company, Sickles, which was a wire company, and any teams up there. The people that played softball was the people that we hung out with, and we knew that they were lesbians, and a lot of these civilians teams, they were. Oh yeah, they were real dykes, you know. They would say that we cheated. "Well, we cheated. You know where to meet us." We'd have a few drinks and usually end up in a fight. [She laughs.] I'm serious! [More laughter.] But they were tough. Well, we were tough too.

We had a coach, and she was a son of a gun—no drinking, no this, and no that. And we had a day room where just women went, with a tv. You could buy

Maurine McFerrin DeLeo served as a nurse in the air force during the Korean War.
Photo courtesy of Maurine McFerrin DeLeo.

cigarettes and beer and stuff. When we were there, she'd come down and smell what we were drinkin'. Everybody knew she was coming. Then, she'd leave, and we'd have a few beers. No hard liquor on the base.

At this point, I asked Maurine if she ever experienced the lavender scare during the Cold War era.

Sure there was a lavender scare. Most enlisted personnel, they had no secrets. They didn't know anything, but there was still a scare. They'd send in this gorgeous blonde as a spy to seduce you, and to me that was a crock. Of course, the reds, with the Red Scare, God, you didn't know what Russia was going to do. But the lavender scare, it was a farce. I don't know of anybody ever told any secrets to spy agents. That's only in the movies! Well, I guess there was a few for money, but not for sex.

I had friends—as I said it was a military transport base—and I had friends, who had special quarters because they came in at all hours of the day and night. There was one particular girl that I was seeing, and there was a party. I was invited, but there was one of these flight attendants that did not like me. I could sense that she didn't like my association with this particular woman. Maybe she set me up, to get even with me for seeing this person.

At the end of the party, someone says to these two guys I didn't know, "Oh, you can drive Maurine home?" They did. They were officers, pilots. We went out in the boondocks before they took me home. We were going home, and all of a sudden we went to this place that was pitch dark. I was young; I didn't know too much about life. So, this guy in the front seat just jumps all over me, and then the guy in the back seat opened the front door, and did the same thing. I was afraid I could be killed. Because I know there was an incident of another person that was raped by a sailor on the base, and he beat her up pretty badly. I didn't want to get beat up. Now, I would fight tooth and toenail. They would have to kill me first. But when you're young, you're afraid. I'm not afraid anymore.

It just happened so quickly. I was dumbfounded. I didn't say a thing to anybody. I was so ashamed, and then, later on, I did tell my commanding officers. They said they would check into it. The major that was head of the 1600th Medical Group, he was a wonderful person. I used to babysit for his kids, go to his house for Thanksgiving and stuff. He was very understanding when he found out. But being raped was devastating, devastating, devastating. I used to have nightmares and see people with no faces, and wake up in a cold sweat. Also it was the anger and the rage taken out on people.

The officers, I don't know how they traced them down, because I didn't know their names. Naturally, they claimed that they didn't. Nothing happened to them as far as I know.

We paused the recorder and took a break from the formal interview. When we began again, I asked Maurine if the air force investigated women suspected of being lesbians.

Oh yeah, we used to outrun OSI [Office of Special Investigations] many times. We'd have a big laugh about it, you know, because we knew where they were. You knew where they were. But we were very careful, very careful. Now there were officers and I used to go to their house, but they lived off base. You would be discreet about it. You had to be discreet and some people just weren't.

We had these two girls that played softball. They would have too much to drink and they would get to feeling good. Then they'd get in an argument and get in a fight. Well, they'd come in with black eyes and everything. They did get kicked out.

But we used to go to places off base. I don't think we went to many gay bars. There was one in Springfield that we went to, but you couldn't go in too often, because you never knew who was going to be there. We used to go to the American Legion and a few other places. They played Polish music. Believe it or not, you could get a pitcher of beer for fifty cents. [She laughs.] Fifty cents! Cigarettes were twenty cents a pack! We used to do the polka and dance with the guys, but we never dated them.

We were a pretty tough group too. I remember after I got out, I went back to visit. We were at the American Legion club. Well my nickname was "Tex," because I enlisted from Texas. I was sittin' there, talking to the bartender, 'cause I hadn't seen him in a while, and these people came in with a motor-cycle gang, a couple of guys and women. This one woman sat down, and she figured we were in the service. She said, "Oh yeah, these women in the service are nothing but whores and lesbians." I said, "What did you say?" She said, "You're nothing but a bunch of whores!"

Well, I had a beer in my hand. I took the beer, set it on bar, and I think the beer jumped up about a foot. A big, fat fight broke out. [She laughs.] We weren't going to stand for that. Even the guys wouldn't stand for that, because they knew us. We were there all the time. They knew we were good people.

Maurine left the air force in 1953, near the end of the Korean conflict. After working for many years in the maintenance department at a Massachusetts hospital, she retired. In her retirement, she volunteered at a homeless veterans shelter. At the time of this interview, she was living in Malden, Massachusetts.

DARKNESS AND FLIGHT

An Interview with Jim Estep

Jim Estep attended the U.S. Naval Academy at the same time that Arizona senator John McCain did. Though they were not friends, McCain and Estep started down similar career paths. Both became naval aviators after graduating from Annapolis, and both would eventually fly missions from aircraft carriers off the coast of Southeast Asia. Then in 1963 and '64, their stories diverged dramatically. In the year before the Tonkin Gulf incident ratcheted up American involvement in Southeast Asia, the navy investigated Jim Estep and discovered that he was gay. Here he talks about the interrogation process—one endured by thousands of gay service personnel during the Cold War—that ultimately led to his dishonorable discharge from the navy at the very point when naval aviators were needed most.

I was born in Bluefield, West Virginia, on the twenty-second of May 1936. My father was a salesman for an ice cream company; my mother was a former teacher and housewife. We actually moved around quite a bit when I was young, and we ended up in a place called Beckley, West Virginia. That's where I really grew up. Beckley was a town of 25,000 people when I was growing up. It was the county seat, but it was small enough for lots of people to know one another very well.

I remember the day that Roosevelt died. I heard it on the car radio because I was playing out in the car, and I ran in to tell my mother. That's about really all I remember about World War II. I do remember my father crying a lot when his youngest brother was drafted and had to go overseas. There was a great deal of rationing. It was difficult to get tires or gasoline for your car. You had to have coupons for everything. There were frequent drives to pick up things like aluminum, so we would collect aluminum pots and pans, and brass, any scrap iron. Everyone had a victory garden. We had one too. We raised our own food and canned it. We had a bunch of chickens and ducks that we raised, for the eggs, mainly. We bartered among neighbors for other things. I remember those kind of things.

I went to the Naval Academy, because my teachers told me I was too stupid to go. My father did too. Come time in junior year to begin to think about college and choices for the senior year, and everybody was picking out the places they were going to go. I didn't know what I wanted to do at the time. I was not really a part of the popular crowd, pretty much of an isolated individual. My uncle had gone to the Naval Academy and resigned. There were about three or four other boys who had gone to the Naval Academy that had not made it through. So I decided on the academy, particularly since they were going to pay me to go there, and I didn't have any money to go to any college anyway. My father and mother didn't want me to go to college. They weren't going to give me any money. I applied and took the field of service test along with three of my classmates and got the highest score. Representative Robert C. Byrd called the house and said, "Do you want the appointment?" And I said, "Yes."

I didn't have any trouble with the discipline at the Naval Academy. I sort of took to it naturally without paying too much attention to it. There were some other kids that had some difficulty. At that time, the men who came in to the Naval Academy came from a very wide range of academic backgrounds, so we had people who were coming in who had already graduated from college who were twenty-one or twenty-two years old and we had people coming in as I was who were seventeen and from all across the country, so there was a terrific variety. We all were subjected to the same training, and we all went through it together.

The first summer cruise after my freshman year was on the USS *Northampton*. It was a control ship in the sense that it had a lot of modern radar and communications aboard. That was the first time that I have ever gotten seasick. It was terrible. I wanted to die. And that's pretty much all I remember about being on board ship. We stopped in Cuba, at Guantanamo Bay; in the navy it was called "Gitmo" Bay. We went to Europe, we stopped in London, we stopped in Barcelona, and from there I took a train to Madrid. It was an eye-opening experience for a boy who was about eighteen years old. Never been out of the hills of West Virginia and was now going around the world. It was as if I was standing there sort of slack jawed and wide eyed wondering if this was a real world. It was a very vivid experience for me.

In between sophomore and junior year we were located mostly here in the States and we went from naval base to naval base to experience different aspects of the navy. That was the summer that we did a lot of flying in airplanes and that was the summer that I decided that I wanted to be a pilot. How could I *not* want to fly? I mean it was just fantastic. It's not one of those things where you weigh the pros and cons and you decide based on all that. They got me in the plane, and I thought, "My God, this is what I love! I want to do this!" It didn't take any thinking about it.

After graduation, I spent some time with my family, and then I ended up in Pensacola for flight training. It was still pretty abusive, I mean I had a flight trainer who would throw things at me, beat me over the head when I made mistakes, so it wasn't very much different from the Naval Academy actually. I really didn't like it that much until I began to solo. I transferred into jet aircraft, and there was a time when I was doing very poorly. I had an anxiety reaction—nearly killed myself in a flight. I didn't have an accident, but it was a close call, and at that time I did something that was almost unheard of for a fighter pilot. I requested psychiatric evaluation and treatment.

I had begun to discover that I was gay. I had had some encounters when I was in high school but passed those off, and when I was at the Naval Academy I always wanted a best friend that I could buddy around with and didn't have one. I was pretty much the loner when I was in the flight training program. When I came home at Christmas—this was probably in '61 or something like that—I had an encounter with another guy and in my hometown, and that really scared me, so when I went back to the flight training situation I was to take a check ride with another pilot, an instructor who was known to be really, really tough. I was scared to death. I had an emergency in my airplane, and during my attempt to handle the little emergency, I was flying pretty erratically around the sky, and I almost flew into the ground. Of course, he was chasing me in another plane and wondering what the hell was going on. When I finally got the radio back and called in, we went back to land and he was more scared than I was. He got out of the plane shaking. I was pretty cool; it just didn't hit me that I almost killed myself. That was when I requested the psychiatric evaluation.

I never did admit that I was gay to the psychiatrist. I kept saying, "I'm going to get married, and Marianne and I are going to be engaged." That was part of what I really wanted, but it wasn't really true. He knew that, and he told me that frequently. He would listen and say, "Well, I understand what is going on." This was in Corpus Christi, and I would go out in town and have dinner before driving back to the base and I'd pick somebody up. I never thought that much about it. At the same time, I was hanging out with a group of gay guys who were in the training program, and I didn't know they were gay. I had no concept of this. None. But anyway, after the psychiatric treatment and counseling, it was a whole different ballgame. I recovered my self-confidence, and I knew what I was doing. Then, I really enjoyed flying. It was glorious.

On the way to Jacksonville to join my squadron, I stopped at Valdosta Air Force Base, and I stayed in the Bachelor Officers' Quarters. It was very much like the YMCA. You had your own room but communal showers, and so I walked out of my door and was walking down the hall with my towel over my shoulder and there was a guy that came out in front of me with his towel over his shoulder. I just sort of watched his ass jiggle, and I thought, "Wow, nobody but a homosexual would look at another guy's ass like this! Gee, I must be a homosexual." That was the first time that I could really verbalize that. I didn't even know what gay meant. So, when I got down to Jacksonville I wanted to do some exploration, and I also wanted to continue my psychotherapy so I made an appointment with the base psychiatrist, thinking that I would have the same supportive relationship with him that I had with my former therapist over in Corpus Christi and the first interview we introduced ourselves, and he said, "Well, what brings you into my office?" and I said, "Well, I think that I might be a homosexual." He said, "Don't say another word. Anything else you say I am required to report to a higher authority." I said, "Thank you very much for your time," and I left.

Then I decided that I had a choice. I could do private psychotherapy or I could be the best homosexual that I could ever be. I chose the latter. I knew when I did that it was going to cost me sooner or later. So it was a conscious choice; it wasn't something that sneaked up on me. I started reading. I found a book called *The Sixth Man* by Jess Stearn. So in this book he's telling me about beaches that you might go to, places in town like the central park of a town or places where homosexuals gathered, like bars. Eventually, I found a bar in Jacksonville, Florida, and everybody cruised around Central Park. I would put 45 miles on my car a night, driving around that park. In the bar, people left me alone and wouldn't talk to me. I was clean cut. I had a military haircut. I came in really crisply and well dressed. They thought I was a cop.

In my squadron, my two best friends knew I was gay. One was Hank Cramer, who was another pilot, and he was a farm boy from Kansas. We were very close. There was another pilot named Art Avor, who is dead now. Both of them are dead now. And there was a third officer who knew I was gay, the press officer, Joe Ziegler. I was a personnel officer in the squadron and the first-class petty officer I had working for me was gay and knew I was gay, and that was it, pretty much. I think several of the enlisted people knew I was gay. In fact, I know they did; they could not, not know.

It was "Don't Ask, Don't Tell" the way it was really suppose to work because people just didn't say anything about it. They really didn't. Nobody asked, and so I just kept quiet. There were times when I was on board ship that I met other midshipmen. There was one of the kids in the squadron that was very open to this. Occasionally we would hold hands with one another when he was getting me ready, buckling me in, and standing on the ladder before I was off on the catapult. But other than that, there was nothing that went on, on board, on ship—that I knew about anyway.

In the early 1960s, Jim's squadron became part of the first American actions in Southeast Asia. We now know that such missions were precursors to American involvement in the Vietnam War, but at the time they were merely part of the larger Cold War strategy to contain the spread of Communism. Jim's reconnaissance missions in Southeast Asia were highly circumscribed. Here, he talks about this and about the harrowing experience of flying night missions from the carrier.

We never flew over Vietnam. In fact, we were instructed—even if we had an emergency—we were not to land our airplanes on any Vietnamese territory. We were to crash at sea before that could happen. So we ran reconnaissance missions along the coast. Those reconnaissance missions were designed to locate and identify enemy radar more than anything else. They were not exactly the most exciting things in the world. You flew out on a certain heading for two hours or an hour and a half, and then you turned around, flew back in, and landed.

Taking off and landing on a carrier at night can be terrifying. The carrier has two decks. Underneath the flight deck, there's another deck that's fairly quiet. When you're doing night operations, there's no white lights anywhere. It's all red light, so that you maintain your night vision. If you're down on the lower deck, you come in, get strapped into your plane and wait for the call.

Then all the handlers will push you to an elevator. They push you onto the elevator backwards. You always hope that they don't push you too far, over the side. It happened to one of my colleagues; they pushed him off the side of the ship one night. He survived but there's always that problem. Your adrenalin level is very high. You're always looking around to see what's going on and keeping track of everything. You're on the radio constantly with the air boss to make sure that he knows where you are. The elevator lifts you up very rapidly to the flight deck.

The flight deck is incredibly noisy because you've got all of these jet engines going, and you've got propeller planes that are turning over. Everybody is moving around, and it's very precisely choreographed so everybody knows where everybody else is and where everybody else is going. There are no accidents up there. Eventually they will light your engine off, and you now have power to move around by yourself. You follow the directions of a man who is standing in front of your plane. He is carrying colored wands, one in each hand, and he directs you onto the catapult itself.

The catapult's about 165 feet long, and it's steam-driven—a big, long steam piston. On the top of the deck there's a hook on this piston. They hook a cable onto the catapult and then they hook the other end of the cable onto your airplane. They attach another cable to tie you down to the deck and in the middle of that cable there's a small fragile metal neck that is designed to break at a specific tensile strength. That will hold you in place until the catapult starts you down the catapult track. You pull your canopy down. Your control panel in front of you is well lit, so you can see all the instruments. You make a final check to make sure that the oil pressure is where it's supposed to be.

All of your navigation instruments and flight instruments are working, and then you watch on the outside for the catapult officer to give you the signal. You run your power up to 100 percent. You can feel the plane being pulled down, getting ready for that catapult shot. You put your head back against your headrest, and you salute the officer to let him know that you are ready. When he brings his arm down, that catapult accelerates you from zero to 125 miles per hour within 165 feet. It's absolutely black. I mean you cannot see anything outside the airplane, so all that you can see are your navigation instruments. You pull your nose up fifteen degrees above the horizon when you go off the bow of the ship. The airplane will sink down a little bit. There's only sixty feet there, and you're never sure exactly how close you are to the ocean. It's a tense time.

Now, if it's a moonlit night, it's beautiful; it's just incredible. If it's a stormy night or overcast and cloudy, it's absolutely black, and it's scary. That's the takeoff. Then, you go out and do your mission.

After the mission, you come back to the ship at 20,000 feet and you go into what's called a holding pattern. You stayed in the holding pattern until the air marshal called you down. Then you started your dive towards the surface. You're all on instruments mostly unless it was a beautiful, clear night. You come down to 600 feet and you're about six miles behind the ship. You're in constant contact with the Central Information Center (CIC) until they hand you off to the landing signal officer who stands on the stern of the ship. Then you drop down to a hundred feet and angle down to the carrier deck. You land on the carrier deck and your tail hook either catches a wire and you are stopped, or in some cases, it bounces across the wire and you go back out into the night to come around for another pass. Sometimes it was absolutely terrifying, and sometimes it was beautiful.

John McCain ended up flying the same kind of plane that I did. I knew John a little bit at the academy—knew him enough to say hello to him. I knew of some of his escapades. I'm not sure if he would remember who I was now any more than he would remember some of the other classmates. When we got involved in combat operations over South and North Vietnam, he was hit by a missile. I never came close to that. I was on my way out way before we started those kinds of air operations.

I had just come out to California when Air Group Sixteen moved from Jacksonville to Lemoore, California, and I was going down to Los Angeles pretty much every weekend to see people down there. I met a guy in Hollywood who took me to a bathhouse in Beverly Hills. He was sort of my contact down there. Then, he moved to Seattle. I had a friend who was the navigator on a B-52 who was stationed in Seattle. His name was Vern, and he was pretty wild. I wrote him a letter that said, "Dwayne is in your neighborhood. You might want to get in touch with him, and sort of introduce him around." Well, Vern left that letter out on his bed. That was a bad thing to do. But he was pretty careless. His roommate found the letter and read it. Vern was already under investigation by the air force, so when they found the return address from a Lieutenant Estep, they put me on the list.

Eventually, they came around to talk to me, and that's when I was arrested. This was in 1963, in the fall. The ship had been damaged, and it was in Yokohama to get repaired. So we were there for like six months. One morning, I got a call from the skipper in our squadron saying that he wanted to see me in his cabin. So I went up to his cabin. There were two guys standing there, and he said, "These guys are from the Office of Naval Intelligence, and they want to talk to you."

There was an interrogation room, which was just a normal room. They were at one end, and I was on a chair at the other end. They had a folder, and I know that they didn't have anything in that folder, but they played it as if they did. They would turn pages and they would ask questions. They asked me if I had experiences with any of the other officers or enlisted men. I said, "No." Apparently they had seen some of the stuff in my cabin. I was doing artwork then. I had done a picture of a nude statue, a Greek statue, and that was hanging on the wall in my cabin. They asked about that, and I said, "Well, it's just a piece of artwork that I did."

They had gone down to my cabin and rifled through everything that I had down there. Earlier, I had asked my roommate to throw everything overboard if I gave him a signal that something was wrong, but he was not on the ship. He was out on liberty at the time, and there was no way I could signal him. So they got a hold of my address book, and they threatened to contact everybody in my address book—at their place of work, if they had to—and ask them about me and talk to their employers.

I thought, "I don't want to be in an organization that treats me this way, and I don't want them plowing around in the lives of the people I know." I said,

"Look, I want out." They said, "Fine, you'll have to sign a confession." I said, "Fine, I'll sign the confession." They said, "You have to be specific." I said, "What does that mean?" They said, "Well, you have to say in your confession what you did." And so I said, "I had sex with an air force officer. I don't know who he was." I don't know what else I said on the confession, and then I had to sign it. My motivation was to get out. I just simply did not want to be in an organization that treated me that way. There was also the idea that everybody knew what was going on. All my squadron mates knew. I mean you can't keep a secret like that in the service. So even if I were exonerated, even if they said, "Well, we don't have anything on you now, but you had better be careful." I'd go back and everybody in the air group would know what was going on. I just did not want to go through that so I signed the confession and I was on my way out.

I felt very isolated. I can remember writing to some people, trying to explain —oh God, how did I put it?—I felt as if the tent ropes of my life had been loosened and my tent was flapping in the wind or some silly thing like that.

At the end of the interview, I asked Jim to look back on his time in the navy to talk about its legacy for his life, and he immediately returned to the topic of flight.

Well, flying is ultimate freedom. When you're in an airplane, you are free. You are free. It's the greatest feeling in the world.

Jim mounted legal challenges to his discharge twice, but they were unsuccessful. Ultimately, he earned a doctorate at the University of Arizona. At the time of this interview, he was working as a professional singer and a writer in Buffalo, New York. He was also challenging his dishonorable discharge for a third and what he hoped would be the final time.

VIETNAM

During the Vietnam War era, everybody wanted to be gay—at least, every man who was eligible for the draft but who did not want to serve in Southeast Asia. Since the Department of Defense continued to view homosexuality as a "moral defect," homosexuals were one of the few groups of able-bodied young men (aside from students, veterans, and reservists) who were theoretically ineligible for the draft during the war. Ironically, one of the few groups of young men who did *not* want the military to think that they were homosexuals were gay military personnel proudly serving their country.

American involvement in Vietnam began during the French Indochina War, when the u.s. government supported the French in a bid to regain control over their Southeast Asian colonies following World War II. In Vietnam, the French were fighting a force led by the communist leader, Ho Chi Minh, and Cold War foreign policy all but mandated that u.s. officials oppose communist expansion in the region. After the French left in defeat in 1954, the u.s. stepped in with aid and military advisers for anticommunist Vietnamese forces. Large-scale u.s. military involvement did not begin until 1964, in the wake of an incident involving u.s. and North Vietnamese ships in the Gulf of Tonkin. Between 1964 and the end of the draft in 1973, the Selective Service brought 1,875,304 men into the military.[1]

Throughout the late 1960s, antiwar groups and underground newspapers printed advice and guides on how to avoid the draft. Many offered tips on how to become a "hoaxosexual." When Pete Zavala was called up for the draft in Los Angeles, he decided that he had seen too many young men from his Mexican American neighborhood taken to Vietnam for a war that he did not support. So even though he was straight, he claimed to be gay. The sergeant said, "Do you like boys?" and Zavala replied, "Well, sir, I used to like girls, but now I like boys." "Good," the sergeant fired back, "because there'll be plenty where you're going."[2]

Draft boards and military psychiatrists heard claims of homosexuality quite a bit, so no one batted an eye during the psychiatric examination when Perry Watkins admitted that he was a gay man who had both oral and anal sex with other men. In fact, Watkins, who had studied ballet and tried out for the cheerleading squad, had been openly gay since junior high school. Here was a young man at peace with himself, despite the intense social pressure against such a proud gay identity in the mid-1960s. Inducted into the u.s. Army in 1968, Perry Watkins never tried to hide his sexual orientation. He even became something of a minor celebrity for his drag shows as "Simone" in enlisted men's clubs. After serving on various posts in the United States, Germany, and South Korea, Watkins was finally discharged from the army in 1981 based on his written acknowledgments of his sexuality in 1968 and in 1971, when he reenlisted. Ultimately, in 1990 the u.s. Appeals Court overturned Perry's discharge, since the Vietnam era veteran had never lied to the army about his being gay.[3]

Most of the gay men and lesbians who served during the Vietnam War era, including the interviewees in this chapter, were not as open as Perry Watkins. At the time, few would have identified as gay. They were simply Americans called to serve their country during a time of war. If they had read pamphlets and flyers printed by gay rights organizations at the time, they would have found very measured advice about sexuality and service. "If you wish to serve," the San Francisco–based Society for Individual Rights warned, "you may do so knowing that countless homosexuals have, but you must at the same time weigh the real danger that you may receive a less-than-honorable discharge that will create serious difficulties for you in obtaining employment."[4]

Despite the dangers, thousands of gay and lesbian service personnel did serve during the war. Combat veterans like Bob Yeargan did not have time to worry about such policies when they were in the field. They and their buddies were much more worried about survival. Bob's two tours of duty, first as a platoon leader and later as a company commander, reveal that combat leadership is not the exclusive purview of heterosexual officers. Like several other interviewees in the book, Bob chose to make a career of the army, though he never found peacetime duty as challenging or rewarding as the leadership and training assignments he tackled during the Vietnam War era.

Unlike Bob Yeargan, Ted Samora and Michael Job began to reckon with their sexuality when they were still in Vietnam. This was especially difficult for

Ted, whose job in military intelligence required that he enforce the ban on homosexual soldiers even though he was struggling with some of the same issues himself. As a grunt with a machine gun and later as a supply clerk, Michael did not have to worry about enforcing the ban, but he did have to spin yarns about girlfriends back home and sexual conquests on R&R to cover his emerging sexuality.

Back in the States, Judith Crosby was coming to a similar understanding about her sexuality at the same time that she began to sympathize with members of her generation who opposed the war in Vietnam. It became hard for her to separate her growing distaste for the war from her bitterness about the navy's investigation into her sexuality. Both experiences were fundamental in shaping her identity when the war and her enlistment ended.

It is impossible to understand the experiences and conflicting emotions of gay and lesbian veterans of the Vietnam War era without placing them in the context of the emerging antiwar and gay liberation movements that became so intertwined in the early 1970s. The rise of social movements and the counterculture during the 1960s inspired young people to question the political conservatism of the early Cold War years, long-standing puritanical views of sex, and traditional Victorian gender roles. Exciting for some, these societal shifts seemed dangerous to others. One older American (a mainstream Democrat from Chicago) famously worried, "We've lost our kids to the freaking fag revolution."[5]

Yet the same countercultural and movement groups that encouraged straight men to fight the draft by becoming "hoaxosexuals" remained quite intolerant of real gays and lesbians in their ranks. For instance, a young, idealistic Tom Hayden prohibited both "homosexuality and marijuana" in a community organizing project he ran in New Jersey in 1964. So even within organizations that were challenging conservative politics and social mores, gay activists in the 1960s faced homophobia and gay baiting. As the historian Ian Lekus writes in his study of gay activists in the antiwar movement, "Harassed for their long hair and their draft resistance, many activist men reclaimed their masculinity by bragging about their sexual prowess with women and by mocking their rivals as homosexuals."[6] If these attitudes created difficulties for gays and lesbians active in the antiwar movement, one can only imagine the alienation felt by gay troops returning from Vietnam to question both their roles in that conflict and their sexuality.

As different as the worlds of the antiwar activist and the combat veteran were in many respects, interesting parallels emerged in terms of sexuality. Lekus argues that an "intimacy of organizing" ultimately encouraged some straight movement men and women to move beyond homophobia.[7] On the front lines of the antiwar movement, they had forged bonds with gay and lesbian comrades that transcended traditional prejudices. The same could be said for some of the straight soldiers, sailors, airmen, and officers who served alongside the gay and lesbian veterans interviewed for this book. There were differences, of course. The counterculture had explicitly challenged traditional gender and sex roles, while people in the military rarely did (at least in the Vietnam era). But in both the antiwar movement and the wartime military, hard work and working together, plus courage and commitment, became more important than whether one was gay or straight.

Few activists at the time could have imagined such a parallel, as the war came to symbolize a whole host of attitudes that divided Americans on more than simply U.S. foreign policy. The gay liberation movement of the 1970s was clearly on the side of the cultural divide that opposed the war and, to some extent, those who fought in it. Gay liberation was not without its roots in the 1950s and early 60s, but the spark that ignited the movement was resistance to a 1969 police raid on the Stonewall Inn, a gay bar in New York City. Out of this resistance emerged the Gay Liberation Front (GLF), a militant organization that quickly joined other leftist groups in fighting for rights, advocating an egalitarian society, and opposing the war. Although there had been stirrings of a movement to lift the ban on homosexuals in the military during the mid-1960s, by the early 1970s, GLF was wholly opposed to the war, demanding that gay troops be given honorable discharges and that gays and lesbians refuse to fight.[8]

The relationship between GLF and the antiwar movement undoubtedly advanced the cause of gay liberation by tapping into a pool of experienced organizers and allies, but there was also a cost. Inherently distrustful of the military, gay liberation activists were reluctant (at best) to fight for the right of open and honorable military service. This only deepened the alienation felt by gays and lesbians who wanted to serve their country *and* find acceptance in their community. Too much can be made of this divide. Some gays and lesbians who served in the Vietnam era found acceptance and peace almost immediately after their wartime service. But for other gay and lesbian Vietnam Veterans—like many of their straight comrades—healing, peace, and acceptance would only come in time.

PLATOON LEADER

An Interview with Bob Yeargan

Bob Yeargan was a mild-mannered accountant, fresh out of college, when he was drafted at the beginning of the Vietnam War. Though he had hoped to avoid combat as part of the finance corps, he found that, to his surprise, he made a damn good field officer. Bob became an infantry platoon leader and later a company commander. This reluctant soldier had a twenty-year career in the military, retiring as a lieutenant colonel, whose last post was in the Pentagon.

I'm Bob Yeargan. I was born in Arkansas City in 1942, May 15. Arkansas City is down in the south-central part of Kansas. Both of my parents were schoolteachers. My mother taught predominantly English and music, and my dad was a biology teacher and then a school administrator. I basically grew up in a little place called Goodland, Kansas. Goodland's a very small town. My dad was superintendent of schools, so I had to behave myself. Everybody knew everybody's business.

Then, I went off to school at the University of Kansas in Lawrence. I wanted to go as far away from Goodland as I could get, and Lawrence is clear across the state. Actually, I had a good time there. I went to school from '60 to '65. Took me five years. Should've taken me four. I found I'd rather have fun than study. I majored in accounting, but I also found out where the beer was. I graduated in 1965.

The very first thing I did after I graduated was got married on graduation day. And then I worked for the general accounting office in Kansas City, Missouri. I worked there for about six months until I got my draft notice for Vietnam. When I got my draft notice I went down to see my friendly local recruiter, and I said, "I have a college degree; there must be something I can do better than be cannon fodder." And he said, "We got just the thing for you, boy. We'll send you to ocs (Officer Candidate School), and since you have your degree in accounting, you'll probably get a commission in the finance corps, and that'll take care of you. But before you get commissioned in the finance corps, you gotta go to infantry ocs, and before you do that you gotta go to basic training."

Basic training was pretty miserable. I didn't think South Carolina was supposed to be that cold. But it was cold and raining. I was a little bit intimidated, but I knew I had to get through that, in order to get to ocs and avoid having to go be an infantry punk. It was stressful. I was not in horrible shape when I went, but I had never been a jock.

ocs was much more intense. The one thing I can remember is flying over from South Carolina to Fort Benning, Georgia. I was totally unprepared for it. It is physically very demanding, and absolutely, totally, more dehumanizing than basic training ever thought about being. You do things because you're told to do them, and you learn that very quickly. If you do things that are at the edge of what you're "allowed to do," you can get into all kinds of trouble. One evening, I'll never forget. The whole platoon snuck out and ordered pizza. We had picked up our pizza, and we were running back with it. When we got back, all the tactical officers were there waiting for us. They threw us all in the shower and we had our pizza in the shower—thirty of us, in one shower, eating pizza. People did push-ups for physical activity, until they could do no more, until you literally fell exhausted. I saw lots of guys cry, because you just couldn't do any more.

I went directly from there to a basic training company at Fort Gordon, Georgia. I started as a lieutenant TAC [Tactical Air Command] officer or lieutenant training officer there. That was my first assignment. As a training officer, you don't do a lot of hazing because all of that is basically taken care of by the drill sergeants. You're mostly there to supervise. In fact, one of the functions that you have as a training officer is to make sure that nobody goes too far.

My next assignment was to Vietnam. By this time, I already knew what the sequence was. You take a basic training unit for anywhere from four to six months and you go to Vietnam, as an infantry platoon leader. That's just the way infantry officers went. So I was prepared for it. When I first arrived in Vietnam, there were no vacancies for infantry lieutenants in the field. So I went and joined an infantry battalion, and I became a support platoon leader. Now a support platoon leader is responsible for getting all the beans and the bullets and the fuel from a base camp to the troops in the field. I did that for about five or six months. Then, there comes a point in time in which they *do* run short of lieutenants. So you get tapped. They say, "OK, you're going to go to the field."

I went out as an infantry platoon leader for four and a half months. One of my first days as an infantry platoon leader, I did something really stupid; I stopped in the middle of a field to make what's called a situation report. As soon as I stopped, a young spec-4, enlisted person, came up to me and said, "Sir, get the hell out of the middle of the field. Your sit-rep's not that important. You can call it in fifteen minutes late, but don't stop in the middle of the field." I paid a lot of attention to him. I got the hell out of the middle of the field. The first thing you need to learn as a lieutenant is you are not God; you listen to the guys who've been out there and survived. This guy was young, he was a good

Bob Yeargan served as a combat platoon leader and company commander during two tours of duty in Vietnam. Photo courtesy of Bob Yeargan.

soldier, and he wasn't meaning to be disrespectful. He just wanted his ass covered too. So we got out of there. I think of all the things I did as an infantry platoon leader the smartest thing I did was listen to kids who were more seasoned than I was. It didn't take very long then before they figured out that I was listening, but that I could also lead. So we had a good time.

My most traumatic experience as a platoon leader there involved friendly fire. I hated the battalion commander at the time, and I worshipped my company commander. He was very good. You always felt he was looking out after everybody in the company. We went up to work on a position in which we knew there were North Vietnamese that were dug in, I mean, they were *very* dug in. We set up a perimeter, put the company on the hill across from them, and then tried to bomb them out. We had a 500-pound bomb drop short. We had called into the battalion commander to say that the flight plan that they had was wrong. They were flying directly over us. A 500-pound bomb dropped short, killed four of my kids. Knocked everybody who was anywhere close flat on the ground—lots of ringing in the ears for a long time. So that was probably my most traumatic experience, getting four of my kids lost because of a stupid error.

At the time, things happened very quickly, and you don't—it doesn't get to ya. When we got back to the rear, everybody got together, and we all hugged, and we cried. That was two weeks later. When you're still out in close proximity to the enemy, you never let up. Not until you get that chance to get back where you are in a slightly more secure area do you let up.

After talking about the friendly fire incident, I asked Bob to talk about winning the Bronze Star. He demurred and said that it was something everybody in the unit earned because they got out of a bad situation without losing too many people. When I asked him how they got out, he laughed and said, "We retreated!"

Relations with Vietnamese civilians were not good. Once you're out in the field, and you start working around populated areas, you're going to lose kids to mines. And I lost kids to mines. I didn't have anybody killed that way, but just like I see in Iraq right now, you send home an awful lot of kids who are going to make it home, but they're maimed. When you are in an area, about the second or third time you have somebody hit a mine, you start to notice if the civilians in the area don't hit them. That tells you that most of those civilians know where they are. Not a happy situation. Ever. So I would say that I know of no cases in which American troops were warm and fuzzy with civilians.

There's a few of them that supposedly are allies, that you're trusting, and that are working with you. But in the field with the people who are living in the villages, it's like you never know where the front line is. I never treated any-body in the field as a friend. Ever. I had the assumption that all civilians were hostile.

After working in the field for nearly five months, Bob spent the last two months of his first tour at division headquarters. Then he returned to the United States, and eventually decided to make the army a career. He ran a basic training company for nine months, but had an unexplained seizure. After a short while in the hospital, the doctors released him.

Three months after I got out of the hospital I went back to Vietnam. I could've avoided that because I could've stayed on a medical deferment, but I chose not to. I wanted to go back to where the combat was. My wife knew I was going. She could tell. She wasn't very happy. My father thought I was crazy. But at that point in time I had made up my mind. I had decided that I was going to stay in the army. People said, "You're crazy. You're going back to Vietnam and you're going to stay in the army?" And I said, "Yes." This was late in '69, and I went back to Vietnam in '70.

I went back, and I was the operations officer for receiving new troops into the division. It's sort of an in-processing center that they go through for about two weeks. The whole motivation of an in-processing station like that is to get the new troops ready and to help them survive. I went through every piece of the program of instruction that we had, and talked with instructors and said, "How do we make it more realistic? How do we help them get better pre-pared?" We rewrote a lot of instruction. The trainees then got to actually see Vietnamese sappers crawl through and breach wire. Pretty impressive. They crawled through three levels of concertina and never got scratched. We put that kind of training in. We tried to give them a little indoctrination of the fact that there were some good Vietnamese. That's neither here nor there, in my opinion. But it was trying to get them conditioned, and ready. After I did six months as a training officer, I went to the field. I took over an infantry com-pany for my last six months, and I stayed in the field until three days before I came home.

When I was company commander, we were working in what we called company-sized operations. That's a large group—eighty, ninety, 100 people. Every once in a while one of those groups would get hit, and we'd lose a bunch of people. So then we had a guy who came in as a battalion commander, he says, "We're going to change how we operate, and you're going to start operat-ing in eight- and ten-man groups." The troops *hated* it, because they were *afraid*. They thought there was the security of being at least in a platoon-sized group of thirty or forty. But we started breaking them up into groups of ten and twelve. And we started to really control the area because we could saturate it. We knew where everybody was, and the bad guys quit moving because we were everywhere. We had every piece of terrain. We stopped getting people killed because they were out in small groups, and they moved silently. In that last five months, we got our troops to be as good a Vietnamese as the Vietnamese were. I never had a casualty in that five months.

We were as smart or smarter than they were. You talk about lots of groups spread out, but at the one point in time when I needed to call forty-five kids together, I got them together in less than thirty minutes. We conducted a hasty ambush on fifteen guys taking a bath in the river. As far as I know, not one of those fifteen guys walked out of the river.

At that point, I asked Bob if he killed anyone while he was in Vietnam.

You betcha! I hope I did. In that kind of a situation, you just draw a bead down and you're going to knock off all those people who are down there, because they're all bad guys, and they were absolutely identifiable as bad guys. I killed a North Vietnamese nurse. I felt very badly about it. But she was walking at night, and we popped a claymore and blew her away. I would do the same thing again. Because she was a female, that probably caused a lot of angst with the troops. My comment to them was "Nice ladies don't take walks in the woods." I think they got over it. It was just that we hit her, and my medic took a look at her that night. He said, "She'll be fine." She obviously had more severe wounds than we thought, and she died. So she died in our perimeter that night. We could have evacuated her. Had I had any indication that she was as serious as she was, I would've evacked her. I think the fact that she died in our care probably caused a little bit of angst.

When Bob finished his second tour of duty in Vietnam, he came back to the United States and attended the Armor Officer Advance Course in Fort Knox, Kentucky. Later, Bob worked as an ROTC [Reserve Officers' Training Corps] instructor at the University of Wisconsin–Milwaukee and then returned to Fort Benning, Georgia, where he helped draft a new combat training program for noncommissioned officers. This was one of the proudest accomplishments of his career. He was transferred to the U.S. Army Headquarters in Europe, and then he returned to the United States to work in the Pentagon as a lieutenant colonel. Administration, however, could not compare to training, combat, and troop command. Bob ultimately grew tired of being what he called "a worthless staff weenie."

I came back from Europe in 1984 to be part of the Deputy Chief of Staff for Resources Management in the Operations Division Headquarters of the army. Basically, I just jumped into a much greater size organization with a huge budget and all the politics of Congress. As far as I'm concerned, it's a whole bunch of people grinding their wheels and gnashing their teeth over nothing. There are people who spend hours and hours and hours in the Pentagon, simply for face time, because the boss is there. Well, they brought the wrong guy back to do that. When I came back to the Pentagon, I had a year and a half left, and I said, "You tell me what you want done, and it gets done." But I didn't play the game, lots of folks did, and that's just stupid. The Pentagon was not very rewarding.

When I was in Washington, I went to the Vietnam War Memorial, and, well, I cried a lot. Out of my ocs class of some fifty odd guys in my platoon, I know that at least forty-two of them are dead. And I know that of the five tac officers in my company, four of them are dead. So the first time I went to the Wall, it was very hard. I didn't go very often. I really only went about three times to spend any length of time there. I would take visitors when we had them, and mostly I would just sort of stroll along behind them. I think it's a wonderful monument, and I can't think of anything better that they could've done, but it's really, really overpowering when you know how many people up there are dead that you know.

Bob's marriage had always been a platonic partnership, and in the mid-1980s he began to realize that he had feelings for men. After he left the military, he and his wife divorced but remained friends. Finally, I asked Bob about the role of sexuality in the military.

Sexuality per se in the military doesn't have any place. It doesn't have any place getting women pregnant in the military by other military people, and it doesn't have any place with a man having sex with another man within the military context. The basic issue is fraternization. If you are not being disruptive in the unit, then who gives a shit? Now if you are being disruptive within the unit—and I don't care whether that's with another woman or another man—you need to get your sexuality under control. That means that the company commander doesn't screw the first sergeant, because that's not appropriate, and it wouldn't be appropriate within the military structure, ever. You leave your sexual preferences somewhere besides the unit that you're with, and it doesn't make any difference, whether it's gay, straight, or whatever.

When I walked out of the door of the military, I hung up my green suit. I still have it with all of its ribbons and rank on it in a back closet, but I never once turned back and looked at it again. My only remaining affiliation with the military is the fact that I occasionally go to them for health care, but I prefer to pay for it myself. I seldom go onto a military post. Maybe I'm a little bit bitter about the fact I didn't go where I wanted. Maybe it's because I'm gay. I don't know. When I got done at the end of twenty years, I said, "I am done."

At the time of our interview, Bob Yeargan was retired, living in Austin, Texas, with his partner.

HOSPITALS AND THE HOME FRONT

An Interview with Judith Crosby

Judith Crosby has a rebellious, anti-authoritarian attitude that bears the distinct imprint of the 1960s counterculture in which she came of age. Befitting the era, there's something of a surreal soundtrack to this interview. During Judith's youth, the regimented rhythms of John Philip Sousa marched in a strange counterpoint to the hip-swiveling rock and roll of Elvis Presley. If many of the men of this era were caught somewhere between Jimi Hendrix and GI Joe, Judith's story lies somewhere between the narratives of Janis Joplin and GI Jane.

I'm Judith Crosby, and I was born in Pensacola, Florida on September 27, 1945. My father was in the army, and my mother was a housewife. My dad's service in the army probably inspired me. He was a musician, so he played in the army band. I used to go watch him play in parades, and I knew all the John Philip Sousa marches, so I saw the inspirational side of the military through him.

We lived in Florida, Georgia, Tennessee, and Germany. We bought a house in Georgia, so I went to junior high, high school, and nursing school there. But Germany had a profound effect on me. We were there for two years in 1957 and '58. We were there when Elvis came over. I went to school with Elvis's wife, Priscilla. We had friends from all cultures and races and then we came back to the South in '58 and everything was segregated, which was real strange to me because I had had black friends and Hispanic friends and Asian friends and I really liked that. It made a real difference in my openness to people and cultures.

After we went back to Georgia, I left the Methodist Church because of the civil rights movement. The church I was going to, my parents kind of made me go, and I felt like they were a bunch of white racists. One Sunday, the preacher got up and said, "We gotta have a meeting to decide what we are going to do if the black people try to come in here to go to church." I got mad. I was like eighteen or nineteen, and I said, "Well, I am never coming to this church again." And I didn't, until my mother died, and I went to her funeral there.

I went to the University Hospital School of Nursing at Augusta College. I didn't want to be a nurse; I wanted to be a journalist. But I won a scholarship that paid for everything, and my parents said they couldn't afford to send me to college. Augusta College was pretty conservative, but then I got into the party scene and majored in partying. I lived in the dorms. All the fraternity guys would come into town on the weekends and call me, and I would fix them up with dates with girls in the dorms. It was great! I loved it.

After I graduated, I worked as a nurse in Augusta at St. Joseph's Hospital. The war was going on in Vietnam, and recruiters had started coming around to our nursing school trying to recruit nurses to go into the military. The navy recruiter had been by our dorm and had taken me out to dinner a few times, talking to me about the navy. The war started escalating, and we kept hearing more on the radio that the military needed nurses. I was getting pretty bored with my hometown, and my mother and sister were nagging me a lot about my partying. I decided to join the navy so I could be free to party as much as I wanted to and see the world.

My parents were pretty thrilled. My father was an enlisted man in the army, and I went in as an officer. There wasn't a big antiwar movement in Augusta. But when I joined I knew a lot of military men, young officers and officer candidates. I was dating an army lieutenant who had been to Vietnam. He was very upset, and he started telling me about Vietnam and how terrible it was, and he was like a career military officer, a West Point graduate or VMI [Virginia Military Institute] alum. And he's telling me, "Hey, this war is stupid, it's terrible over there. Don't go in."

I went to Women's Officer School. I did a month in Newport, Rhode Island, in July of 1969. Basically I was out at the Junior Officer's Club every night drinking, except for one night when I had to do the barracks watch or something. They just sort of indoctrinated us and got us the uniforms. I mean we didn't have to march or stand at attention very much or things like that. We just learned about navy customs and traditions—who to salute, what forks to use at the dinner parties, and things like that. [She laughs.]

My first assignment was to St. Albans, Long Island, New York. They put me on the neurosurgery ward. It was a big, open ward with young guys that were either paralyzed from the neck down or the waist down or they had shrapnel in the brain and they were vegetables, so to speak. They were all combat vets. All the guys we were taking care of were all just back from Vietnam. I had the ones that were in really bad shape.

I started really thinking about the war and how stupid it was and how all these young guys were coming back just blown away. They were all angry, and they started telling me how stupid the war was. They didn't want to go over there anyway. They got drafted, and then they got severely injured and also came back with jungle rot and malaria and all kinds of things like that. They were pretty bitter and physically messed up. I started listening to what they were saying and agreed with them that it was a stupid war.

There was a big morale problem. There were the reservists like me and then there were the hardcore military people—what we call the "lifers." A lot of people had joined the navy to keep from getting drafted. They were just doing their time in the navy rather than being in the army and going to Vietnam, so we were all pretty rebellious. There were a lot of mistakes being made over there, and it could have been ended a lot sooner than it was, plus I thought the draft was pretty ridiculous. People got drafted that were basically pacifists that weren't interested in going over there and killing people. I just don't think the draft works. I think if you are going to draft people, then let those people who don't want to fight serve their time in other areas besides a combat zone. But most people just didn't want to go into the military, and they got drafted and they were pretty angry.

We had protesters that would hang outside the gate—the mail gate to the hospital carrying protest signs and stuff. I started reading their signs, and one day it dawned on me that they were right and we were wrong. So I started doing more rebellious things, like I would drive into the front gate and instead of saluting the marines at the gate, I would give them a peace sign. They didn't like that.

Judith didn't remember facing much sexism, because she worked in a predominantly women's field. But she did run into trouble because of her emerging sexuality.

Well, I think I started questioning my sexuality when I was in nursing school, in psychology class. Back then being homosexual was considered deviant behavior. It was written up in the textbooks as an illness or deviancy or something, but, anyway, it was abnormal. I had already started thinking that I probably was gay, but then when I got in psychology class and started reading about it in the books, I realized it was abnormal. My biggest goal in life at that time was just to be cool. That's all I cared about. I wanted to be a party person; I wanted to be cool. I didn't want to be deviant or an abnormal person, a crazy person or a sick person. So I tried to just squelch any feelings I had for women.

They told us in women officers school that they did not tolerate homosexuality and you would be put out on a dishonorable discharge if you were caught doing any homosexual acts. I pretty much said, "That's not me. I don't have to worry about that one." I'm too busy partying and having a good time and having sex with men. But there was an instructor at women officers school that took a liking to me, and I did spend some time with her even after I got out of the school. I went back to Newport, Rhode Island, for a few weekends to stay with her and she started coming on to me and that really frightened me so I stopped going to see her.

I started hanging out with a bunch of enlisted people that I worked with in the hospital. We all started partying together. They were having softball games right outside their barracks, so I started going over there in the afternoons and evenings and playing softball with them. This particular group, they were the best workers, the smartest, the most attractive, so I started hanging with them. There was a guy in the group named Rick, who was a corpsman, and I kinda liked him. I thought he was cute, and one night we were all drunk, and my friend Edie said to me, "Don't get a crush on Rick because he's gay." I just looked at her, and I had never heard that term before, so I said, "Well, I am pretty happy myself." [She laughs.] She said, "No, you don't get it. He's a homosexual. He likes boys." So, I said, "Really?" I couldn't believe it. I thought she was just telling me some gossip, but then she said, "Yeah, he's not the only one. A lot of us are."

I used to get called into the chief nurse's office at least once a week about my conduct unbecoming an officer. They didn't want me hanging out with enlisted people, but I used to go to the enlisted club rather than the officer's club because I worked on the wards with corpsmen who were all enlisted, so I would hang out with them. We could go to their club and drink beer and listen to Janis Joplin songs where at the officer's club you had to get all dressed up and be nice to the senior officers and their wives. It just wasn't for me. I mean my dad was an enlisted person, and I had always been around enlisted people, so I started getting in a lot of trouble for fraternizing with enlisted people.

In my last week or two at St. Albans, I had gotten orders to go to Spain, and I was up on my ward working one day, and the supervisor came and said, "They need to talk to you downstairs." They took me down to the NIS [Naval Investigative Service] office, and then they started interrogating me. They said, "We have reason to believe that you have been doing homosexual acts and hanging out with a group of homosexuals." They started asking me all these questions and asking me about people I knew, and what I had seen. I lived in a house with three other navy nurses out at Atlantic Beach on Long Island, and we used to have a lot of weekend parties. We'd start partying Friday afternoon

*Judith Crosby survived an interrogation about her sexuality by the
Naval Investigative Service while she was a navy nurse during the Vietnam War.
Photo courtesy of Judith Crosby.*

and go until Monday morning. NIS had names of people that were there and something about how they said that I got drunk and put my hands in some-body's pants, another female. It made me think that there were people that I was working with that were spies.

I hadn't even come out to myself yet. I had never even been to a gay bar at that point. I had never even kissed another female. But I was just starting to find out that some of the people I was hanging out with were gay. I had just reached a point in my mind of thinking, "You know, maybe I am gay and maybe it's not so bad after all." Because that was the sharpest group at the hospital, the group that I hung out with, and like I said, they were the best workers, the smartest, the most attractive, the best party people, and it was the gay group.

So NIS just kept on and on and on. I remember I was thirsty, and they didn't give me anything to drink. They had me under these lights and I was pretty freaked out, I mean, I was really upset about it. They said, "You seem nervous. If you weren't guilty, you wouldn't be nervous." I said, "Well, anybody being accused of something that could lead to being put out of the military on a dishonorable discharge would be nervous." I could see myself losing all my benefits, and I had been there two years taking care of the guys coming back from the war. I would have lost all of that, and plus my family would have been horrified. They wanted me to sign a confession, and I kept saying, "I can't sign a confession. I am not guilty. I haven't done anything except party with these people." Anyway I wouldn't sign their confession. I held out and didn't sign it.

Other people did. The guy, Rick, that I had a crush on, had been a corpsman in Vietnam, and he was about to get out of the service. He got called in, and he just flat out told them yes he was gay, so they gave him a dishonorable dis-charge. He lost all his benefits and everything. I think he had been in the navy three years and he was just about to get discharged.

I was very traumatized after that and very paranoid. It really changed me a lot. I no longer went out and partied. I would stay at home and drink. I was just a loner and very isolated then. I just decided to go to Spain, do my time, and get out, and that's pretty much what I did. I was stationed in Rota in 1971. That's the name of the naval base down in southern Spain. I did make a few friends, mostly with some of the other nurses that I worked with and a couple of the dental techs that I found out later were gay. I did a little bit of traveling, but I could have done a lot more. I was really angry at the military and very paranoid. I felt like they were watching me.

I had a hard time relating to other people who hadn't had the military experience when I got out in 1973, because a lot of people that I had gone to college with didn't have a good understanding about Vietnam, and then that whole interrogation thing changed me. So I had a hard time relating to people that I had once been friends with and that I had known well. Mostly, I found that a lot of people were unaffected by the war, and they didn't really understand. I was real angry. I was angry about the war, about getting interrogated when I hadn't done anything, but I was really angry about the war. And I was shocked that more people weren't involved in protesting the war or they just didn't seem to care one way or the other.

I went back to Augusta for a couple years, and then I went to Atlanta. My parents said I had changed a lot. I was very depressed, angry. Now, my father was a career military person, very pro-military. In fact, he still flies the flag for every national holiday, that kind of thing. I was very angry, antiwar, and probably appeared unpatriotic to them.

After Judith left the military, she finally felt free to explore her sexuality. She talked about that at the end of the interview and also about her views of "Don't Ask, Don't Tell."

After I got home, I said, "Well, if they are going to accuse me of it, I need to find out whether I am and what I want to do about it." In Augusta, I started working at a local mental health facility, and I developed a close relationship with a mental health tech, a female that I worked with, and one day there was a *Cosmopolitan* article about bisexuality. We were sitting having lunch, and I said, "Oh, by the way did you read that *Cosmo* article about bisexuality?" And she said, "No, it sounds interesting. Can I come over to your house tonight and read it?" [She laughs.] So that's how it started.

"Don't Ask, Don't Tell" is ridiculous. We should be more like some of the countries, like Holland, that allow gays to serve in the military. I think there should be more gays in the military. I don't see anything wrong with it. I think it's better to have gay people in the military rather than taking married couples and parents away from young children and making them go serve on a ship and stuff like that. So I don't see anything wrong with having gays in the military. I am working with somebody now who just got out of the navy. She was a lifer, and she is very openly gay. But she said as long as she did her job, and didn't get in any trouble and obeyed all the rules and kept her shoes shined, that they didn't give her a hard time about the fact that she lived with a female off base.

I think probably if they don't like you, if you're a little bit rebellious or smart [laughs], and ask questions, then, if you are gay, they will probably go after you. I am a free thinker, and I don't like a lot of rigid rules and regulations. I like to be more creative, and I like to be able to ask questions. I don't like authoritarian systems. There have been moments when I thought, "Oh, I think I am going to sign up and go help out." But that passes pretty quickly.

At the time of this interview, Judith Crosby was a licensed nurse, working as a disability claims examiner for the state of Florida and living in Jacksonville.

HEALING

An Interview with Ted Samora

Tedosio Louis Samora was born during World War II in California's Central Valley. As he explains, there were few role models in rural California of the 1950s for a young Mexican American boy with questions about his sexuality. But there was no shortage of community and family support. Whether working at his mom's restaurant or palling around with his three brothers, Ted was rarely at a loss for companionship. In many ways, Ted experienced an "all-American" childhood, attending schools named after early presidents like Washington and Jefferson. He volunteered for military service out of a sense of patriotic duty. Eventually, all four of the Samora boys would serve in Vietnam.

I was born in Madera, California, in 1943. My dad was a volcanizer. He worked with tires. And my mom owned a restaurant—Mexican food. It was called the Mexican Kitchen. After I graduated from high school, I volunteered for the service. My dad and my uncles were in World War II, and we always thought that it was our obligation—a tradition, I guess. So I was the first of my father's sons that joined. At first, I tried to join the Marine Corps, but they told me I couldn't because I had a cyst on my lung. I was kind of disappointed. They removed it, and then two years after that I joined the army. They took me during the Vietnam conflict. I guess they were taking anybody.

My dad and mom were happy and proud that my brothers and I joined the service. Since my dad served, they were proud that we served. Plus, they wanted us to do something to stay out of trouble. Of course, after the other three sons went, I'm pretty sure it took a toll on them. When I joined, it was pretty early, and there were no bad things said about the war. My friends and family were just concerned. They would tell me, "Ted, you know if you join, you're going to Vietnam." And I'd say, "Oh, no. I'm going to go into administration. I'll work in an office and all that." But that wasn't the case.

Basic training was hard, but I enjoyed it. I liked being with all the other soldiers at Fort Ord. And I liked my lieutenant. They were very friendly to me. There was one instance in basic training where we were running towards the rifle range, and I couldn't handle it. So I dropped out and got into the truck.

When we got to the rifle range, I jumped off of the truck. There were about four of us. The lieutenant—I think it was Lieutenant Day—he kind of singled me out, and says, "I want you to see this 'girl' in the platoon. He had to get into the truck." He called me a sissy, and I felt kind of bad. We were going to ride back on the truck, but I didn't. I ran. I did it to prove that I could. That was one of the things in basic training that I remembered. I was very happy when I graduated. My mom and dad came, so it was kind of nice.

My first assignment when I got out of basic training was to join this MI battalion in Fort Bragg, North Carolina. I didn't know what "MI" stood for. I thought it was a missile battalion or something like that, but when I got there, I found out it was military intelligence. They were supposed to send us to MI school. But we didn't ever see a school. We did see a lot of jungle training. They'd take us out into the woods and teach us how to survive.

Then I had a feeling that I might be going to Vietnam. The orders came down that we were going, and it kind of bothered me. I never expected it. Because at that time we were hearing about it—you know, bombing and people getting killed—and I think I called my mom. I *did* call her. "I really don't want to go, but I guess I have to." As they say, "You're in the army now." That was it. I didn't want to, but I went. And that was it.

The first thing that hit me in Vietnam was the smell. It was wet, dirty. It didn't feel like the United States. And it was dark when we landed, and then we saw all of these Vietnamese. Basically, we were waiting for a truck to take us to our compound. Mostly what really stood out was the smell. There was some particular smell about it.

Our base was outside of Saigon. It was a small military intelligence compound. We had, I think, two battalions. They had the "spooks" and then, of course, they had MI, our group. I think the "spooks" were the ones that went out to the jungle. They would gather the intelligence. We remained back. They took us to Tan Son Nhut Air Base, and that's where our Quonset huts were. That's where all the equipment was, where we did our data processing. We gathered intelligence. That's when I got into data processing and computers.

We got up in the morning, got into formation, and we had breakfast. We got on these military buses, and they took us to Tan Son Nhut, which was about three or four miles away. They'd drop us at the Quonset places, and we worked until about six o'clock. It was scary being at the Quonset hut. We used to hear the bombs falling on the outskirts. It used to scare us. But at the end of the day, we got back on the buses and went back to the compound. That was basically it. At work, it was mostly keypunching, handling the sorters, and other collators, and other IBM [International Business Machines] equipment.

*Ted Samora served in a military intelligence unit
stationed near Saigon during the Vietnam War.
Photo courtesy of Ted Samora.*

The information that we were compiling and analyzing was all Top Secret at the time, because we all had Top Secret clearances. Mostly we had to do imagery interpretation (with airplanes taking pictures of the jungle and villages of Vietnam). There was the order of battle, and that was basically how many troops were on the other side. There was another one, but I can't remember what it was called. It was basically the weapons that they had and different coordinates in the area. I was there for three months, and then, even though I was an E-4, I became the head of the MI keypunch handling. We had Vietnamese that came in and did the keypunching for us. I used to watch over them to make sure they were keypunching the information into our computers.

Intelligence didn't tell me that much about the North Vietnamese or the Viet Cong, but I knew that they were very good military rebels. They knew the jungle. That was always mentioned. When we were in Saigon, we didn't know who was the enemy and who was not. That was another thing. We had to watch our backs. We knew that the Viet Cong had help and equipment from the North Vietnamese. We had that in the intelligence too. Me, myself, I considered them very strong. That's why I was scared. Because at that time, I really thought that this war was never going to end, that it would be inconclusive and it was going to be a long war. The Vietnamese love their country, and that's why I left it. Those were the thoughts I had, but I didn't tell anybody.

There was one instance, when I was out in the truck. We were going to the new MI battalion, and our bus ran over a Vietnamese. I was sitting with all of my soldier friends, and they all yelled, "Hey, gook! We killed a gook!" You know. And I was just shocked. I just sat there quiet. They were all happy that they saw us run over this Viet Cong, I mean, Vietnamese head. They were all happy and screaming, "Gook! Gook!" I looked at everything differently at that point because that was the first time I had ever seen a person die. That's what changed me.

When I went to Saigon, I tried to get to know the people and talk to them—mostly in the bars. I was very friendly, even on the streets. I met this one family, and I went to their home. It was a poor family, but they served me soup. While they sat on the floor, they got me a chair because they didn't want me to get on my knees like they were. They wouldn't give me nut nam, which was a sauce that smells horrible, so I didn't partake of that, even though I wanted it. But the dinner was friendly, and I took their son to the Saigon zoo. They wouldn't let me take their daughter. I used to teach them algebra because they wanted to learn some math. I wish I would have got their names or address because when I went back to Vietnam recently, I didn't have their address. I was hoping maybe that someone would recognize me, but they never did.

When my brother Arthur arrived "in country," he flew into Saigon and he called me. I talked to my commander and told him my brother was here. They were always so good about me and my brother Arthur. The commanders always did something special. An aide got me a jeep and a person to drive me to the airport to pick up Arthur and bring him back to the compound. I introduced him to all of my friends. Of course, that night, he had to fly to where he was stationed at Na Trang. He was an air traffic controller.

Two months before I was supposed to go back to the United States, since my brother was in-country, I asked my commander if there was some way that I could go visit him. They were going to send some military intelligence to that area, so they gave me a .45, some handcuffs, and a briefcase to take this intelligence up there. That's how I got to Na Trang. It was beautiful. The beaches, that's what stands out—the water and the beaches. I really loved Na Trang. I don't know how to explain it. It's just nice. I love the beach and the ocean. For my brother and I, being together and sharing that was really nice. Me and my brother visited for three days, and then I came back.

Before the interview, Ted told me that he received a commendation when he was in Vietnam. The troops unofficially called this award a "Green Weenie". Ted had mixed feelings about the commendation because of the way he received it. After he returned to the United States, he destroyed the medal during an antiwar protest. Part of him wishes that he could get it back; part of him is glad that it is gone.

The commendation was given to me because I had this room full of intelligence that they wanted onto the computer, and I was able to get it on in the time frame that they asked me to. So I got a medal. But at that time—you know, I told you about the incident with the truck—I was drinking more, so I started having a problem with drinking and smoking marijuana.

The night before I got the medal, I got drunk. I didn't know I was going to get the medal. I had no idea. I got drunk with my friends and went to the compound where I slept and started throwing up. The officer of the day saw me, and he told me to stop. He got very angry. We almost came to blows. I was arrested. Me, being drunk, I kept on saying, "I have one phone call." But I wasn't in the civilian world. I said, "Call up the naval commander of military intelligence." So he did. The officer of the day told the commander everything that happened to me, and then they hung up.

A little while later, the officer of the day got another phone call, and they told him that I was going to get a medal the next day and to let me go. Even at that time I didn't know that I was going to get a medal. The next day, they told me, "Ted, you're going to get a medal." After I got my medal, I was walking toward where I slept, and the officer of the day came up to me and said, "You don't deserve that." I can't answer for why I got it, but he was very upset. And there's where that story ended.

When I asked Ted to talk about his sexuality and his time in the service, he started again from the beginning.

I didn't have any role models in Madera. I knew there was something different about me. Every time I heard "faggot" or "gay" or "queer"—especially the word "queer"—I didn't want to be that. I knew that I liked men, because when I used to go to the swimming pool, even when I was younger, I used to watch the older men undress.

When I was in the military, there was a common bond between the guys. We were all friends. In Vietnam one time, my friend and I got drunk, and there was some kind of playful thing that happened. I remember it, but I don't think he does. I'm just glad that nobody caught us, because I was mostly the instigator of it. I wish I had known more about sexuality back then. I kept it to myself, which caused a lot of problems. I was homophobic within myself.

When I came back from Vietnam, I went to the Nineteenth Battalion in Fort Gordon, Georgia. At Fort Gordon, I used to handle cases of homosexuality. This guy would come in and say, "This other guy was hitting on me. You better watch out for him." Then we'd call the other guy in, of course. When that happened, both of them got kicked out of the service. I felt sorry for them. I wish I could have told them, "You're both going to get kicked out. Even though you were both drunk and you claim that he did this to you, you're both going to get kicked out." It was kind of hard also, me having some of those feelings too, and kicking some of those guys out. It was very hard. I disagree with it very much, because I know that it has been going on since the military began. They've always had "don't ask, don't tell."

There were gay people at Fort Gordon that I knew. One day, we went out to the parking lot to do some drinking. They knew that I worked in MI. They worked somewhere else. We went out drinking in the parking lot, and they started feeling me out. I said, "I know you guys are gay, but I'm in military intelligence. But I won't tell anybody." When I was stationed in Georgia, I did go to gay bars. Nothing was said. I saw other military people there. Everybody knew it was a gay bar. The way I look at it, the military is saying, "Just keep quiet and don't say anything." But you can't express your feelings. That's what's hard about it, keeping it inside. There may be a group of guys who know each other are gay and who go to the gay bar, but then, there's the other side. And there's a conflict there.

There's a lot of homophobic military people. My idea is that most of these straight soldiers don't know their sexuality. Sometimes I don't like to put labels like homosexual, straight, or bisexual. I just say that if a guy doesn't under-stand his sexuality, he's going to have a problem. I have straight friends who understand and don't have a problem with me being gay. They go out with me and would probably even hold my hand and touch me and hug me, but there's no sexual problem with that to them, even though they may be straight and they go out with women. Those are the type of people that I like to know. There are some gay people who don't understand the sexual part, and they don't like straight guys. But that's the deal with understanding your sexuality. If you understand it, you won't have any problems. I only got that idea after I started getting clean and sober.

Getting clean and sober was part of a healing process that took nearly two decades for Ted and his brothers. Before we began the interview, he told me that he wanted to talk about how the war affected his family, especially the four young men who served. Though this was clearly painful for him, it was something that he felt he had to do.

Well, when my brothers and I got home there were many problems. All four of us were alcoholics. We were all drug addicts. And this was basically because of Vietnam. I wish there was a way that the Veterans Administration or the army could have helped us out more to understand what we were feeling when we got back. We were taught to hate, and we weren't hating people.

So me and my brothers had a lot of problems. A lot of them were connected to me being gay and them knowing I was gay. It used to come out when we'd get drunk. One of my cousins got married, and at that wedding we were all drinking and my brother Leonard came up to me. I don't know what the argument was, but he put his cigarette out on my forehead and called me a faggot. It was a big ordeal. After that, none of us were invited to any weddings or parties. That really hurt my mom and dad, because they were invited, but we weren't. After that, we didn't really talk to each other.

I was the first one to go to AA [Alcoholics Anonymous] and clean up my act. Arthur kind of cleaned up his act because I did. Leonard was a heroin addict. He was stealing from our parents, which caused a lot of conflict. Eventually, five years after I was clean, he became clean.

Ricky continued. Me and my other brothers confronted him and said, "You can't live with Mom anymore." He was doing speed. He started hallucinating a lot like he was still in Vietnam, getting a gun. He scared my mother. We talked to him, and he did get help. For six months he was ok, but then he fell back. And then he committed suicide. It was a big blow to the family, especially my mom. She thought she was at fault because she asked him to leave. I told my mom not to feel that way. It was his addiction, basically. It was hard.

Now, me and my other brothers are talking. They know I'm gay. They come up here to visit. They've met some of my partners. I have pictures of them over there. I'm glad that we're able to talk now. It took many years for us to be able to do it. I think that this thing right here. . . . [He holds up a framed newspaper article.] We all got together because the Unitarian Church wanted us to speak about Vietnam. We all spoke. I think another thing that kind of brought us together is our nephews and nieces. They look at us, and they don't want to be like their crazy uncles.

Ted returned to Vietnam for a visit in the late 1990s. It was time, he finally realized, to close that chapter of his life. His brother Arthur went with him.

Well, me and Arthur kept on talking about going back to Vietnam because my brother had post-traumatic stress disorder. I had a little of it too, but I had dealt with it because of my aa. I told my brother Arthur that I was going to go to Vietnam to see what it's like now. And he says, "Well, I'd like to go too." So we made arrangements and we went back.

When we landed in Tan Son Nhut airport, I saw where I used to be stationed at the Quonset hut. When I got off the airplane, the difference that I noticed right away was that there was no smell—the smell that I remembered when I first got there during the Vietnam conflict. Along the Saigon River, there used to be a lot of sewage. It seemed like the Vietnamese government cleaned that all up, and there was no smell. Saigon was changed. I went to all the places I used to go, but, of course, some were not there.

The people were very friendly. Because of our age, they knew we were Vietnam veterans. There were Vietnamese soldiers who were often very friendly to us. It kind of made us think. We're back in the United States thinking the war is still going on. But for the Vietnamese the war is over. That kind of shocked us somehow. The Vietnamese were very friendly, and they treated us very nice. It was like they forgot about the war. It didn't exist. But to us, it did. When we went to Na Trang, where my brother was stationed, it was an experience for him. I remember my brother came up to me when we got there. He says, "Ted, I'm ok with it now. The war's over in my head."

At the time of the interview, Ted Samora worked as a computer programmer in San Francisco, California.

An Interview with Michael Job

There is a wooden peace sign on Michael Job's door in San Francisco's Haight-Ashbury neighborhood. It is hard to imagine that the man who greets visitors at that door with a warm smile was once an integral part of a machine gun team in the hill country of Vietnam. Today, Michael is an ardent advocate of peace and human rights. But Michael's path to peace was not an easy one. He traveled from Detroit to Da Nang, San Francisco to San Salvador, Nicaragua to Iraq. As he says several times in the interview, he feels very lucky to be alive and, finally, at peace.

I was born in Detroit, Michigan, in January 1945. My father co-owned a bar. Then, he became an ironworker. My mother basically was a housewife. There were a total of five children—three sisters, one brother, and me. I only lived in Detroit until I was seven years old. From there, we moved to a small farming town called Gladwin, Michigan, about 150 miles north of Detroit. There were about 2,000 people in the city limits, so it was a very small, rural, farm, vacation land kind of area. It was a good place to grow up.

I think rural areas and small towns tend to be more conservative. The words "gay" or "homosexual"—honest to God, I had no idea what any of that meant. You heard the words back then like "fruit" or "fairy," and you knew from people that it wasn't good. It was something that you shouldn't be. It was just innuendo. I'm one of those who firmly believe that you're born being gay. It's not something that you make a choice at some point in your life. Here I am, growing up in this highly religious, rural environment, with no source of information. I had my first sexual experience with another boy when I was like fourteen and then again at sixteen.

I graduated from high school in 1962, and then I went to college. Everybody in our graduating class was going to college. That was what you were expected to do. If you were in college, you got draft deferred. I attended Eastern Michigan University in Ypsilanti, Michigan. It was mainly a teaching college, and I went for teaching. I was a speech and drama major and a French minor. I can't read, write, or speak French today, but the speech and drama I loved.

When I graduated in '66, I was twenty-one years old. I taught speech and drama at a school in Pontiac, Michigan, for like two years. There was no gay scene there. There was just clandestine sexual activity at various times. But, still, there was no way to work through it. At the end of the second year in 1968, one of the other teachers came right out and asked me, "Are you a homosexual?" People have no idea how frightening that can be. "God, no, I'm not!" But that was enough to scare me. "Are people noticing?" I hadn't come to terms with it myself, and now I'm scared and confused.

I decided to quit teaching. Because teachers were deferred, I knew that as soon as I quit teaching, I would get drafted. The way I was reasoning it—well, my father had never been in the military. So I want to go. It'll make a man out of me. It'll prove I'm not gay. That's how I had it wired, even though I couldn't say that to anybody. In hindsight, I know that I was really running away from myself, trying to prove that I was not gay.

I can remember leaving that morning. First, they take you to Detroit for a physical. My parents wanted to drive me into town, and I said, "No," because I am one of those people who cannot say goodbye without crying. I walked from my home—it was less than a mile from town—just so that I wouldn't be crying and all of that kind of stuff, getting myself calmed down. I went to Detroit and passed the physical. Then we went in and swore our oath of allegiance, and they put us on a bus for Fort Knox, Kentucky.

As soon as you get off of the bus, all of the yelling at you starts. "Line up! Get over here!" The first three days, we didn't do anything. We were in these barracks. The drill sergeants would come in at 2:00 in the morning, turn all of the lights on, take everything out of your locker, and throw it on the floor. Then you have to get up and put everything back. You go to hand-to-hand combat, bayonet training, and this idea of blood, kill—getting into everybody's face. Those are the things that really stand out. I don't think that it was basic training, but probably advanced infantry training. The drill sergeant was mad at us, because we weren't being aggressive enough, so he made us take a handful of sawdust and put it in our underwear. Now you got to walk around with this sawdust, and it's like, "What is this craziness? Is this what men do to each other?"

I realized very, very early that I had made a mistake. I realized that if this is what it means to be a man—the yelling and screaming and putting down other human beings and being as crude and as crass as you possibly can be—if that's what it means to be a man, I was perfectly fine the way I was. But now, I've got two years to serve.

Then, my orders came for Vietnam, and I had a forty-five-day leave at home. Oh, God! I wish I could explain to people who may read this what it's like right before you go to war. It was one of the most scary times of my life. It was not fear exactly, but those last two days, I don't know if I stopped crying for forty-eight hours. Knowing that when I say goodbye to these people, it may be the very last time that I say goodbye. That's the hardest thing. [He begins to cry softly.] Sorry. The last thing I can remember was the ride to Detroit, which is like a two-and-a-half-hour ride, and I must have cried most of the way down. But once I hugged my family at the airport, turned my back, and started walking on that ramp, I wiped my eyes. That's when veterans—or I at least speak for myself—I started stuffing the feelings and not allowing them to come back for another year.

As you're getting off of the plane with the new soldiers, the old guys are lining up ready to go home. Boy, you see how dirty and worn they are, and they're laughing as they see us coming with our brand new uniforms. I was sent to the 101st Airborne up to Camp Eagle, up to I-Corps. I was with Company D of the 1st Battalion of the 327th Infantry Division. My company was near Phu Loc and Phu Bai, which were small villages.

On the very first night I was in the field, the position next to ours, the guys sent out their team to put out the trip wire. We'd put up trip flares and set up claymore mines. And we'd try to do things sort of like a triangle, so if the enemy tried to get into our perimeter, we'd know they're coming. Usually one guy goes out to set the wire, and then another goes with him with his rifle to post security. The other three guys are back at the position. One of those guys must have got scared. He fired on his own guys. It's dark, and everyone can hear the gunfire. We hear the guy screaming, "Mom! Mom!" This guy is just screaming, because he's in pain. Well, now we have to set up flares. We have to bring in the helicopter. It's like: "Welcome to Vietnam."

I was on the front lines for the first four months, and I consider myself very lucky, because most of the guys in my outfit spent the whole twelve months on the front lines. We didn't stay in the Low Lands. They would also send us up into the hills for a couple of weeks at a time. They would send us to this one place called the A Shau Valley where we'd get five or ten of our guys killed, over fifty of our guys wounded. Then they'd have to bring in reinforcements, new people coming in country who aren't trained. I remember bullets going right by me in the grass. Every day your life was in danger when you were there, but as we got into various firefights, it was a really horrible place.

I'm one of those who can't say that I've looked somebody in the eye and pulled the trigger. Again, I'm lucky that way. I'm very fortunate. My heart aches for every veteran who knows for sure. And the thing is, being a high school teacher, the very first thing teenagers always ask is: "Did you kill anybody?" Why is that the very first thing that people want to know? The only thing I can say is—and this is going to sound funny and maybe it's my mind blocking it—but I remember this tree moving across this field. I shot at it, and the tree stopped, but we never went to see, so I don't know if I have killed anybody. A part of me is glad that I don't know—that I can't say, "Yes, I did."

I still remember the feeling of being in a firefight. You're not really nervous while it's happening, or at least I wasn't. You're in this heightened state where all of this adrenaline is rushing and pumping. You've got to move. You've got to react. I had to load the ammunition into the machine gun, get the rest of my team behind me. So I constantly had things to do, which was for me, the best thing. It gave me something that I could concentrate on doing. It saved my life. I can remember the sergeant that carried the machine gun, especially up this one hill. We'd go from tree to tree, and he happened to be a Catholic also, and I'd say a prayer before we moved from tree to tree and then we'd move. We made it up the hill. Immediately after it's over, that's when you start to shake. That's when I'd have to get my nerves to spring back together.

After four months on the front lines, Michael got a transfer to the rear area as a clerk. There was still the danger that his base would come under attack, but he felt much safer than he had on the machine gun team.

Our first sergeant would pull guys from the field when guys in support positions rotated home. So we were always trying to get these rear area jobs. If you got one, you'd be called a REMF, a Rear Echelon Motherfucker. But we all wanted to become REMFs. I still say that I was pretty useless in the field, although I did help to bring comic relief to the group. I'm not a very big person, and humping an eighty-pound pack on my back up and down those hills, I got heat exhaustion. But as you build up stamina, you're OK. The company would look to me because if I got tired, I'd just start yelling, "I'm stopping!" And I'd just sit down, which means that everybody else would have to sit down. Then, pretty soon, as I built up my stamina, the other guys would say, "Job, aren't you getting tired yet?"

I can still remember the first sergeant telling me that I was going to be sent in. I thank my lucky stars that I became the company supply and mail clerk. The nice thing was that I had been in the field with some of the guys. The supply sergeant had been in the field with me too, and we knew what the guys needed. So if we had to steal, borrow, beg—whatever we had to do to keep them resupplied, we'd do it. Whereas if you get somebody who is trained stateside as a clerk, what the hell does he care? He's never been out in the field. So on a lot of levels it really did help, because we had the compassion. We knew how they were suffering, and we knew what we could do to alleviate their suffering.

When Christmas came, I decorated one of the back rooms that we had. My mother had sent a package that had all kinds of little toys in it and stuff. I took a barrel to make a fireplace and made stockings for the guys that were able to come in. I'll probably never have a better Christmas than that Christmas I had in Vietnam, not because of presents, but because we had to make it ourselves. I remember the first sergeant almost had tears in his eyes, and he was this real macho guy. I had made him a stocking and put this little plastic bugle on it for him to call the troops to attention. He was really touched that he was included and that somebody had thought of him.

I'm sure that you've probably heard this before. There is a bond that goes on that cannot be explained other than in war. At that time, before women were in the ranks, it was a very strong male bond. Nowhere in our lives usually do we have to depend on each other for our lives. Even my close friends now, I don't count on them to save my life, nor do they count on me that way. But in this war situation, if you screw up, it could cause me to get killed. If I screw up, it could cause you to get killed. And we're both here on a one-way ticket. You can't get out and I can't get out until the military says that we have permission to go home. My life depends on you. Your life depends on me. It builds this kind of bond that you could never ever experience in normal life. You're never going to forget the guy. If that's friendship, I don't know. But it's strong.

The guys from my unit that died and got killed were acquaintances, but the ones that I was closest to did not die. One did get wounded. This happened after I was working in our rear area as our supply clerk when he got wounded. I remember going to the medevac hospital and seeing him brought in. He wrote in a letter after he got home that the one thing he remembered was seeing my face. To this day it kind of makes me feel special. Even though I didn't know him really well, I still feel that connection. I hope that some day, before we die, I get to talk to him again.

R&R brought the possibility for relief from the fighting, but time off brought its own challenges.

I took my R&R to Sydney. R&R is a time when being gay or questioning your sexuality is really frightening. Because every guy who goes on R&R comes back with these fuck tales about how many women they screwed. Now, as a gay person you have to make up these stories. I made sure that I was seen with women and took pictures with women. I remember signing up to go on this dance contest that I ended up winning with this woman. My partner and I won a boomerang. I did no gay stuff. I was still closeted. Even though, I was going on twenty-four or twenty-five, I didn't even know that there were gay bars. So it wasn't like I was going to go on R&R to do gay things. Instead, I spent most of my time trying to find a woman that I could take a picture with, so that I could go back and tell these stories to cover my ass.

Then I went on a leave to Bangkok, Thailand. That's where I lost my virginity to a woman. Here I am like twenty-five years old. In Thailand they have these bars set up and the women are all dancing with numbers on them. It's like: "I'd like number eighteen." So number eighteen would come and sit at your table. You can talk to her and if you don't like her, send her back dancing. "I want to see number twenty-three." Whatever woman you pick, you buy her drinks and you pay her I think it was $15. Then she was yours for the night. I can remember how frightened I was. I had never seen a woman naked. I had no idea what I was doing. I was so drunk. I still had my rosary on, and as I went to take it off, it broke. [He laughs.] I thought, "Oh, God!" I threw the rosary into the closet. "I'm going to go through this thing no matter what!" I can remember the song playing on the radio was John Lennon's "Come To-gether." [He laughs.]

Actually, the thing that people are not aware of is that when we were in the field, the military would bring us Vietnamese women. They'd bring like three of them, line them up behind trees, and the guys would line up to go screw the women. That was sexual activity. A lot of guys would do it, but then there'd be a whole lot who didn't because they were worried about disease and then there were those who had more of a religious background. The idea of one guy climbing on right after another one, I'm sure that it turned some off. But I don't think many people are aware of how the military plays into heterosex-uality and basically forced the guys to have sex, forced the women of these countries to get into that position.

As the antiwar movement heated up at home, American soldiers in Vietnam had varying reactions to the protests. Though he later became a staunch antiwar activist, Michael remembers his initial ambivalence about the demonstrations.

You do have somewhat mixed feelings. When you hear people putting down the vets, it was like, "Well, let them come over here and see what it's like." But at the same time, I can remember writing home and telling my parents, "Whatever people can do to bring us home, that's what should be done. Call Congress." So I never really opposed the demonstrations. I was always for them. I can't remember any conversations that I had with the other guys in my unit, but we were aware of the demonstrations.

After Michael left Vietnam, he felt that people back at home really couldn't understand what he and other veterans had been through. Being gay in a small, conservative community did not help matters. Eventually Michael moved to California. In the 1980s, he found solace and support with other veterans who had become pacifists.

I just happened to find this flyer one day for the Veterans Peace Action Teams. This was during the Reagan years, and somebody had called and told me that they were going to do this march on the western White House. That was basically my first involvement with peace veterans.

They were putting together this veterans delegation to go to Nicaragua. I think it was in November of 1987. My roommate at the time said, "Oh you'd be crazy not to go." So I signed up. I think it was a one- or two-week delegation, and we traveled all the way up into the north area of Nicaragua. We took school supplies and got to meet with a lot of people. Then about six months after that I went on a construction brigade with the Veterans Peace Action Team for six weeks to help build a school up in a small cooperative there.

That's when the war was still going on. It was in like '88. I remember we were on a hill one day when shooting broke out with the Contras. We weren't directly involved. Other people were scared. Me and this other Vietnam veteran were just standing there looking around like it was as natural as all day. He and I were just laughing like it didn't really affect us. "Oh, what an old familiar sound that is to hear the guns going off in the distance." But you gained a deep respect for the people to understand that it was United States money and munitions going to kill them. So that was empowering.

I became the chairman of the board of directors for the Veterans Peace Action Teams for like two years in the late 80s and early 90s. Then I went to El Salvador when wounded FMLN were held up in the cathedral in San Salvador.[9] Through Veterans Peace Action Teams, we sent American veterans to live with them, because they would be less likely to shoot the El Salvadorans. What they were trying to do was seek safe medical evacuation out of the country as guaranteed by Geneva Conventions. So we went in solidarity with them. That was scary, because our very first night there was a threat of rocket attack on the cathedral. We could have been killed. But I did it because of the Vietnam experience, learning that we've got to stand up to our government and halt this damage that we cause around the world for money and greed and big corporations.

Later, I went to Iraq with a group called the Fellowship of Reconciliation, which is out of Nyack, New York. I don't know if you remember that before the first Gulf War was started, there were prisoners of war taken. So various groups were going to see if they could get some of them released. But our delegation was going with 1,500 pounds of medical supplies, because the United States had put sanctions against Iraq. We were going in friendship, to let them know that not all Americans were in favor of this war against them. So we took the supplies. Everything was guarded, and we were driven everywhere. It was controlled, but we got to meet the people, got to go to the university. We could tell that they were determined to stand up for themselves as much as they could. There was talk that they might release a couple of prisoners to our group, but they didn't. We did deliver our supplies. Iraq had reasons to invade Kuwait. Kuwait was slant drilling and stealing Iraq's oil. Our media doesn't tell us those things. I think most of these things were to test our military preparedness. Could we mobilize a force quickly enough? We hadn't tested weapons really since Vietnam. There was a whole bunch of lies to bring on the first Persian Gulf War—or massacres as I call them.

At the conclusion of the interview, Michael explained that he was conflicted about the ban on openly gay servicemen and servicewomen.

As a gay person, I don't want anybody from my community to go into the military, so the longer the ban against gays in the military, the better it is for my community. I wish that, on some level, they hadn't even passed "Don't Ask, Don't Tell." Keep the ban on forever, on one level, so that men and women don't have to experience what I did in Vietnam. This goes for all minorities. I say, "Why do you send your children to fight in our military? You're not going to benefit." African Americans serving, what does it gain them to send their sons and daughters to die in Vietnam, to die in the Gulf, to die in Iraq today? It's going to get them nothing. It's not going to get the Latinos anything. It's not going to get the Asians anything. It's not going to get the gays anything. All we're doing is protecting the interests of American corporations.

I'm not opposed to all militaries, because I think that if we have to defend our shores, we will. I think that's a survival instinct. But what our military has come to—going around the world and launching preemptive strikes—I am not for it. We will become a better society and a better world when we build monuments to peacemakers and war resisters rather than monuments to war veterans. We should be striving for a world with no more veterans.

At the time of this interview, Michael Job had just retired from his job as a schoolteacher in San Francisco, California. He remained a proud member of Veterans for Peace.

THE ACADEMIES

       The idea for a United States military academy is almost as old as this country. In 1799, George Washington suggested the creation of such an institution in a letter to his friend and fellow Revolutionary War veteran Alexander Hamilton. "The establishment of a military academy [has] ever been considered by me to be an object of the highest national importance," Washington wrote.[1] West Point was founded in 1802, and there are few national institutions more steeped in tradition. The "Long Gray Line" of West Point graduates reads like a "who's who" of American military history: Lee, Jackson, Grant, Custer, Pershing, MacArthur, Patton, Bradley, Eisenhower, Westmoreland, and Schwarzkopf. Along with West Point, the u.s. Naval Academy (founded in 1845), the u.s. Coast Guard Academy (founded in 1876), and the u.s. Air Force Academy (founded in 1954) produce the leaders of our nation's armed forces, the men—and more recently, women—who value honor, duty, and country above all else. Cadets and academy alumni embody this sense of tradition, but they don't lose their sense of humor about it. "West Point represents two hundred years of tradition . . . unhampered by progress," they joke.[2]

       Grounded in a proud traditionalism, the academies have nevertheless evolved a great deal over the last two centuries, adapting to changes in military strategy, technology, and American society. John Lovell, a West Point alumnus and scholar, who wrote a synthetic history of the academies in the 1970s, found that this evolution has often been spurred by a creative tension between the Spartan model of military leadership and the Athenian ideal of intellectual inquiry. Being "neither Athens nor Sparta," the academies have exhibited a flexibility one might not expect from such traditional institutions. Between World War I and World War II, the academies first limited plebe hazing in response to congressional pressure. During the Cold War race for scientific supremacy with the Soviets, the academies strengthened what were already nationally recognized engineering curricula while simultaneously allowing cadets more choice of academic coursework, majors, and concentrations. Finally, in response to the civil rights and feminist movements, the academies expanded recruitment of racial minorities and opened their gates to women cadets in the 1970s. Change was gradual and (in the best military tradition) hard fought, but change did come to the academies.[3]

One way that the academies have been especially slow to change has been in their policy on homosexuality. Although "Don't Ask, Don't Tell" prohibited the academies from asking about homosexuality on admissions forms, open acknowledgment or evidence of homosexuality remains grounds for separation. Still, there are and have always been gay cadets at the academies. The gay academy alumni whose interviews are included in this chapter represent academy classes in every decade from the 1960s to the 1990s. They too are part of the "Long Gray Line." They too speak with reverence about the initiation rites of plebe summers and Beast Barracks. They too are loyal to academy tradition.

Tradition was especially important to Tom Carpenter and Steve Clark Hall. They attended the Naval Academy during the Vietnam War era. They chose careers in the marines and the navy during a period when many young Americans were fighting against the military, not in it. Officers who attended the academies during the Vietnam War, one journalist recently wrote, "have the same narrow-eyed disposition as civilians who survived the Depression."[4] This is not quite true of Tom and Steve, but they did have to deal with many of the antimilitary prejudices that other service personnel faced during the war years. Yet because they realized that they were gay only after they left the Naval Academy, they did not have to fear separation or harassment any more than their heterosexual classmates.

Jeff Petrie came to understand that he was gay while he attended the Naval Academy during the 1980s. As if this were not difficult enough, the growing knowledge and fear of the AIDS epidemic increased homophobia during the era that he served. One of the academy initiation rituals is that plebes must always be prepared to answer questions from upperclassmen about both history and current events. For Jeff, discussions of AIDS and homosexuality were painful and fraught with danger. The only saving grace was that he knew he was not alone. Jeff's quest to create a gay USNA alumni chapter and more general academy alumni group would create a support network for gay and lesbian cadets. When Stephen Boeckels graduated from West Point after the passage of "Don't Ask, Don't Tell," there was no such support network. If there had been, he might have made a career of the army. Instead, he works in the private sector and serves as a West Point alumni interviewer.

Beth Hillman did not attend an academy. Instead, she went to Duke University on an ROTC [Reserve Officers' Training Corps] scholarship and served as an officer in the air force, before returning to the University of Pennsylvania for an M.A. in history and ultimately taking an assignment as an instructor at the U.S. Air Force Academy. In Colorado Springs, Beth helped the air force address issues of gender discrimination and sexual harassment that have plagued all of the academies since the admission of women cadets in 1976. Although they have taken a lot of heat for ignoring sexism and harassment within the corps of cadets, the academies have come a long way on these issues. In the 1970s, William Westmoreland, a former superintendent of West Point, said, "Maybe you could find one woman in 10,000 who could lead in combat. But she would be a freak, and we are not running the Military Academy for freaks." No longer seen as "freaks," women make up 15 percent of the corps of cadets. As one female officer who served at West Point told a reporter in the 1990s, "In a non-nurturing environment, [women cadets] are kicking ass, and that is the bottom line."[5]

Though difficult, the integration of women and minorities into the corps of cadets appears to be part of the continuum of change at the academies. Most of the interviewees in this chapter believe that the traditions of equal opportunity, merit advancement, and fairness embodied by the academies will ultimately lead to changes in the policy toward gays and lesbians. Some faculty members at the academies share this view. It is a question of liberty, according to Lieutenant Colonel Allen Bishop, a West Point faculty member. "Despite our government's claims of liberty for all, we leave homosexuals out," Bishop wrote in 2005. "When we deny their right to military service, we improperly restrict the franchise of citizenship and give in to homophobic prejudice very like the unreasoned racial and gender prejudices of the past."[6] With faculty members like Allen Bishop and academy alumni like these interviewees leading the way, the tradition of change continues.

TWO HUNDRED YEARS OF TRADITION

An Interview with Tom Carpenter

I met Tom Carpenter for our interview at a hotel in downtown San Francisco reserved for marines and veterans of the Marine Corps. Tom attended the U.S. Naval Academy in the late 1960s. He realized that he was gay after he graduated, but while he was still in the service. In the 1970s, he met the man who would become his lover for more than two decades. Quick to smile, Tom had a serious side that emerged when he talked of the difficult choice between service to his country and love for his partner.

I'm Tom Carpenter, and I was born on February the eighteenth, 1948, in New York City, actually in Queens. My father was an army paratrooper during World War II. My mother joined the Red Cross, and they sent her to the Pacific theater. She ended up going to the Philippines, New Guinea, and Okinawa. She met my father in Japan, at the end of the war, as the Japanese surrendered. Theirs was one of the first American weddings in Japan after World War II.

Most of my childhood was spent in the Southeast at army bases. Dad spent thirty years in the army and retired as a full colonel. One of his most interesting duty assignments was as the inspector general for special investigations in Vietnam. He was one of the people that investigated the My Lai massacre. I was at the Naval Academy, but he did talk to me about that. Said that it was a terrible thing.

My family has a long tradition in the military. We've traced back the family history and realized that men on both sides of my family served in the Revolutionary War. You probably saw the movie *The Patriot*. The British colonel that led that group in South Carolina is apparently related to my mother's family. And on my father's side, they fought with Francis Marion. Two or three times they were in battle against each other. My father's family fought during the Civil War, or as they call it in the South, "the war between the states" or "the war of Northern aggression." [He laughs.] All those sons fought in the Civil War. Then my grandfather on my mother's side was in World War I. Ended up joining the Canadian artillery, and he got sent over to the Battle of the Somme, fought out there, got mustard gassed, lost this toes. Kind of a remarkable guy. My uncle retired from the air force as a two- or three-star general. He led the first and last B-52 strikes against North Vietnam during the Christmas Offensive directed at Hanoi. He's still alive today. My cousin is a brand-new brigadier general in the Air Force, flies F16s. My brother-in-law was my Naval Academy roommate; he went into the marines afterwards. The whole family is wrapped up in the military.

So there was no question that that was what I should do. The only controversy was that I was an army brat going into the navy. In South Carolina it was a competitive process. You took the civil service exam, and they combined the results of that with your high school record. The senator makes the choice. When I graduated from high school, I was president of the student body. I was in the National Honor Society, top 5 percent of my class, and captain of the soccer team. Believe it or not, I was appointed to the Naval Academy by none other than J. Strom Thurmond. Now there's a picture I should get for you, a picture of him handing me my appointment to the Naval Academy in '66.

The Naval Academy was, I think, like most service academies. It's a transforming experience. They get these young people from all around the country and they're usually selected because they're the best and the brightest. They put you together. They take away all your personal identity. Literally take the clothes off your back, the money out your pockets. They shave your head, and they put you all in this one uniform. It's like the beginning of a race. They say here we are. Here's the starting line, everybody even. We don't care how much money you have. We don't care what schools you went to. We don't care how good looking your are. You're going to compete against these other people and it's all going to be on merit, which I think is a good way to do things.

Then the education—it was an excellent education. At that time it was very engineering oriented, but it was going through a transition where they were bringing in more liberal arts. The stuff was very hard. I didn't have a great math background, and it was difficult for me. The first summer I was there they sent me to "Stupid Studies," because I hadn't taken physics and calculus in high school. All these other kids had. To level the playing field, they said, "Okay, while all these other people are out doing whatever they were doing, you have to go to 'Stupid Studies,' so that you were even with everybody else." I did very well at the academy. I graduated, I'd say like in the upper third of the class. I was a battalion commander my senior year. Actually, I was regimental commander for part of it then a battalion commander for graduation. I received a distinguished military graduate award. There are about twenty of us who got that because we excelled in the military.

After his third year at the Naval Academy, Tom was sent on a summer cruise to live the life of an enlisted sailor in the surface fleet. Though he loved the navy, this was a disillusioning experience for him. When he returned to Annapolis, he decided to become a marine.

The marines really were people-oriented because they recognized the fact that their greatest assets were their people. The navy's got these ships; they've got airplanes, they've got big toys to play with. That's really their assets. But in the marines your assets are your troops. As a general proposition, they have received the garbage that nobody else wants. I remember the first time I saw marine 105 howitzers—this was still at the Naval Academy—I looked at these things and they were just worn down. They were old. They should have been cashiered a long time ago. That's the stuff they had; that's what they had to work with. So you recognize that really your people are your biggest asset. You have to take care, protect them. If you do good by them, they'd do good by you. That was the whole emphasis, but it was tough. The marines were really demanding. There's no slack. You stand up and you do what you're called to do. And you better do it because you've got this whole tradition, this institution behind you that has such a tremendous reputation. You think, "I would do nothing to foul this institution's reputation." That's the way it is.

While I was at the Naval Academy, many of my friends went over to Vietnam, and a lot didn't come back. So that was kind of expected, but my class didn't lose too many in the war because we graduated in 1970. Then, flight school takes two years—that's why I didn't go over there. The navy guys would go over, but they were off coast, unless they were commanding Swift boats. If you were a Seal, that took like three or four more years of training. We were all at the tail end of that stuff. I don't know of any of the pilots that ended up going into combat in Vietnam, the navy pilots or the marine pilots, that were my class-mates. It was the classes before mine—men like John McCain and others in the classes of '65, '66, '67, '68—those were the ones that had the most of the casualties, because they were combat ready. We were still being trained. Then, the war ended. I was right there at the doorsteps, in Okinawa, when Saigon fell.

At home, we were aware of the antiwar movement. We had to have platoons on each side of the National Colors—the flags—at the parades to protect the colors from the protesters. When we marched in Nixon's inaugural, they sent a battalion of midshipmen to march in that parade, and the protesters were standing alongside the parade route. They were yelling, "One-two-three-four. We don't want your fucking war!" They were taking urine and feces and putting them in plastic bags and throwing them at us. We were marching with bayonets so it would hit them and go all over us. Yeah, we knew the protesters were there. [He laughs.] You know, it was always a constant discussion with us, because we would get angry, particularly since people are dying, but then we would say, "Yeah, but this is why we're fighting. People have to have the right to dissent and to protest and do the things that these folks had chosen to do, even though it's trouble." You looked at them and they were kids that were our age basically. We had just taken this course, and they'd taken that course. They thought that the war was wrong; we felt that it was right.

After going through basic infantry training in Quantico, Virginia—a require-ment for all marine officers, regardless of their specialty—Tom went on to become a marine aviator. Though he was engaged to be married, he realized that was a mistake when he met the man who would become his longtime partner.

Let's back up. Early on in my life I had an attraction to boys. Then I realized what it was, and I stopped it. I thought it was just a period I was going through. When I was at Annapolis, I dated women. I was engaged to be married. It was just very, very suppressed. Maybe that's why I was as hard on people as I was, because I just had to bite that. Then, after I graduated and I went into infantry school, I saw people get married, have lives. I had met this women who I was in love with. She and I were together for maybe about a year and a half. About that time, I was stationed at Cherry Point, North Carolina. My initial assignment when I got there was Pool OIC, officer in charge. I was in charge of all the new pilots coming through. They all came in and reported to me.

This guy walked in one day. I took one look at him and said, "Wooh, is this guy a looker." He looked very much like Tom Cruise. He walks in, and I go, "Wow!" These deep stirrings came through me, and I said, "What the hell am I doing? I'm engaged to be married!" To make a long story short, we became friends. He was an F-4 radar intercept officer, back-seater in an F-4, and I was in an A-4 training squadron at the time. One day, there was a great big snowstorm. The whole base was shut down. That evening, it was his wetting down party. That was a tradition back then where they would take the difference between your present pay grade and the new pay grade that you were being promoted to, the difference in salary in one month. All the people on the list that were going to be promoted the same time as you would put their money in a pool. And they'd go down to the officer's club and open up the bar and drink until the money was gone.

So that night I went down there. He was sitting across the bar—it was a circular bar. Thing was just jammed pack. Everybody was in there in the world. All ranks from the second lieutenants to the colonels were in there. We're all hanging around, smoking and drinking, all the stuff that people don't do anymore. He kept looking at me, and I kept looking at him. He had been promoted from second lieutenant to first lieutenant, and I was a first lieutenant already. So I walked over to him, we started to talk. Then, the next thing I knew, I found myself with my hand in the back of his pocket. He goes *bang* like that, pushes my hand away. And I said, "Uh oh, I'm in trouble now." Then I did it again. I was just being persistent as hell. So he says, "You know, I think I better get out of here." Our mutual friend said, "I'll drive you home." So I turned to him and said, "Wouldn't you rather me drive you home?" He looks at me, and he smiles and says, "Yeah, why don't you drive me home." We got in my car, and he just turned to me and said, "Are you with the Naval Investigative Service?" I said, "No, I'm not." He said, "Are we going to do what I think we're going to do?" I said, "I think so." That was the beginning of a twenty-year relationship.

Throughout their relationship, Tom and his partner, Court, were not always stationed in the same place. For many military couples, particularly gay and lesbian ones, having to endure long-distance separation was par for the course.

When we were stationed far away from one another, we used to have these marathon telephone calls. We were running up phone bills like three or four hundred dollars a month—each of us talking to each other constantly. We were just very depressed and lonely. So we decided a way to fix it was get an assignment that nobody wanted. We went to our detailers to see if we could get sent to Vietnam or some place far away. Court was in Hawaii at the time, and the detailers thought he was nuts, but it was something they could do. So both of us ended up getting orders to Japan. He arrived there before me, and it was funny, because when my flight arrived it was in the evening and this limo pulled up, staff car. All the colonels and majors on my flight thought it was for them, but it was Court and a driver for me. He took me to our hooch—that's what we called it. We had our own rooms, two separate rooms but obviously we were together for all intents and purposes. I was there for like three or four months and the orders came in for me to go to Okinawa.

Then, we'd plan little rendezvous. I had to get my flight time while I was in Okinawa, so I'd fly out, and he would get in his F-4, and we'd pick a place to meet. We met in Korea. We met in Taiwan. We'd meet down in the Philippines. It was very romantic. Incidentally, while we were in the Marine Corps, we confided in friends that finally figured us out. They knew about the fact that we were gay and had a relationship. They were totally cool with it, but they were our contemporaries. As I always said, never tell anybody who has less to lose than you do about this situation.

One day, I got a telephone call from a good friend of ours. He tells me there's a problem. I asked him what it was. He says, I can't tell you on this phone. You need to get up here from Okinawa. So I flew up, and Court had been placed on house arrest. He had been charged with bringing an enlisted man, a lance corporal, over to the house we had off base. The kid accused him of grabbing his crotch. Court said, "No way, no how. It didn't happen." I said, "Well, you have to decide what you're going to do. You have to either fight this or not."

Court's father was a retired air force colonel, and he said, "I couldn't put my father through this, and I don't want you drug into this. If they do an investigation, they're going to start snooping around." My answer to him was: "Listen, they've investigated the hell out of me. I'm one of the few nuclear weapons delivery pilots in the Marine Corps." At the time, I had the highest clearance available. To get the clearance, the marines had checked my friends and neighbors and family, and I cleared through all of that stuff. So I figured I was safe. My other argument was the fact that I went to the Naval Academy, so this could never happen to me. Of course, I've learned since then they don't care much about that. In the end, Court said, "No, I'm not going to put people through it." They gave him the option of resigning his commission with a less-than-honorable discharge or going through a court-martial. So he decided to resign. They sent him back to Camp Pendleton and then cashiered him.

Tom and Court were together until 1992 when Court died of an AIDS-related illness. Having served as a legal assistant to one of his commanding officers, Tom knew that he had an interest in the law. After leaving the marines in 1976, Tom decided to go to law school. He got his J.D. in 1980. As co-chair of the board of directors for the Servicemembers Legal Defense Network (SLDN), Tom is an outspoken opponent of "Don't Ask, Don't Tell." Here, he explains why in terms of his Naval Academy experience.

In "Don't Ask, Don't Tell," they say everybody keeps silent about this thing. We're not going to ask them on the induction form. We're not going to ask while you're on active duty. At the time it was being debated, I said, "It's never going to work." I said, "The military is really built around small unit leadership and small units. You live in close conditions. You find out things about people. You get to know about their families, about their love lives, their lack of love lives, what they do, their hobbies. You really get to know people very, very intimately, and so what are these people going to say about these things? Are you just going to make up lies? So you weave this web of lies, which in itself is completely contrary to the core values of the military. We're taught at Annapolis, West Point, the Air Force Academy, the Coast Guard Academy, and throughout the military, an honor code. You live and die by the honor code at the service academies, and you never lie, cheat, or steal. That's part of the core values of the military, so you're creating an environment where you bring these people up, you teach them to be honorable and honest, have integrity, but then you tell them that they have to lie about the most intimate part of their life. It's never going to work.

A year or two after the policy was put in place, I was approached by Michelle Beneke, who was one of the cofounders of SLDN, and she asked me if I'd be on the board of directors. I took her up on that offer. About four years ago, I was elected to be the co-chair of the board. I've been co-chair of the board since then.

Initially, SLDN was created to provide legal assistance to people who are caught up in "Don't Ask, Don't Tell." And we've done that to the tune of over 6,000 people to date. It was a legal aid society where we hooked people up with lawyers, gave them advice on how to make statements that would get them out with their honorable discharge if they chose to do that. We're still providing legal aid, but in the last year we've taken on the primary responsibility for the lobbying effort to end "Don't Ask, Don't Tell."

Today, there is an argument about unit cohesion. This is very similar to the arguments you heard about African Americans before Truman signed his executive order. They said that black and white troops won't serve together. They won't shower together. White troops won't take orders from black officers. It all affects unit cohesion. We have to keep them separated like we have since the Civil War. That fell when Truman signed the order, and look at the military today. It's probably more colorblind than civilian employers are. The military has always been a leader in that. I wouldn't say it's because they voluntarily decided to do it; they were forced to do it. There's one thing with the military: when they're given an order and they're told, "You're going to make this work," then they're going to make it work. And they've been able to do that with both of those cultural changes within the service, integrating African Americans and women.

I'm absolutely convinced that if tomorrow they said, "Okay, the ban is lifted," there would be no difference. As our European allies have said, and Australians and New Zealanders, when they lifted their bans, it was a "non-event." Nothing changed. The services didn't crumble and fall apart. People didn't resign in waves. It just happened. Nothing changed, and the reason for that is real clear: the military is still going to remain homophobic to a degree. The people who want to have good careers aren't going to talk much about it, but you've taken away the sword of Damocles and gay troops can't be thrown out just because someone finds out they're gay. Then people are going to want to stay in.

If they didn't have this ban, I would have stayed in. I've had two other careers since then. I was an airplane pilot for Continental Airlines, and I've been a lawyer now for twenty-two years. But the marines was my first love. The thing I liked about it the most was that the people you were with were really, really wonderful people. They were doing things that were bigger and more important than themselves. Money was not an issue. I'm always amazed in the civilian world where everybody is worried about how much money you make. That was not their attitude at all. They did this because—and it may sound corny—they loved their country. We were surrounded by a band of brothers back then and sisters now that all shared common values, that were moving toward a goal or a common purpose that was bigger than us. You see that in the military and the tradition.

I go back to the Naval Academy now, and it's one of those institutions that doesn't change much. The only thing I see different is women, because there weren't women back then. The structures are the same. What do they say about the Navy? "Two hundred years of tradition unhampered by progress." [He laughs.] That's kind of what the Naval Academy is like. But it's one of those places. It's something very special.

At the time of our interview, Tom was a practicing attorney in Los Angeles, California.

COMMANDER

An Interview with Steve Clark Hall

I met Steve Clark Hall after I learned of USNA Out, a gay Naval Academy alumni group. Steve rose through the ranks to become a nuclear submarine commander despite the fact that many of his fellow students at the Naval Academy and his later superiors and subordinates knew or suspected that he was gay. He became the commander of the USS Greenling just as "Don't Ask, Don't Tell" was being debated. But Steve Hall and other gay officers could not participate openly in the debate without risking their careers.

I'm Steve Clark Hall, and I was born 9 November 1953 here in San Francisco. I spent a few years here when I was really young, and then I moved to the Pacific Northwest and went to high school in Eureka, California. My dad was in the paper business. My mom was a housewife.

I had an older brother who attended the Naval Academy, but I had no desire to go there until my parents went to visit him and brought back pictures. I had seen the UC-Davis campus and the campuses at Humboldt State and Oregon State, but I just loved the architecture of the buildings at the Naval Academy, and said, "I want to go there."

We all had a time of day that we were supposed to be brought into the academy that first summer. I was one of the later groups to come in. Basically, people were yelling in your face, telling you to do this and this and this. Made you line up here and get your uniforms. It was a hot, humid, long day, but it was nothing traumatic. Of course, you didn't want to object to anything, and when they're handing you uniforms that are already too tight and you're showing up at a place that's going to make you big, it was a bad idea not to object and say, "Hey, don't these need to be a little looser?" So I basically outgrew all of my uniforms within two months.

There were two to a room in Bancroft Hall. It could house 4,200 people easily. I had a roommate, who was my roommate all summer long. We were on the top floor of a six-story building. It was the "Fourth Deck." There was a basement, there was ground level, and then zero level was the next one up. These were levels on a ship. My roommate was from Tahlequah, Oklahoma. There were people from all over the country. One of the neat things about the Naval Academy is that all fifty states are represented proportionally in terms of population. There were a lot of people who grew up in Manhattan and New Jersey and other places, so everybody had different experiences growing up, and they all sounded a little different too.

I knew from day one what I wanted to major in, because it was something that was right up my alley, control systems engineering. It involved quite a few different aspects, analog computers, digital computers, simulating things with computers, optimization was a branch, so a lot of it was doing mathematical models of things that move either electrically or mechanically or electromechanically and design. It was the new thing back then. Now, your home computer does all of that.

First year is a plebe year. A lot of people probably thought that it was hellish, but I was too busy worrying about my grades. I also picked up rowing and was on the freshman rowing team. That got me out of some of the stuff because we had our own special table to eat dinner. So I didn't have to eat with the upperclassmen. I didn't have to march on the parades every Wednesday. We were out rowing in the river, which was a lot of work, but lower stress.

The Naval Academy was this place where they're supposed to be forming officers, but where I really got my formation was from my crew coach. His name was John VanAmering. He was a Yale ROTC grad, and a surface ship driver. He was also fairly brilliant. He rebelled against authority. He was like, "Screw 'em. I'm doing the right thing because I want my team to do well, and not because of this military stuff." That played out in my whole career later on. I know what the rules are, but this isn't the best thing for my team, so I'm going to do it my way. It all really goes back to my days with Coach VanAmering.

Steve decided to become a submariner while he was still at the Naval Academy, because "submarine officers ran the navy." When asked about missions, he said, "I definitely remember them, but talking about them is a different matter." Eventually, Steve rose up through the ranks and became commander of his own boat.

By the end of his twenty-year career in the navy,
Steve Clark Hall had commanded two nuclear submarines.
Photo courtesy of Steve Clark Hall.

When they made me captain of the *Greenling*, this was a ship that I knew every pipe and valve and switch. My whole career had been learning these things. I knew what could happen and what could go wrong. I show up as captain, and most of the other captains had never been on these things before and many of the enlisted people had never seen these things before. So it was kind of an unusual thing. Someone would tell me that something was broken, and here's what they're doing to fix it, and I'd think, "That's not the right answer." But they don't know that I'd know the right answer, because why would the captain know this little piece of minutia about the ship. But I did. It wasn't long before the crew knew that I knew this type of boat.

Your relationship to the boat is one thing, but what really brings the boat to life? It's your crew. When you become captain, you're told, "You can do with your boat whatever you want to do." It's like, "What?!" "Yes, if you want to go somewhere, just go ask the commodore." It's like, "Has it always been this way? How come my former captains never got to do this?" "Well, they were afraid to take the ship into a new place, because if anything goes wrong, their career's over." Well, it's like I'm not going to have anything go wrong to start with. My guys are really well trained, and I want to go see the world, which I hadn't gotten to do on other submarines because we'd just go to ports that we were familiar with. So I was like, "Hey, can I go to Bermuda?" And the commodore was like, "Sure." So we'd go to Bermuda for Memorial Day weekend. The crew started to appreciate these things that you'd do for them. Looking out for the sailors was important, because if their quality of life is good, they feed it back and their performance goes up.

When we decommissioned *Greenling* in '94, it was a sad thing [sighs], because the boat was brought alive by its crew, and it's like you're killing the crew. A lot of people spend their whole youth, the best years of their life, maintaining a boat to keep it running, and when you lose the boat due to a decommission, it's kind of a sad thing even though it's an inanimate object. But you're really basically discussing the life you had there.

At this point in the interview, I asked Steve to back up and talk about how his sexuality affected his time in the navy. Steve remembered that during the 1970s and 80s, it was understood that there were gay sailors and officers.

Back in my early days in the navy, being gay was seen as a sickness or a lack of moral turpitude. They [gays] were considered to be bad people. I certainly wasn't one of them, so I couldn't have been gay. So all these comments that I was hearing behind my back weren't true. [He laughs.] But it didn't really become apparent to me until I got to my first boat, out of the college environment, hanging out with a bunch of my peers in the real world. That's when it became apparent that maybe there was some truth to all of these things that I was hearing behind my back. Everybody else figured it out before I did. So I just kind of thought, "I'll pretend it doesn't happen and keep working hard and doing my job." It resulted in me working harder on the boat, spending more time on the boat to have an excuse of why I wasn't out doing what everybody else was doing.

I knew of some sailors who were gay, only because they'd come out or somebody would tell me about them. There was one enlisted guy when I was on a ship we were rebuilding. He was fairly out of the closet and the whole department knew about him. It wasn't an issue until he decided that he didn't want to be on the ship anymore, and he pulled the gay card out. We had to get rid of him.

In 1982, I was training 160 people in a combined blue-gold engineering department. I was up there talking and we had a few minutes before class, so I was talking about when we get to Seattle, here are all of these things to do. And of course, this guy raises his hand and says [in a high pitched voice], "Where are the bars that *I* would be going to?" I said, "Well, the bars for you are on Capitol Hill. So you look at this bar, this bar, and this bar." Of course, I knew the names of the bars. So not only was he totally out, I was also pretty open to my department in the early 80s.

My third job was being on the flag staff over here in Alameda. I bought this house in San Francisco in the middle of the Castro. Everybody on the staff knew it. At this point, I wasn't planning on staying in the navy. I was going to be an architect. But I had this great job working for the admiral. I was really enjoying it, so I just did my own thing. And it turns out the admiral loved it. I was always the top-ranked guy. It didn't trash my career like I thought it was going to. I didn't hide anything on that staff. I had a staff party with other officers here in my house in the middle of the Castro. There were a lot of jokes about stuff and where I lived.

I didn't really have to take my career and put it in the closet until I went to be executive officer of the *Permit* down in San Diego where I felt that it was not cool to be gay anymore. I hid everything again and had no gay friends—didn't do any gay things. I basically just worked hard. My boss in San Diego was an alcoholic, and this is why I ended up having to spend much more time on the ship. I was making up for him not being around. I think he was trying to blame some of the failures of the ship on my homosexuality. He would make homophobic comments to me over dinner in front of all the other officers. Everybody else knew what was going on. If I'd get up and leave the evening movie, he'd say, "What's the matter, not enough dick in this movie for you?" Basically, this went on day in, day out. Any opportunity he had to throw a jab at me: "Hey, you going to go on leave to see your boyfriends up in San Francisco?" It was pretty demeaning, and it was blatant sexual harassment, but, of course, I can't turn him in for sexually harassing me. That would have trashed my career. There were two years of that, but I got through it.

I took over as captain of the *Greenling* two weeks after Clinton won the election, and I was getting ready for gays in the military. So I started from day one on my ship, preaching, "It's ok to be different. Not everybody's the same. Don't be afraid of things that aren't like you." I had two black officers in my wardroom of fourteen officers. I could disguise this as being about tolerance of racial minorities when in reality it was also about being gay. I was sensing that my crew didn't seem to object to what I was saying. I have since been told that my entire crew knew I was gay. I don't know when they found out or how they found out, but I didn't sense a problem with that with my crew.

So along comes "Don't Ask, Don't Tell" after these horrible hearings that went on in the summer of '93, and they come up with this policy. This was a step backwards, I felt. I was basically coming out to my crew at the time I took over as captain, letting them know that it's ok to be different. Don't be afraid of me because I happen to be gay. Then this policy comes out and makes it more difficult for me, because I already didn't flaunt too much. I didn't want people telling me, "Hey, I'm straight." It's like why do I care? I don't care if you're gay either. Just do your job. I didn't have the problem on my ship where they were pulling the gay card to get off the boat. You do that when you hate where you are.

We had women in the military, and there are some people who don't like women in the military. When I started doing midshipmen cruises, the women midshipmen could only go out from the morning to the evening and only for informational purposes, since they weren't allowed to serve on submarines. The question that I kept getting asked as a captain was: "Why does the submarine force have this policy?" It's like, "Well, it's because some people don't want women on submarines." That was all I could really say. They'd say, "We don't see a big deal with this. We go out on a cruise—four guys, four women on a sailboat. There's only one restroom. We all sleep in the same area. There's not a problem with this. Why is it a problem with the senior people?" But that's where the problem is.

It was the same thing with gays. The officers who were significantly senior to me were the ones brought up to think of homosexuality as this deviant behavior that causes loss of morale. Young kids these days grow up with kids who are gay. They know that they're real people. They know that they're not the "deviant" people who have always been portrayed as being bad for morale. In fact, I think it's quite the opposite. The younger troops didn't have a problem with the gay thing.

That's another issue of "Don't Ask, Don't Tell." The military is really hurting itself. They spend several hundred thousand dollars training a person to fill a job on the submarine, and it takes a year and a half to get him to the position where he can fill that billet. When you lose him because he's gay, and you have three guys who were on a watch rotation of six hours on twelve hours off, now, you're missing a person so they're on six and off six, on six and off six. It takes months to get a replacement. Talk about something that's bad for morale. That kills morale to lose one of your team members because they happen to be gay.

During the hearings before the passage of "Don't Ask, Don't Tell" in 1993, Senator Sam Nunn took the Armed Services Committee to visit a submarine to show how limited privacy would be if gay sailors were billeted with straight sailors in those close quarters.

I was so disappointed that Sam Nunn didn't come to my boat. Unfortunately, I was up in New London, but had Sam Nunn come to my boat with the TV cameras running, I would have said, "Senator, it's not a problem. About 10 percent of my crew is gay, sir, and it's not a problem down here." I think that the three-star at the head of the Atlantic fleet at the time knew I was gay based on a few private conversations that I had with him where he made some snotty remarks to me. I don't think they would have brought Sam Nunn down to my boat.

Let's talk about the privacy issue with women and the restrooms on the submarines. There's only one officer's head on a submarine, and if you want to make a women's restroom, you flip the sign outside so that it says "women" over it. How is that so difficult? Only one person can fit in at a time. So it's crazy to hear that we have to spend millions or billions of dollars configuring a head to handle both men and women. A lot of it was justification to keep women out. It'll be the same thing with trying to keep gays out. But gays have always been there, and it's not a problem, or it shouldn't be a problem.

At the time of the interview, Steve had retired from the Navy. He was working as a general contractor, restoring old homes and dividing his time between San Francisco, California, and Provincetown, Massachusetts.

An Interview with Jeff Petrie

Jeff Petrie is the dynamo behind the creation of USNA Out, an alumni group for gay graduates of the United States Naval Academy. Like many academy alumni from the late 1980s, Jeff served in the Persian Gulf during Operation Desert Shield. After facing discrimination and harassment in uniform, he resolved to build a support network for gay academy alumni, who could then serve as role models for the gay cadets and midshipmen currently attending U.S. military academies.

I was born on August 6, 1967, in Ellensburg, Washington, which is about eighty-five miles east of Seattle. At the time, my dad was a student at Central Washington University and my mother was putting him through school by selling shoes at J. C. Penney. From Ellensburg, we ultimately moved to Eugene, Oregon, where we finally settled down.

I was about nine years old when I got involved in gymnastics. That was because the PE coach in my elementary school really pushed handstands. My PE coach saw that I had the body type and the drive to maybe take handstands to the next level. [He laughs.] He found a place for me at a gymnastics academy in downtown Eugene, which was actually one of the nation's best gymnastics academies for many, many years. I became the Oregon State champ and the Pacific Northwest Regional champ for several years.

Somehow, at the Naval Academy—the coach there, Peter Korman—heard that I was considering going to West Point. So he got on the phone to call me to see if he could lure me away. He thought if I was serious about a military future, then I would be a great recruit for the Naval Academy. People know about the Army-Navy rivalry, so to have this gymnast who had done really well at national championships when he was a junior, was quite a threat, I think, to him. So he had a few other important people at the Naval Academy get involved in recruiting me.

Probably the biggest reason that I ended up choosing the Naval Academy was that when I was a senior in high school, my grandfather was failing rapidly of cancer. He was beyond even going to the hospital, so he was just at home in bed, waiting. He was such a wonderful man. He had really loved me growing up and had showed me the wonder of the world. I wanted to talk to him about my college choices, and I remember thinking to myself, "He's not going to be around much longer." I said, "E. A.," which is what I called him, "of these colleges, what do you think my best option is?" He had been a dentist in the navy during World War II, a lieutenant commander. He said, "I think that the Naval Academy will really open some doors for you. You'll be set for life, and you'll be able to serve America at the same time." There was no way that I could say "no" to that. It seemed to be my grandfather's wish that I go there. I'm sure that if he knew all of the facts, he would probably have taken other things into consideration, but he didn't know that I was different yet. In fact, he never did. So I think that he was just giving me the very best advice that he could with the information that he had. So with his recommendation, that was the school that I chose.

That first day at Annapolis, I remember meeting the other kids who had ended up there and hearing a little bit about them. I remember getting my hair totally cut off, and that put us all on level ground except for the females who just got their hair cut really short. We all converged near the academic buildings for our swearing-in ceremony. It got hot again during the day, and I remember sweating a lot. I remember hearing a buzz of insects in the air and humidity and heat and this sense of patriotism really starting to kick in. We raised our hands and said the oath of the midshipmen together, and we were sworn in.

Then, we dove into all of the things that are involved in that plebe summer, which are not entirely pleasant. Plebe summer was the baptism of fire, especially for me. It's basically the officer's boot camp, which instead of being as physical as most boot camps, there's mind games thrown in there too. There were a lot of times where we'd be lined up in the hallway and we'd be getting yelled at for who knows what reason, and we'd be getting asked questions that we knew nothing about. But it was teaching us respect and discipline and feeling one of the team, because we were really going through this difficult time together.

As a plebe, I had been required to read the paper every day. I was reading about AIDS and how it was decimating gay populations in the nearby big cities of Philadelphia, New York, and Washington. It was mysterious, and no one knew what was happening to these people. In the lunchroom, when I was asked about what I was reading in the newspaper, I would say that I had read about AIDS. The comments that I would get were that "the homos were getting what they deserved," and they hoped that AIDS would just kill all of them. These comments were things that I heard almost on a daily basis. I think that I set myself up psychologically in a way that those comments would just flow right off, but I realized later that they didn't.

So Thanksgiving came, and being the kid from Eugene, Oregon, I wanted to see the Capitol and I wanted to see the Washington Monument and the White

House. At the same time, because I had been reading about AIDS, I knew where the gay neighborhood was in D.C., so I also went to Dupont Circle. I came out of the Metro station and I was going along the street in front of a bookstore that was called Lambda Rising. This kid who was about my age was walking the other way, and he really gave me an intense look. Being kind of shy myself, I just wasn't sure what to do, but I did turn around. He walked back up to me and said, "Do I know you?" I suspect that that was his line, but I wasn't sure. I couldn't really look him in the eye, so I looked down, and I noticed that he had a blue Naval Academy duffle bag in his hands. I said to him, "I don't think you know me, but it looks like we go to the same school." His eyes got really big, and we went and had coffee some place. We actually became instant friends. I think he was a little freaked out that he had just made a pass at another midshipman, and I was really surprised that on my very first day away from Annapolis, I had met another gay midshipman. I was really kind of excited about that. He was very handsome, so I was really excited about that too.

It turned out that he actually lived very close to me in Bancroft Hall. After coffee, he went on his way and I went on my way, but we were planning to stay in touch. He was a sophomore. In most cases, for a plebe to have any kind of relationship or friendship with an upperclassman is pretty taboo, unless you are a varsity athlete. So the fact that I was able to go back to Bancroft Hall and have a rapport with a sophomore, no eyebrows were raised, because I was an athlete. I would use the term dated very loosely, but we sort of dated and hung out for about a week.

I was still the star gymnast, and we had a meet that Friday after Thanksgiving. That night, I punched off the ground to do a front flip after a double twisting layout, and my knee just snapped off to the side. It didn't really hurt so bad, but it didn't work anymore. I sort of hobbled off the floor. There was always a navy doctor at those gymnastics meets. He tested my knee immediately and saw that I had torn ligaments in it. He told me right then and there, "I don't know if you'll ever walk regularly again." So for someone who had been a gymnast from age nine to eighteen that was pretty huge.

The Army-Navy game was the very next day in Philadelphia. I had been cheering, "Go Navy! Beat Army!" since July 2. There was no way I was not going to go to this football game. Plus, Curt Hughes (class of '88), my friend, he had gotten an apartment for us to stay at, and plebes were allowed to either go back to Annapolis after the Army-Navy game or stay the night up there. Curt said, "I've got a place for us to stay, so will you stay?" And I said, "I'll stay." So even though I was on crutches and couldn't march in with the rest of the brigade, I went to that Army-Navy game, darn it! Navy won. Good news for the plebes, so after that game, until Christmas vacation began, our lives were much, much easier. It's called "Carry on." You don't have to be subjected to the same stuff that had been going on from July 2nd up to that very day.

Anyway, after the Army-Navy game, Curt and I went back to the apartment where we were staying, changed clothes and went to downtown Philadelphia, to a gay bar down there called Key West. I had never been to a bar in my life. But there I was on crutches. It was a three-story place with stairs, so it wasn't the greatest evening for me, but at the same time, it was my first trip to a gay bar, and I was able to see: "Wow! There are all of these people that are like me!" Curt introduced me to another guy from the class of '88, Vann Vickers, and he also introduced me to two first-class midshipmen, two seniors. So I went in one week from knowing no one to knowing four others. I knew that I was not alone and that made things much, much easier for me.

After several months of arduous physical therapy, Jeff was able to compete again for the Navy gymnastics team, though not at the level he hoped to achieve. As a senior, he was voted team captain. His first assignment after graduation was as assistant varsity gymnastics coach at the Naval Academy. Then after Surface Warfare Officers School, he began duty aboard a ship that would eventually head to the Persian Gulf for support operations during Operation Desert Shield.

Being in the Persian Gulf War was our duty. It was what we were sent to do, and I had raised my hand, saying that I was prepared to give my life in defense of the Constitution and our way of life, and I was.

We left in September of 1992. We went with a carrier battle group, but because the USS *Kirk* was a small ship, we were able to pull into the Persian Gulf ports that the larger ships weren't able to get into. So we had sort of a diplomatic mission. We went port-to-port, holding receptions for the government and business leaders, whoever the people in the city or town were that we wanted to solidify a friendship with, to help them feel good about the United States being there. So we went to Kuwait City. We went to Jubail, Saudi Arabia; Manama, Bahrain; Jebel Ali in the United Arab Emirates, and Muscat in Oman. Sometimes we would do exercises with the other ships, but for the most part we would be on our own. We got back in February of 1993.

When we were in Kuwait, the port was beat up. You could see bullet holes in some of the buildings. No one was working in those buildings. And the city itself was pretty beat up. The fairgrounds was where all of the captured Iraqi tanks were, and there were just lines and lines of them, so the signs of battle were still pretty fresh. But when we were there, I never really felt unsafe.

When we were just finishing up our tour in the Persian Gulf, I had been on

After graduating from the U.S. Naval Academy, Jeff Petrie served in the Persian Gulf during Desert Shield. Petrie is pictured here on graduation day with Naval Academy superintendent Virgil Hill Jr. Photo courtesy of Jeff Petrie.

liberty in Muscat, Oman, which is just outside the Gulf. I stepped back on board the ship, and there on the podium, on the quarterdeck, was a letter. It was from my boyfriend back home. He had written a pretty juicy letter to me, and it was open and sitting on the quarterdeck for anyone and everyone to read. I figured that the postal clerk had something to do with it, but there was nothing I could say because the captain would want to know, "Well, where's the letter?" So all I could do was grab the letter off of that podium and take it to my stateroom.

I had not even read it yet myself. It got intercepted before it had even got to me, and I thought to myself, "Who has read this? What do they think of me now? Is the captain going to find out? Does he already know?" We were just starting our trip across the Indian Ocean to Perth, Western Australia, and I got really paranoid, because if you are in the middle of the Indian Ocean and you find yourself going overboard in the middle of the night, you're not going to be coming back. I was truly afraid for my life. I was afraid that somebody who had read the letter would want to get rid of me. And what easier thing to do than get a couple of guys together to come into my stateroom at night and just throw me overboard. So I was really truly afraid for that whole transit. Once we got to Australia, I started thinking to myself: "They've had a chance to do something now, and no one's done anything. No one's said anything."

Jeff made it to Australia and then back to San Diego, but he never felt entirely safe again. Homophobia was on the rise in response to the Clinton campaign promise to lift the ban on gay troops. Jeff was offered an early out during the downsizing of the u.s. Navy in 1993, and, after four years of active duty, he took it. But the navy was all Jeff had ever known, and he struggled to adjust to civilian life. Founding USNA Out gave his life direction once again.

In April 2003 my roommate from the academy was killed in a plane crash in Iraq, and also the *Lawrence v. Texas* Supreme Court decision came out, which legalized gay sex. I remember on that day, the big rainbow flag that flies over the Castro was taken down and the Stars and Stripes were put up. I couldn't believe it, and I had to see it for myself. That really got some patriotism stirring in me again, and it got me to thinking: "What can I do now?" So in August 2003 I sent an email to all of the gay alumni from the Naval Academy that I know, saying, "I would like to start an official alumni chapter from our school. Will you join me? I need 25 people to submit the paperwork."

Very slowly they trickled in. I think immediately eight people said yes. Then, I had to network through them and locate people who I had not seen in years and ask them if they'd join me. Sometimes, I just coincidentally crossed paths with people. I was eating lunch in the museum where I work one day, and there was a guy sitting next to me who had a really big ring on his hand. I looked really closely, and it was the same as mine. I said, "Did you go to the Naval Academy?" He said, "Yes." I could just tell by the way he carried himself that he was a candidate for USNA Out. I've found some people that way.

Anyway, by October we reached twenty-five members, and so I put together the recognition request paperwork to start an alumni chapter at the academy. I flew to Annapolis last Veterans Day to deliver the paperwork. As I was driving out to Annapolis, I felt my pride just slipping away. I was wondering, "Gosh, can I even do this?" But I thought, "I have to do this!" That was a really, really big deal.

At the time of this interview, Jeff Petrie worked at the Legion of Honor Fine Arts Museum in San Francisco. The Naval Academy had still not formally recognized USNA Out, but the group had more than seventy-five members and it has continued to grow.

THE FACULTY

An Interview with Beth Hillman

Beth Hillman is both a scholar and a veteran. Though she was not much interested in academics when she went to Duke University on an ROTC scholarship, she went on to do graduate work in history and taught at the Air Force Academy for two years in the mid-1990s. Serving on the faculty gave her a different vantage point of academy life than the other veterans interviewed in this chapter. As a female instructor, she was in a unique position to observe and aid the air force in combating sexism and sexual harassment. Her interest in the law and emerging identity as a lesbian inspired both a professional and personal commitment to military justice.

I'm Beth Hillman and I was born 10-18-1967 in McKeesport, Pennsylvania. My dad was in the Army Air Corps during World War II and then went to school on the GI Bill and worked for U.S. Steel. He worked in the mills for a while. Then he computerized their payroll and worked as an accountant and systems analyst. My mom mostly raised kids but also was a dietitian. I grew up in the suburbs of Pittsburgh, a place called Pleasant Hills. I'm one of five kids; I have a twin sister and three older brothers.

I started ROTC at Duke in 1985. I decided to do ROTC because I wanted to go to an expensive school and I wanted a scholarship. My parents didn't have a lot of money, but they had enough that I knew I wouldn't qualify for a lot of need-based financial aid. I was an athlete in high school and a good student, and I was not intimidated by male-dominated things. I felt that I would do fine in ROTC, but I didn't have any particular interest or connection to the military. Eventually, I became a very gung-ho cadet and officer. I was very much seduced by the military once I got into it.

ROTC is a sort of part-time military thing. You wear your uniform once in a while. You have some training. But it's not the culture shock of basic training or the service academy in terms of acculturation to the military. ROTC was my primary extracurricular activity, and I spent a lot of time doing the things that would help me get ahead in the detachment. But because I taught at the Air Force Academy, I recognize the difference between being in an ROTC unit and being immersed in a military culture like the service academies. In a way, I think ROTC prepared me better than the folks that were at the service academy. There's this sense that once people graduate from West Point or Annapolis or the Air Force Academy they're suddenly free to have the lives that they want. So, actually, I think in terms of living and having the mature sort of life, I think that ROTC is better in many respects.

I went into the air force because my dad was in the Army Air Corps, but I also had some sense that the air force was a service where opportunities were open to women and it was a service that was technologically advanced. Since I was interested in science and I majored in engineering, it seemed to make sense to me to go into the Air Force.

First, I went and worked at the Pentagon. I worked as a cadet at the Strategic Defense Initiative (SDI) Organization. That's the Star Wars program. I had worked there the summer before I graduated from Duke, and they asked if I wanted to come back. So right after I graduated I went to the Pentagon. At the end of that summer in September, I went out to Lowry Air Force Base in Denver and went to the first training for space operations officers, which is the career field that I went into.

At this point, I asked Beth to talk about the politics of SDI, since it was one of the more controversial programs undertaken by the military during the 1980s.

I don't think that most of the people who work in that program make a decision whether or not to be involved based on the bigger political picture, especially when they're at the beginning of their careers. To me SDI was a rigorous, exciting assignment. It was a place where there was a lot of money to fund interesting and exciting programs, and there was a lot of technological excitement. It was what's called a "Purple Service Environment." There were people from the different services, and there was this connection to the space world and the space business that I thought I was going to end up working with in the air force. So for me it was a place to get some experience. I wasn't political. I didn't think about national politics in a way that I considered how I might influence them as a second lieutenant in the air force.

I worked with very senior people. Like most places in D.C. and certainly in the Pentagon, it was staffed at a high level. There were a lot of lieutenant colonels and colonels and navy commanders and captains who were trying to make decisions about programs. I helped them work with contractors. I helped them write memos to assess things. I did some research for the historian at SDI on some different ballistic missile defense things. You know, it was fun. I learned a lot.

After several months working at the Pentagon, Beth went through the training in Colorado to work with the Air Force Space Surveillance Center. She was working there when the first Gulf War broke out.

I went to Cheyenne Mountain Air Force Base in Colorado Springs, and I worked on a Space Surveillance Center crew. The Space Surveillance Center was one of the different operational centers in the mountain that operates on a twenty-four-hour rotating schedule. People rotate in on shifts and run it all the time. I was part of a center that tracks everything that orbits the earth—watches what goes up and what comes down, helps individuals, countries, and organizations who are launching satellites to keep track of what's up there, and identifies the potential threats to the United States. We watched when objects reenter the atmosphere to see if they might come down some place that's dangerous or that might cause a false alarm.

During the Gulf War, that was the big thing. When a rocket body, which is very dense and large, reenters the atmosphere, it looks bright to many different sensors that are looking at it. It might look like a reentry vehicle from a missile coming into the atmosphere, and if it comes down in the wrong place, it might trigger a reaction from ground-based missile defense systems. We might know or might be able to predict that it was a harmless rocket body. This was an issue during the Gulf War, so we occasionally identified things that looked like they might be Scud missiles, but they weren't.

During the war, I worked shifts at the Center and in many ways our job was the same, but like everyone who was part of the support structure in the military, it was a different tempo of things once the war was on. The intelligence briefings were different; the stakes were higher. It was clear the stakes were higher.

We also helped the space shuttle. That was the sexiest job that we had, identifying any objects that might intersect with the orbit of the space shuttle, because you clearly don't want the space shuttle to run into anything that you can identify. So it would occasionally maneuver to get out of the path of an object that was big enough for us to track.

After I had been in like three years or so, I applied for different scholarship and fellowship opportunities. The one that came through was with the Air Force Academy, so the Department of History at the Air Force Academy sponsored me to study history full time and get a master's degree and come back and teach. I was excited to do that. I convinced them to send me to Penn, and I came to Philadelphia. I was in Philadelphia for about ten months from '93–'94. I did two semesters of course work, and then I wrote a master's thesis, and then I went back and started teaching at the Air Force Academy the next year. I taught at the Air Force Academy from '94 to '96.

Graduate school changed me dramatically. I often tell my students when they say they've learned a lot from a class that they took with me that it's about who they are when they came to the class and not so much what I do in the classroom that makes it possible for them to learn. When I got to Penn I was really ready to be intellectually, emotionally, and personally engaged in a way I hadn't been before. I wasn't an especially good student as an undergrad. I did fine, but my interests were really elsewhere. When I got to graduate school I was excited about the professors I was hearing in the classroom. I was excited by the other students, and I was just ready to listen to people.

For the first time, I saw people who were gay and were unafraid about it. I certainly realized when I went back to Colorado Springs I had known people all along who were gay. Many of them had thought that I was a lesbian, which was a surprise to me. So graduate school was a coming-out experience for me in all kinds of ways including in terms of my sexual orientation. That is when I fell in love with a woman. I had been married, and I left my husband back in Colorado Springs. I came to Philadelphia and I met all these graduate students, and I fell in love with a woman and we had a torrid affair. I thought I was going to leave it behind and that would be the end of it, but it wasn't. Even as I was driving back across the country to teach at the Air Force Academy, I knew that things were not going to be the same.

That first semester at the Air Force Academy, I taught four sections of world history. And world history at the academy was from the Greeks to Gorbachev; it was a large course. There was a lot to cover. It was very strange to teach four of the same classes. I couldn't always remember what I had said to the class the previous time, you know. I taught at nine, ten, one, and two o'clock in the afternoon. I had to keep looking at my notes to make sure I hadn't just said what I was sure I had just said to them.

But it was exciting in the way that teaching is always exciting. Students come prepared in different ways, but they're captive to you. They're going to listen to you for the period of time that they're assigned to that class. They come in with their own ideas about what is right and isn't. Since I studied American history in graduate school, I actually had students that had studied more world history than I had. In world history, someone can always tell you something that you don't know. It was fun.

This was a first-year course, so we had students who had been at the academy since right after the 4th of July. When they started classes in late August, they were very tired. They had gotten through one of the most difficult parts of their training and now they were trying to turn their minds to the academic part of it, but they were still very much under duress; they were tired. In the afternoon classes I taught after lunch the first year, they fell asleep all the time. I got them on their feet like everybody else did, but I certainly understood why that was happening; they weren't getting enough sleep, and they were really taxed.

Beth was very happy with both her students and her colleagues in the history department, and she very much enjoyed her time teaching at the academy. She taught an honors class and received an instructor award. Though I feared it might be a sore spot, I asked her to talk about sexual harassment and the scandals that rocked the academies in the 1980s and 90s.

It was a big issue. I was involved in different efforts to try to "improve the social climate." I was on a committee that studied this. I developed and administered a survey to all the cadets about the social climate, asking them questions about it. I was a participant in the first sexual assault awareness week. All the cadets had to sign up to go to one event during that week in addition to some things that they all had to do within their squadron. I gave a lecture on rape and war in a historical perspective. I had a thousand cadets attend. In terms of what all of these young men are going to be willing to go see, that sounded much better to them than how to hear when someone says "no" to you or what are common date-rape scenarios—the "softer" topics that were being discussed by psychologists and sociologists and other experts that were talking during that week.

I also got a little money from the commandant to do some oral histories of some women cadets, and so I enlisted some other faculty members and we interviewed at great length some female cadets. We put the transcriptions in the library archives. They talked about harassment. I got to know enough of the female cadets to get a sense of what they were going through. As the assistant coach for the basketball team, I worked with the junior varsity, and there were several women who had had different experiences with sexual assault and harassment. It was very much a part of their understanding of the institution. It was certainly not something that somebody didn't know about if they were paying any attention.

There were individuals who genuinely sought change in the culture and in the institutional mechanisms that tried to respond to this, but I think that the problems of misogyny, homophobia, and aggression that are such a deep part of the military—even the air force, which is the least martial of the services— they make it very hard to solve the problems that women faced. There were individual failings of leadership and individual decisions that went awry involving particular cases. But the air force leadership did try to address these things.

I always thought that I could manage sexism, and I felt that I could use it to my advantage. Inside the military and outside the military, I saw discrimination all over the place. In terms of what I experienced personally, I never thought it was going to be a barrier to my career advancement. I had never been a woman who challenged men. I got along with them. I liked sports. I could talk about these things. You know, we got along fine. I was married for Pete's sake.

But I did see how sexism changed the way that people responded to me. In particular, it was more about the choices that I made, about what to study for instance. When I went to graduate school, I realized I was writing about some things that were going to draw some fire, and they did. I wrote about how women's uniforms were dysfunctional and unattractive specifically because the people who designed them couldn't imagine what a woman soldier should look like or how a female military uniform should make its occupants appear. I had a boss who was the director of the American history section. When I got to the academy's history department, he said, "What? You study women's history? Is that like the study of redheads? Is that the history of people who ride motorcycles?" He was joking, but it reflected his real discomfort with women's history.

One of the reasons why I haven't become a more committed advocate of lesbians and gay men in the service is that I don't have uncomplicated good feelings about military service. I can't separate who I am from my service in the air force. I don't regret what I did, but I have doubts about what the military teaches people—especially men, but women too—about violence, about what it is to be an American, about authority, about autonomy.

Sometimes, when I talk about "Don't Ask, Don't Tell," I say that I'm not somebody the air force should have lost. I was somebody they would have liked to have on their team. You would want me on your side, and the air force certainly did for a long time, but I didn't want to play anymore. If somebody had found out that I was involved with a woman and I was discharged under "Don't Ask, Don't Tell," I knew that I would fight that discharge because I felt like if anyone has a record to stand on, I do.

After Beth left the air force, she entered a joint degree program at Yale University, earning a law degree and a Ph.D. in history. At the time of this interview she was teaching at Rutgers University Law School, and she was about to publish her first book about American military justice during the Cold War.

WEST POINT

An Interview with Steve Boeckels

When Steve Boeckels started at the West Point preparatory school, he described himself as very, very conservative, a Rush Limbaugh type. But the United States Military Academy taught him to be a critical thinker, skeptical of ideological extremism on either side of the political spectrum. West Point also taught him survival and leadership skills. Though he never fought in a war, he would need both sets of skills to endure the homophobia he faced once he came out as a gay lieutenant in the army.

I was born in Live Oak, Florida, April 22, 1974. My dad was a social worker, and he did a lot of nonprofit kind of stuff. My mom's a hairdresser. She's Colombian, so they met when my dad was doing a polio project in South America. After they got married, they moved up to Florida, and he worked on a Boys Ranch there to help homeless or disenfranchised teenagers. Then we all moved to New York, actually the New York City area. Every year, until I was about maybe twelve, for the whole summer, we'd spend the time in South America. So a lot of the summers we used to spend overseas.

A lot of my interest in the military had to do with the influence of Desert Storm. But really, it's just my calling. I knew I wanted to do military service, and I had this calling to do it. It's really hard to explain. My dad was in the Korean War, but he only spent four years in. My uncles were in the military also, but they weren't lifers. So it wasn't really like they had huge influence, but when I said that I was interested in going into the military, they started trying to find references for me, people that were in the military to talk to.

In Desert Storm, what really impressed me, and I think helped me decide between the air force and the army was that they had forty-five days of air campaigns, just constant bombings. Then all of a sudden we had this ninety-six-hour war with the ground force. That had a huge influence, seeing Schwarz-kopf—he went to West Point. So it was just the media influence that basically said all these key leaders that actually made the war successful were West Pointers. I think a combination of the locality, geography, what the media was saying about the military, and then also George Bush's comments about West Point. Those several different things ultimately made me decide to go to West Point.

Steve was so sure that he wanted to go to the United States Military Academy, that he first attended the United States Military Academy Preparatory School for a year, before his admission to West Point.

The prep school was great because it exposed me to the regimen of getting very little sleep and just trying to balance your academics, your military re-sponsibilities, military life and sports, which is what West Point did too. So when I was actually admitted into West Point, I started R-Day, which is sup-posed to be the worst day of your life, but for me it was a good day because I was calm, cool, and collected. I was actually able to go in and do pretty well. Whereas a lot of people were getting that big shock right there, I already went through it the year before. I was a little bit more mature and able to deal with it. Our class started out with maybe 1,250, and we graduated just under 900. The first year we lost quite a bit of people.

The first year is called Cadet Basic Training. That's when you get indoctri-nated with how to shine shoes, learn about the history and the traditions of West Point, learn about table duties, which are basically ways for upperclass-men to haze freshmen. You learn how to work with others. There's a lot of teamwork skills. There's basic first aid, combat, and marksmanship. Then the second summer is Cadet Field Training. That's really the first summer that exposes you to the different branches of the military. You go through the combat skills, you go through self-defense courses, you go through all these obstacle courses. I had a great time; for me it was like summer camp. It was really just a blast. I was a squad leader at West Point for the first field summer.

When I was at West Point, I had quite a few leadership roles. I was a first sergeant for the company H-3. Then I was also the training officer at company level and the second semester my senior year was for battalion level. I tried to use positive leadership. For me, I was motivated by people who said, "Hey, can you do this, work together for the benefit of everyone?" I never want to be a person that is going to use yelling and negative leadership to influence people because the result ultimately is they're just going to do the bare minimum of what you tell them. I always liked to try to inspire people to do things in the right way and not what's required. They finish a job right.

When I was first sergeant, if the cadet screwed up, I'd definitely hammer them down, but I wouldn't necessarily yell at them. I would kind of get them in a group together and it's like, "This is what you're doing right; this is what you're doing wrong. I don't want to keep you guys in here. I don't want to waste your time and waste my time. I want to focus on how to correct these deficiencies and then how we can work together to not have me constantly getting on your back." So if people were doing the right thing, I wouldn't get on them. I would actually go in and say, "You're doing a good job. This is great!" I'd compliment them. But if they did things wrong, then I'd basically bring down the hammer.

Graduation, that's one of the happiest days of my life. It so happened that that day the commencement speaker was President Clinton. It was May 30 or 31, 1997. He came out, and he gave a speech about new foreign policy initiatives. It was a big thing. That day it was actually supposed to rain. There were clouds in the sky in the morning, and then all of a sudden, before graduation, as we were marching out to the stadium, the sun just came out and it was just the most beautiful day. My family was there. It was very vivid. To see the light at the end of the tunnel after five years—one year at the prep school and four years going through West Point. It was just the most amazing feeling.

I branched Armor, so I went to Fort Knox, Kentucky, for training. I was super motivated. In February of '98 I ended up going to Fort Wainwright, Alaska. At that point, we were getting ready to deploy to the Sinai Peninsula for a peacekeeping mission with a multinational force. It was a peacekeeping mission that was going on between Egypt and Israel. The UN mission that was supposed to create a demilitarized zone there after the Arab-Israel war of the seventies failed, and these nations that wanted peace in the region basically got together and created this multinational force.

As you remember, that was actually the time that Clinton was trying to forge the peace between the Palestinians and the Israelis. So really there weren't any car bombings; there was actually a lot of peace. I was very, very fortunate to be down there during that time because I got to see all of Israel and a lot of Egypt and some of Jordan. There was a positive feeling within the area that there was actually going to be a peace, and there was a lot of positivity towards Americans.

After talking about his Middle Eastern deployment, I asked Steve to back up and talk about how sexuality affected his time in the military.

In '92 in the prep school, I remember going through the DODMERB [Department of Defense Medical Examination Review Board]. They actually had a question there saying, "Are you homosexual?" This is when I was seventeen or eighteen, and I had no clue about it. "Are you homosexual? Have you ever engaged in a homosexual activity?" I'm like, "What the . . . ?! [He laughs.] Didn't even cross my mind. I was like, "No, no." When I got into West Point, the "Don't Ask, Don't Tell" policy had just been implemented. We were the first class to go into West Point and not have to answer the question about sexual orientation. That year they had that question crossed out because the forms hadn't been updated yet. When we were marching in from our basic training, from Lake Frederick, we were marching into the campus at West Point, and they had what was called "the gauntlet." It was this huge line of all of the upperclassmen on either side, and they were just basically screaming and yelling at all the freshman coming in. All kinds of things were being said, but one thing I remember consistently being said was "Clinton's army." They kept calling us "Clinton's army." I heard a couple epithets of "faggots" and things like that.

Even when I was at the prep school, I kept a whole bunch of things that came up that were pretty derogatory, making fun of Clinton. They had this one fax that I kept that I think was "Clinton's Queen Berets."[7] It had the song "The Green Berets," and they basically modified it to make a spoof out of Clinton and his accepting of gays in the army. So there was a lot of blowback from Clinton trying to open or change the policy. He tried to do a lot in the beginning of his term, which got a lot of negative press. And it eventually ended up, I think, hurting him in Congress. But that was something that I remember vividly.

There was a big scandal in my company between two women, two lesbians. It actually got in the newspapers. There were always rumors about these two girls that were lesbians, that they had this relationship. But never with guys, it was always the lesbians, the women, that were always being harassed—the ones that were always in the spotlight. So one night when they were doing a bed check, the cadet on duty was checking all the rooms and caught the two girls in the same bed. Nothing came of it, but then they split the room apart the second semester my junior year, and one of my classmates actually went through and took a diary of the girl, read through it, then turned it in. Both girls were kicked out. One was a junior so she was kicked out a year before she graduated, and then the other one was kicked out of West Point the week of graduation. It was a witch hunt, in hindsight.

I was dating girls at the time still, but going to West Point was mostly

*When Steve Boeckels entered West Point in 1993 after the passage of
"Don't Ask, Don't Tell," some upperclassmen derided the new plebes in "Clinton's
army" as "faggots." Boeckels met President Clinton on graduation day in 1997.
Photo courtesy of Steve Boeckels.*

focused on survival. I really focused on work too much, and there's definitely a disparity between the amount of time I put into work and the amount of time I put into developing my social skills. I had done that my whole life. I was always a workaholic at school, very studious. When I was like around twenty-three through twenty-five, that's really when the wall started coming down and that big disparity between focusing on work and social life collapsed. I would say that that was the turning point of my life.

When I got back to Alaska after the Sinai deployment, I was starting to think that maybe this army career isn't working out because there were rumors starting to circulate saying that I was kind of feminine, but I really wasn't. There was this club called Club G. It had really good dance music, and there were straight people who would go to the club. I went with a couple of friends of mine. When you're up in Fairbanks, Alaska, where the metropolitan population is 70,000 people you can't help but get rumors starting to fly around, because everyone knows what everyone else is doing.

At that point I was becoming very disillusioned with the military. I was just becoming very unhappy with my life. All my vacations were to go down to California. I went down to San Diego for Thanksgiving of '99, and when I came back from that trip, I came out to my roommate. I told him I kind of was a bisexual. [He laughs.] He basically said, "Alright." When I saw his expression, the floodwaters opened up, the dam broke, and everything just came out. Seeing his reaction was totally the opposite of what I was expecting. I thought he was going to move out, but he didn't. He was like, "I kind of had a feeling you were, but I wish you would have told me sooner." He was one of my classmates from West Point.

This was 1999, what Steve calls his "year of enlightenment." Even though his roommate and other peers from West Point were supportive of his coming out, his superior officer in Alaska was not. He could not challenge the homophobic environment in his unit without endangering himself, so Steve requested a transfer. Knowing that it would mean his discharge from the service, he openly admitted his homosexuality.

The transfer down to Fort Knox was a lot better because the colonel up in Alaska was very antigay and there was a lot of antigay sentiment up there. There were always a lot of gay jokes, not directed towards me, but there were a lot of gay jokes in the room or in the units. You could never say anything, like "Don't say that because it offends me," because people are going to start questioning.

The colonel was always like, "Oh, I can't understand these homosexuals." I think it was the year when the Barry Winchell beating occurred.[8] We were in a staff meeting with the colonels and captains and everyone else, and they said that we had to go through the "Don't Ask, Don't Tell" briefings. The colonel began: "I don't understand these homosexuals. Now, we have to do this stupid briefing." Throughout the meetings, it wasn't just antigay; it was also anti-woman too. It seemed like it was anti-everybody. The culture was not accepting of anybody really.

When I did finally get all my thoughts collected, I created this three-page memorandum on why I wanted to get out—or why I was coming out to the military. I gave it to my command down in Fort Knox, Kentucky. I basically realized that at Fort Knox the command was a lot more professional. But still, you don't know what can happen, so I was sleeping with a loaded handgun next to my bed.

I submitted my statement to the army on the army's birthday. I remember it vividly. It was in the afternoon. It was at two o'clock, and my commander, Captain Jenkins, was getting ready to go to the parade, the army birthday parade at Fort Knox, and I was supposed to go with him. Captain Jenkins was a black officer. You could tell he cared for the troops. I was like, "Sir, I have to tell you something." I went in, closed the door; we both sat down. I said, "Here's the statement," and I pulled it out of the envelope. "I need you to read this." While he was reading it, he was just in complete shock, because he realized that he was going to have to initiate the process for me to get out of the military. He was like, "You're one of the best officers that I've seen. You're highly motivated. It's a shame that I have to kick you out." I said, "I know." But that's what I wanted at that time.

I couldn't really get nicely divorced from the army because I had loved the military so much when I was at West Point. I enjoyed my time there. I really loved the camaraderie, the fact that everyone works together. It's basically a community of its own, and for me to feel like I wasn't part of that community anymore in my time in Alaska just made me feel terrible.

My colonel at Fort Knox was a guy from Montana. You could tell he was uncomfortable with gay people, just wasn't exposed to it or whatever. But for the few months that I was there, he always treated me like a human being, and he was very professional dealing with the whole process. I appreciated that, and I realized that it's not everyone in the military; it's a policy. Sure there are conservative people in the military that don't think that gay people should serve openly, but the fact is that more and more people are starting to realize that there are gay people in the military, and they are more accepting of that fact.

At the time of our interview, Steve was working for an international pharmaceutical company in San Francisco. He was also a local admissions coordinator for West Point.

THE WOMEN'S WAR FOR INCLUSION

Even though women had supported, fought, and even been wounded in every American war since the Revolution, they did not actually become integrated into the regular armed forces until the 1970s. In that decade, as the Women's Army Corps (WAC) and other auxiliary forces gradually gave way to a gender-integrated military, women who served felt as if they were fighting a war in a time of peace. This was a war for respect, a war for equality, a war for inclusion in the "band of brothers." For gay rights advocates, and some of the interviewees in this book, who argue that lifting the ban on openly gay service personnel will be a quick and painless process, the stories from the front lines of the "women's war" in the 1970s and 80s provide a cautionary tale.

On the second day of navy boot camp, one female recruit recalled, the company commander had said, "Welcome to the fleet. In the navy's eyes, you're either dykes or whores—get used to it." This woman happened to be a lesbian, but the message was targeted at all military women during the 1970s and 80s. As the sociologist Melissa Herbert has observed, "Gender and sexuality are intertwined in such a way that notions of appropriateness in one are used to reinforce the other."[1] This was especially true in the military of the 1970s and 80s as many women found themselves in a catch-22: either they "proved" that they were heterosexual by sleeping with men (often in their unit) or they risked being investigated or kicked out as lesbians. To understand why sexism and homophobia were so endemic during those years, we need to examine the historical context of women's integration into the armed forces.[2]

Some commentators look back on the Women's Army Corps and other auxiliary services that existed from World War II to the 1970s as sanctuaries of female empowerment and tolerance of lesbian leadership. There is some truth to this. From 1954 to 1978, the WAC headquarters at Fort McLellan, Alabama, had an entirely female chain of command, providing equal advancement opportunities within the corps. "We had no need to conform to an artificial standard," one former WAC officer later recalled. "Women were entrenched at Fort McClellan, with *real power*."[3] In terms of sexuality, Fort McLellan seemed to be a place where lesbian service personnel found not only tolerance but even acceptance and support. When Brenda Vosbein was assigned to the post for WAC basic training in the early 1970s, she found that many of the officers were lesbians. "When I first went in, women couldn't be married and couldn't have dependents under eighteen," she explains. So "the ones who tended to be careerist seemed to be gay."[4]

As much as the WAC might have been an empowering organization for women in the military, it still bore the hallmarks and deficiencies of a segregated institution. Until 1967 the proportion of women in the military was capped at 2 percent, and women were unable to achieve the rank of general or admiral. Women were also barred from most military occupational specialties (MOSS) other than administrative, clerical, and medical ones. While Fort McClellan was not a military ghetto, it was clearly a junior sister to most of the predominantly male posts throughout the country.

Women's roles in the armed forces began to change in the 1970s as a result of both military necessity and social pressure. With the end of the increasingly unpopular draft and the advent of an all-volunteer force in 1973, military officials realized that they were going to have to broaden their recruiting vision. Junior ROTC (Reserve Officers' Training Corps) was opened up to female high school students for the first time in 1972, and women gained entry into the military academies in 1976. The army even experimented with integrating basic training from 1977 to 1982. The WAC and other auxiliary services were dissolved in 1978, sending women officers and enlisted personnel to units throughout the country and the world. That same year, women were first allowed to serve on noncombat ships (though they had earlier sailed on hospital and transport ships). These milestones brought new opportunities for women joining the military and held a sense of promise for recruits.[5]

All three of the women whose interviews are included in this section joined the military during the heady days of the 1970s. Brenda Vosbein, Barbara Taylor, and Patty Duwel joined up for many reasons: to get away from home or please their parents, to flee from dead-end jobs or find new and exciting career paths, to challenge themselves or change what society thought of them. All three of them had questions about their sexuality, but none were out—even to themselves—when they joined. Gender and sexuality would complicate each of their enlistments, but these factors were not enough to keep two of the women from choosing careers in the military.

Brenda Vosbein saw the transition to an integrated army firsthand after enlisting in 1970, but the positions available to her remained limited because she was a woman.[6] Still, Brenda loved the military, and she spent nearly a quarter of a century in the reserves after leaving active duty. Before retiring as a lieutenant colonel in 1999, Brenda joined a challenge to "Don't Ask, Don't Tell" as the lead plaintiff known by the pseudonym "Jane Able" in the case of *Able v. United States*.

Barbara Taylor joined the army at the end of the Vietnam era, only one year after Congress did away with the draft. She was one of the first waves of recruits in the new all-volunteer army. Perhaps the drill sergeants forgot to tell the soldiers that volunteers have better morale than conscripts, because FTA— Fuck the Army—was still being scrawled on bunks, barracks, and even the maps that Taylor drew as a cartographic drafter. In the all-volunteer force, women like Barbara were a small but growing minority, and their resolve was still being tested even when she left the military after her enlistment ended in 1977.

Patty Duwel also decided to join the marines in the mid-1970s, but the training in etiquette, makeup, and ironing did not fit with her expectations of a military career, so she joined the navy.[7] Enlisting in 1980, just two years after the navy began assigning women to noncombat ships, Patty engaged in a campaign to get a ship deployment that was in some ways a metaphor for women's struggle for full inclusion and equal opportunity the navy. Yet Patty had a realistic vision of the navy as a "man's world," and she was actually surprised by the opportunities and support that she found as a woman. The navy's position on sexuality was another matter entirely, as Patty weathered witch hunts and investigations, watching friends and acquaintances lose careers because they were gay.

Dubbed witch hunts by both the press and military women themselves, collective investigations and discharges of lesbians on bases across the country and around the world were especially aggressive in the 1980s. High-profile purges took place on bases in San Diego, Puerto Rico, Okinawa, Pensacola, and the Memphis Naval Air Station in Millington, Tennessee.[8] Captain Brenda Hammer tried to explain why women seemed to be targeted so often in such witch hunts, especially during the 1980s when she was drummed out after a four-month investigation. "I sometimes felt that it was because [men] felt we didn't belong. We shouldn't be here. We were invading their territory," Hammer later told the writer Zsa Zsa Gershick. Women "had a particularly hard time. If you were here, it was because you were a whore or a lesbian."[9]

Yet the same armed forces that were investigating these women for homosexuality had also given them training, self-confidence, and survival skills. In her book *Camouflage Isn't Only for Combat*, Melissa Herbert details several of the survival strategies employed by women in the military to appear either more feminine or more masculine as the situation required. Based on a survey with 285 women (212 heterosexual and 73 bisexual or lesbian) who served between the 1950s and the 1990s, Herbert found that when military women felt the pressure to appear more traditionally feminine, they wore dresses or more makeup, grew out their hair, and dated men. When they felt the pressure to appear more masculine, they swore, drank, or worked out. It was hard, Herbert learned, for these women—gay or straight—just to "be themselves."[10]

The two interviewees in this chapter who made a career in the military camouflaged their identities for so long that they found it difficult to be completely open even in the 1990s, when the military policy toward homosexuality was revised. For Brenda, Patty, and many other lesbians who had entered the armed forces during the promising but difficult days of the 1970s, "Don't Ask, Don't Tell" changed very little. It was simply a new paint job on an old closet door. As in the 1980s, women continued to make up a disproportionately high percentage of service personnel kicked out for being gay. Though they made up only 12 to 15 percent of the armed forces in the decade after the passage of "Don't Ask, Don't Tell," women constituted between 21 and 33 percent of service personnel discharged for being gay.[11]

With the continuing threat of expulsion hanging over the heads of both gay and straight women, scholars have argued that lifting the ban on openly gay service personnel might lessen the pressure on all women in the military. As Melissa Herbert concludes, "The link between gender and sexuality situated in an institution that formally regulates sexuality insures the subordination of women. To eliminate such formal regulation would greatly enhance opportunities for the more equal participation of women."[12] If the struggle of women integrating the armed forces during the 1970s and 80s is any indication, lifting the ban will be no panacea for the ills of homophobia and sexual harassment. Still it will be a further step along the journey begun by trailblazers like the women veterans interviewed here.

CITIZEN JANE
An Interview with Brenda Vosbein

Brenda Vosbein joined the WAC in 1970, and she served during the transition to gender-integrated armed forces. Vosbein left active duty in 1975, but she stayed in the reserves. Over a twenty-nine-year career, she balanced the demands of family life with a commitment to service. By the 1990s, Lieutenant Colonel Vosbein was tired of what she saw as a hypocritical policy resting on the "open secret" that most gays and lesbians in the military served with honor and distinction. As noted above, she joined the first legal challenge to "Don't Ask, Don't Tell" as Lieutenant Colonel "Jane Able"—a citizen and a soldier.

My name is Brenda Vosbein. I was born and raised in New Orleans, Louisiana. My mother's family had been there for two or three generations. My father's family had migrated from Germany in the late 1890s. I think I had one uncle who served in the coast guard during World War II, but my father didn't serve during the war. He was working in a shipyard, doing defense work.

Going back to my childhood in the fifties, I had organized the kids on the street. I ordered uniform stripes from a catalogue. I put sergeant stripes on me. I made all of the boys—it was all boys except for one other girl—I made all of the boys privates and corporals, and I drilled them and did the Manual of Arms. I read *Marines at War* and lots of other comic books. I just lived by those.

As I got older I began to realize that what I was reading about and really wanted to do was something that I would never be able to do in the Marine Corps. At the time I enlisted, the emphasis still was more on trying to make women look pretty in uniform than it was in training them to really be soldiers. I knew that it was even more that way with the marines, because of their image. So I figured, "I have to find something that I can enlist to do, because I'll never be a combat soldier or a combat marine."

In high school, I found an interest in health care. So I enlisted in the army in 1970 to be a medical corpsman. I went to basic training at Fort McClellan and then advanced infantry training at Fort Sam Houston, where I became a medic. I went to Fort Knox, and from there I applied to Officer Candidate School (OCS). After I was accepted to OCS, I went back to Fort McClellan in '71 and was commissioned as an officer in December of that year.

Timing was such that female medics were not being sent to Vietnam. Mostly it was male medics. Most of the women that were going to Vietnam were in personnel and supplies. Timing-wise, you had to have at least a year, I think, of stateside service before they'd even consider a woman for Vietnam. By that time, I'd gotten the application started for Officer Candidate School.

When I was going through the enlistment papers, there was something about: "Have you ever had sex with someone of the same sex?" I was basically asexual when I went into the military. I had never had sex with anyone. Some kids get in touch with these things a lot earlier. I was into sports. I was into activities. At that point I wasn't interested in either sex other than someone to play sports with. So, in all good conscience, I could say "no" because it was true. There was never a time again when I was asked that question.

I liked the army. I fit in very well with the discipline of the military, and I thought that a career as an officer would be something that I'd really like to do. As time went along, my mind changed for two reasons. One is that I was in during a time of transition when women were being assigned outside of traditional WAC companies or WAC units. But they didn't know what to do with us when they got us someplace else. I was assigned to Fort Huachuca in 1973, which was the first time I left a WAC unit. I'd always been either an enlisted woman or an officer in a WAC company. I got into a regular unit, and I found myself getting bored. I spent most of my time at my desk trying to figure out, "What job can I create for myself today?" No one really kept me involved in anything. So that first got me thinking.

Another thing that had come along was that while I was stationed at Fort McClellan, I had formed a very strong platonic relationship. I didn't know what I was or what she was at the time. But we had formed a relationship that was more than just friends. She had decided that she wanted to leave the military. Her reason was that at the time the role of women was changing, and women were beginning to fire weapons and be more combat proficient. She had decided that she wanted to be a conscientious objector. I said, "All you have to do is shoot at a target." She said, "A target is shaped like a human being. I cannot fire a weapon—period. I will not fire a weapon." She had decided that she was going to leave the service, and she was going to come to California.

So given the fact that I was bored stiff, and she was moving out to California, I thought, "Well, it sounds like a good deal." It was a combination of both of those things. We moved out to California and lived together for a while. She got in touch with the fact that we were playing house, but there was nothing else there. She moved on with her life. Last thing I heard, she's a Ph.D. psychologist at a VA hospital.

Even after we moved to California, I definitely wanted to stay with the reserves because I really loved the military. I served in the reserves for another twenty-four years. Throughout the rest of my reserve career, I had a few commands that I really enjoyed. One was a personnel service company and a personnel service battalion. I enjoyed the command time there. It was not that you had that much real power, but I really enjoyed that feeling of being responsible and being respected.

As an officer, I would always look out for my soldiers. I would always look downward rather than upward. One of the problems that I think is common in the military is that officers look at who is writing their efficiency report and who is rating them, rather than looking downward at the people they lead. I always felt that my primary responsibility was to protect my soldiers even if it meant getting the higher-ups mad at me for something that I did. I would not let fear of a higher-ranking officer make me do something that I didn't want to do.

After talking about leadership, Brenda talked about her gradual awareness of sexuality.

When I was stationed at Fort McClellan, I was not out to myself. Everybody else took it for granted that I was gay. They knew before I did. I was originally assigned there as a training officer, and I'd have female drill sergeants sit down next to me and start talking about problems that they were having with their girlfriends. Then one day, this gal I was telling you about, with whom I had this platonic relationship, she came into the office, and she needed something adjusted on her boots or something like that on her field uniform, which she didn't usually wear. So I fixed it, and she leaves. The company clerk said something to me about my "girlfriend," and I said, "That's not my girlfriend." She looked at me and said, "You gotta be kidding."[13]

When the women first started off in the army, they were very segregated from the men. Women served in WAC units that were commanded by women. You lived in a barracks where everybody else was a female. You may have gone out to work at the hospital or some other job on post, but you always came back to be under the command or supervision of other female NCOs [noncommissioned officers] or other female officers. Back in the days of the WAC when I first went in, military women had to be unmarried with no children, so the majority of careerists were lesbian. Some of those regulations eventually changed, so women could be married, but they couldn't have dependents. Then they could have children. As the requirements were eliminated, you saw a much broader spectrum in the military.

But at Fort McClellan, when I was there, you had an entire battalion of female basic trainees and officer trainees. Women outnumbered men. It was the WAC center, where all WACs were trained. So consequently, everybody around there, the senior NCOs and senior officers were all either lesbians or at least people who were sort of used to being around lesbians, because that's the way it was at the time. The regulations made it that way. So I got exposed to it then.

But I was fighting a lot of religious issues with myself. I felt, "This is wrong. This isn't natural. This isn't right." So I didn't actually come out until after I came out to California with the reserves. I had my first lesbian affair at that time. It was a brief coming-out affair. Then a short time later, I met my present partner, Diana, who was never in the military. We met in '77, got together as a couple in '79, and we've been together ever since.

The open secret was that a lot of people kind of knew. But it's a secret that no one talked about. For instance, one time I was a captain with this other fellow who was a major and we were at a meeting in Los Alamitos, California, and Diana came to the unit for some reason. He met her. Then, years later, I was a lieutenant colonel and he was a colonel, and we were sharing an office. She called, and he answered the phone. It was Diana calling for me. After I hung up, he said, "Oh, are you two still together?" Another time, I brought her to a family day and the xo [executive officer] said something like, "Oh, is this your partner in crime?" I mean maybe he didn't know what he was saying, but she said to me later, "I was tempted to say: 'No, it's legal in California now.' "

I've always looked kind of butchy, so a lot of people would drop hints to me—other lesbians and gays and not necessarily straight folks. They'd say, "Oh, I went to see this movie" or "I went here or did that." By dropping names, you could tell. I had a number of friends who were gay or lesbian that I met while I was in the military. But like I said, a lot of the straight people knew Diana was important.

One night, I was at my unit, and she got a call at home from a general. Diana told him that I was at the unit, so he called me there. When I get home, she said, "Did the general reach you?" And I said, "Yes." "Well, what did he want?" I was just about to rotate out of command, and I had told her I was going to retire as soon as I finished this tour. She said, "Well, what did the general want?" I said, "Well, he offered me a job on his staff." She said, "Well, what did you say?" I said yes. She went, "If I'd have known who he was, I would have said, "No, she's not home, but this is her lesbian lover, do you want me to take a message?!"

When we first got together, I had nine years of service at the time, and I said, "In eleven years, I can retire." Diana was never happy about the amount of time that the military took away from other things. But then, twenty years came, and I wasn't ready to call it quits, so I said, "Well, after this battalion command." Diana would say, "Well, you miss everything that's important because of the army. The army always comes first. You're always off at some exercise. You're off at drill. You're at the unit doing administrative stuff. Whenever there's something important going on, you're off with the army. The army and its mission always come first." That's probably something you hear from anybody in the military. It's the culture. I missed an awful lot of things in her life or our shared life that I should have been there for, so she really was very happy when I finally did retire.

After Congress passed "Don't Ask, Don't Tell" in 1993, Brenda joined a suit to challenge the constitutionality of the law.

At that time, I was a battalion commander. Lambda Legal Defense and Education Fund determined that they were going to challenge "Don't Ask, Don't Tell" using people who were still in the military, not people who had been discharged. So they advertised in a number of publications what they were looking for. I saw the ad, and I called them, and I said that I was still in the service and I would be willing to participate in this lawsuit.

I can't say exactly why I wanted to do it, but I just felt that I had to do something. We had a policy in place that was ridiculous. I had served for so many years with so many people that I knew were gay and were outstanding soldiers. Officers, enlisted—they ran the gamut. I mean, yes, there were some that I wasn't fond of and would never want to be friends with, but in general most of the gays and lesbians that I served with in the military did a good job, and I would have been proud to call them a friend any time. So I did want to do something to change the policy.

When I called Lambda, they said, "Well, the first thing we're going to do is get a court injunction that says that while this suit is in progress, that no action can be taken against any participants." And they said, "We'll use pseudonyms to protect your identity." I said, "OK, that all sounds good. No problem." They made me "Jane Able." When the briefs started to appear at the house, I noticed that there was "Jane Able" and all of these other people with real names. I called Lambda, and I said, "I notice that everyone else is using their real names. I have no problem using my name." At that time, I was planning on retiring in '94, which would have been the end of my battalion command tour. When I said that to them, they said, "No, we don't want to use your name. We listed all of the plaintiffs alphabetically, and you would have been second to last, but because you're the only woman and the senior person in the lawsuit, we want to use you as the lead plaintiff." They wanted a name that would sound capable and strong. "Able" was the name they came up with. So the case became *Able vs. The United States of America.*

*Brenda Vosbein became "Jane Able" to challenge
the "Don't Ask, Don't Tell" policy in the 1990s.
Photo courtesy of Brenda Vosbein.*

I think it was in the spring of '94 that we actually had the trial. It was held in New York, in a courthouse in Brooklyn. Four of us were from the West Coast, but we had one coast guard fellow who lived in New York City. Lambda filed there because of the court's history. They felt they had a very favorable court to work with. We had a judge by the name of Nickerson. He wrote a very good decision on our behalf, in which he said that the "Don't Ask, Don't Tell" policy was based on nothing but prejudice and ignorance.

We had a lot of good testimony to that effect from people like a retired general who was not a lesbian, Evelyn Pat Foot. She testified on our behalf, because she was at Fort McClellan as a battalion commander and battalion xo back when we had the wac, and she knew that most of the drill sergeants and many of the officers there were lesbians.

The military just presented their stack of rules and regulations and their opinions as to why gays shouldn't serve in the military. After we won in the u.s. District Court. It went to the appeals level. At the appeals level, they kicked it back and said, "Well, we want some more information." So again the lawyers filed briefs back and forth. Then it went up to the appeals court a second time. The appeals court finally just admitted, "You know, we don't really want to touch this." The courts usually do not like to interfere with the Congress's running of the military. "That's Congress's job, we're not going to interfere."

The lawyers for Lambda Legal Defense and Education Fund decided not to appeal to the Supreme Court at that point, fearing a negative decision from a conservative court could prove a permanent setback to efforts to lift the ban.

A few years later, I was coming up on what in the military is called MRD— mandatory retirement date. As a lieutenant colonel you could have twenty-eight years of division service. If I had been a full colonel, I could have had thirty years of service. But because I was enlisted before I was commissioned, I ended up serving twenty-nine years. I retired in 1999.

I'd like to say that common sense will finally end the ban on gay and lesbian service, but I don't know if I can be that bold. On one side, I want to feel positive that it will change, but the other side of me is saying that it's going to take a longer fight than people think. We think we're close, and, yes, they've introduced a new law in Congress to repeal "Don't Ask, Don't Tell," but I'm not real optimistic that we'll see something happen real soon.

Gays and lesbians have always served. We've been there in every war throughout the history of this country. The number of gay vets is large. There are still gays serving. The problem doesn't seem to be on the day-to-day basis. Because there are a lot of folks who will tell the same story I did. It was an open secret. You didn't talk about it openly with straight soldiers, but yet everyone just kind of took it for granted. Nothing was ever said. Nothing was ever done. Yeah, this person is gay.

I would have pretty much continued to live the way I did with or without the ban, because I didn't really try to hide. It's not like I tried to tell people I had a boyfriend. I would have lived the same way, but there wouldn't have been the fear that someone could say, "I know what this relationship is. Let's do an investigation to find out more." Because it wouldn't have taken much investigating to discover my sexuality, if you went through my mailbox and saw who I got mail from. If you went to every gay pride parade, you'd see me. I usually drove a convertible. My partner was the president of a large lesbian organization, and I was usually her driver. It wouldn't have taken much if someone had wanted to do an investigation. If they had lifted the ban, I wouldn't have changed.

I consider myself a patriot. I remember when I first got off of active duty and I was being interviewed by the commanding officer of this reserve battalion. He said, "Why did you want to stay in the reserves when you left active duty?" I said, "All I have to do is hear the opening bars of the national anthem and the hairs on the back of my neck stand up. It just sends a tingle down my spine." It's something that I relate to—pride in the flag, pride in people in uniform.

At the time of this interview, Brenda Vosbein had recently retired from teaching nursing at Cypress College in Orange County, California.

FTA

An Interview with Barbara Taylor

Barbara Taylor joined the army in 1974, primarily for access to the GI Bill. But she felt that it was also empowering to do what women were not expected to do. An academic, peace activist, and folk musician, Taylor said that most people are surprised when they find out that she is a veteran.

I'm Barbara Taylor, and I was born on May 19, 1953, in Tripler Army Hospital, Honolulu, Hawaii. My Dad was in the navy. He just did one enlistment during the Korean War era. My parents got married while he was in the navy. They were both from Sacramento. Then he came back and went to college on the GI Bill. He ended up getting an M.F.A. from Mills College. My parents actually split up when I was five, and my mother worked as a drafter for the state of California, mapping and that kind of thing.

I went to high school at Luther Burbank, a high school in South Sacramento. Doesn't that sound like "South Chicago" or something? It was lower middle class or working class and ethnically mixed. It is so weird that I'm going into a Ph.D. program. I was the world's worst student. I absolutely hated school. They decided I was an underachiever, and so I was like, "Fine! You want me to be an underachiever? I'll be an underachiever." I think I was a bright kid who was bored, and if I'm bored at something, I do lousy at it. If it challenges me, I'm interested and I excel.

I graduated from high school in 1972. I worked at McDonald's [laughs] and learned how to make change. I had a brief interlude at Sutter General Hospital Food Service. They tried me in the coffee shop, and I was a lousy waitress. I figured these obnoxious old men could keep their ten-cent tips. [She laughs.]

I don't know where I got the idea, but I decided to join the army in 1974. In my mind, even though this was not accurate, the Vietnam War was over. I didn't support the Vietnam War. I really wanted time to figure out what I wanted to do and money to go to college. It wasn't coming to me from my family. So the motivation in my mind for joining the army was to get the GI Bill, because men could, and I wanted access to that too. It was a sort of protofeminism idea.

I was sent to Fort McLellan, in Alabama. I was a backpacker and so I went into this, and everybody's like, "Oh, basic training you have to do a six-mile march with a twenty-pound pack." And I'm like, "So?!" I was used to doing eight- or ten-mile mountain hikes with a thirty- or forty-pound pack. Basic training was a joke in a way; it was pumped up to be this really hard thing, and in some ways it wasn't. There's a lot of psychological stuff, but it wasn't difficult to do any of the physical things.

We had female and male drill sergeants. I think the senior drill sergeant was a man, and then there was a drill sergeant who actually had a room in the barracks. There were two of them. It was supposed to be about having to do things just right and having fatigues starched and how to stand in line. But it was only eight weeks. I don't think I particularly distinguished myself; I just got through it.

If you enlisted for three years, you could choose what you wanted to do. I chose cartographic drafting because I saw my mother support herself in that field and 'cause I loved maps. So I went to Fort Belvoir, Virginia, for that school, and I really liked the subject. But it just moved way too slow for me. At any rate, from there I got assigned to Fort Hood, Texas.

I was assigned to a unit whose job was mapping, and that's what we did. We had these vans with light tables, drafting tables that open out—big, like four-by-six glass. We'd do what's called scribing. We had a sheet of Mylar that's got this orange coating, and you have these little special tools that you use to etch away the orange coating. I would say that in the three years that I was in the military as a cartographic drafter, I did maybe, maybe a year's worth of actual work. The rest of the time was spent sitting around doing bullshit.

Let's back up to Fort Belvoir. I was there for sixteen weeks. Now up to this time I considered myself straight. I really hadn't had any successful relationships with boys or men. I'd been sexually active for a few years, but I was pretty unenthusiastic about the whole thing. I'd be interested in somebody, and then we'd have sex, and it'd be like, "Ughhhh!" [She laughs.] I thought there was something wrong with me, and everybody else knew how to do this thing.

But when I was at Fort Belvoir, I fell in love with a woman, and it was like really sudden. We were friends. We were playing music, partying, and going to school. I always have the image of the cartoon character walking down the street and somebody drops a flowerpot on their head. It was like that. It wasn't one of those slow warm fuzzy things. It was like "Whoa! Oh?! Hello!" Now I didn't act on this till I was out of the military. But from early in my experience of the military I had this awareness of myself. So I had two reactions to that. One is that this is a really good thing and I shouldn't deny it. And the other reaction I had, which was every bit as strong, was: "There's absolutely no way in hell I could ever do anything about it."

At Fort Hood, Texas, I had a friend who was a lesbian. She was an older woman. She had reenlisted; she was on the lifer track. I remember one time, she and I and this straight guy went down to Austin. That's when I went to my first gay bar, but we also went to a strip show. She was really into it, and he was really into it. I thought it was pretty dreadful. [She laughs.] It just looked like exploitation to me, but I remember going to the gay bar. There were men dancing together and women dancing together, and I was like, "Whoa!" [She laughs.]

When I think about my time in the army, I remember the sexual harassment—dealing with just being a woman. There were like two infantry divisions in Fort Hood. The place was crawling with testosterone-driven, eighteen year-old guys. You could not walk down the street without, "Hey baby!" "Hey Baby!" "Hey Baby!" "Wanna Fuck?" "Hey Baby." "Hey Baby." "Hey Baby." You know? It was like relentless sexual harassment, and it was a lot of "Oh well, they're just lonely." I thought that was bullshit. It was sexual harassment.

It was interesting the way that worked. In my unit, the guys I actually worked with were fine. For one thing, most of them were younger than I was, so there was this little brother feeling. Once they got that I wasn't going to play "boy/girl" games, I was going to show up and do my part, they liked me, and we got along on kind of a buddy level. That all worked.

When I very first got to the unit, there was man there who was an older sergeant. And see, I did identify as straight, as heterosexual, but I had this other awareness of myself, this very new awareness. I was walking into this context where the assumption was: if you're a woman and you're in the army, you're a dyke. That was a big question. "Is she a dyke, or is she straight? Is she gonna be available, or is she a queer?" I walked into this unit and it felt like that was what everybody wanted to know. And that was the last thing I wanted to discuss with anybody.

This was right at the beginning of the women's movement and the gay right's movement, and all of these dialogues are coming out. There is this sense of a shift from an older way of having women be in the military to a newer way and a discomfort with it. Like they're trying to figure it out, trying to work it out, how's this going to be? There was a lot of concern about whether women were going to be a drag or whether they were going to hold up their end and do their work. In fact, this was not a problem, except in certain guys' minds.

The other thing about the particular historical time period was that I got there just after the last of the draftees had gotten out. So the guys in my unit that had been there for a while had known draftees, and there was this whole bad attitude thing about the military, you know, "FTA: Fuck the Army." Scratch it on the wall, write it on the latrines, FTA, FTA, FTA. In fact, dear God, I can't believe I'm really remembering this. In mapping, the symbol for a river is a long dash and three dots, long dash and three dots. Well, we used to take incredibly fine scribing points and for the dots inscribe "F-T-A." [She laughs.]

After I had been at Fort Hood about a year, I just really got that the values of the military and my values had absolutely nothing to do with each other. I really got fed up with it. In retrospect, I was actually becoming a conscientious objector, but when I decided that I no longer wanted to be part of this institution, I tried to convince them I was crazy. It was actually one of the saner decisions I had ever made in my life, so I wasn't terribly convincing.

I went down to Austin quite a bit and would go to the bookstores. During that period of time I read *Against Our Will: Men, Women, and Rape*, by Susan Brownmiller and *Women and Madness* by Phyllis Chesler and a little book put out by the Furies—an early radical feminist group—called *Lesbianism and the Women's Movement*. I took that little booklet home and I started reading it, and it scared me so bad I couldn't finish it. I literally could not finish it because I agreed with it. In terms of getting radicalized, that period of time was absolutely pivotal for me. People were saying, "Did being in the army turn you into a lesbian?" I said, "No, it turned me into a radical feminist and a pacifist." I don't think it's possible for anybody to turn anybody else into any sexuality. So it didn't turn me into a lesbian directly, but that's when it started.

Barbara's radicalism made her rethink the concept of military service. Thinking back on her time in the military, she considers it to have been, more than anything else, a learning experience.

To tell you the truth I don't like the word "served." I don't think it's service. I think it's disservice. All we have to do is take a look at what's happening in Iraq. That is not service; that's oppression. That is service to corporate interest. That's serving their desire for world domination. It's not serving anybody; it's not serving the American people, it's not serving the Iraqi people, it's not serving the world. I guess I should just say that I am not proud of having been in the military. I am not at all proud of it. It was extremely educational. It was a very valuable experience, in which I learned very quickly how the world really works. But I don't think it's service.

At the time of this interview, Barbara was living in Guerneville, California, and about to begin a Ph.D. program in ethnomusicology.

WAKE ME UP WHEN YOU MAKE CHIEF
An Interview with Patty Duwel

Patty Duwel joined the marines in 1977 looking for a challenge. In boot camp, Patty found the spit and polish of the military without the rigorous physical challenge that she had expected. In other words, the marines weren't tough enough for her. So she enlisted in the navy, the service that her dad had joined when he was a young man. Although the expectations of her father were clearly an important driving force behind Patty's twenty-year military career, she was also inspired by her mother to push the boundaries of what was possible for women.

I was born October 5, 1959, in Long Beach, California. My mom was a homemaker, and my father had been in the navy. I was born in '59, my brother in '58. My mom was disabled. She was in a wheelchair from the time I was probably about ten, so she really couldn't be much more than that, but I'm sure she wanted to be. It was always a kind of a joke between my brother and I that my mom was smarter than my dad, and if she hadn't have been disabled, she probably would have been a working mom way ahead of the current working moms. She was very bright.

My dad worked. It was a typical family. We were raised in traditional roles. My brother was always outside with my dad out in the garage learning how to use tools. I was inside, doing the dishes, learning how to cook, doing the laundry, cleaning house, that type of thing. You know, never the twain shall meet. I wanted to get away from home as soon as I could because I was responsible for helping my mom. When I became sixteen, seventeen, that wasn't what I wanted to do with my life.

First stop was the military. I knew that I didn't have the grades to get a college scholarship, and I knew my parents couldn't afford college. So I went in the military. I was in three years of navy ROTC in high school, and I thought I knew everything there was to know about the navy. I wanted something different, so I thought I'd go in the Marine Corps.

There were only about five or six girls in my class who were really active in high school ROTC, and the unit had about 110 cadets. This was 1974 through '77, and my senior year I was the first female to achieve the rank of cadet lieutenant in the position of operations officer. Normally, the operations officer, the CO, the xo, and the bugler were what they called marching staff at end-of-year review. But because I was a female, I was told I wasn't going to be allowed to be on marching staff because I was going to be in a skirt. My uniform had a slip skirt. I told them I was willing to wear slacks. I had done it before. We'd worn men's—the boys'—uniforms, so we could blend in for a color guard, but then I was told that I couldn't be on marching staff because I was too short. Here I was, the third-ranking cadet in the unit. It hurt. I remember coming home and crying. Of course, my father didn't know how to handle his daughter crying. My dad did give me a good piece of advice, though. You know, "You've got to realize you're going into a man's world, and you can either work with it or work against it." I wasn't quite sure what he meant, but I just used that throughout my career at times when things might not be going so good.

Parris Island, South Carolina, was not what I expected it to be for a female going to Marine Corps boot camp in 1977. At that time, there weren't that many women in the marines. I thought boot camp would be rough and tumble, equal opportunity, the whole bit. It wasn't; it was totally segregated. We spent three hours in the squad bay learning how to iron our shirt waves and all of our uniforms. I thought we'd be out on the obstacle course and learning how to fire our weapons. You didn't hear one cuss word out of the drill instructors, which was totally alien to me. I really expected to get called every name in the book. It was just that we were women, we shall act like women, and we will be treated like women. It was just so alien from what I thought it was going to be. So I got out after thirteen months. I worked and decided I really did enjoy the military, and I wanted to go back in. So I went down and talked to the navy recruiter.

When I was first contemplating the military in the summer of '76, my family took a trip back east where I have a cousin who had just retired from the navy. She had been in over twenty years. My cousin pulled me aside and says, "You know, there's people in the military who tend to lead"—What did she say?—"a different lifestyle, and you just need to be careful because that's not acceptable in the military." A lightbulb went off in my head, and I remember thinking to myself, "Well, you're a hypocrite, because you're one of them." It was just one of those things that everybody knew but never talked about. After that, it was like, "OK, so you gave me your story. Great, I'll be careful."

My dad did four years active, '50 to '54, during the Korean War, and then he went into the reserves and he did another six. He separated from the reserves in 1960, so he could devote more time to a job and get better medical benefits for my mom. But he always was a vet. He would always remind us of his time in the navy, and he used to have this habit where he'd come home from work. He'd lay down on the couch to take a nap, and he'd always say, "Wake me up when you make chief." I didn't understand it then. I understood it later, once I joined.

Patty really wanted to serve on a ship, but when she joined, the navy was just beginning to allow women to have tours of duty at sea. It took many years of administrative shore duty before she finally got her chance.

I didn't plan to do twenty years. Every time I reenlisted, it was like, "Let's see where this goes." I only came in for two years. I made third class. Then I made second class. I made first class the first time up in March of '85. Then I thought I might want to be a master at arms. It turned out to be very bureaucratic, which, in a way, was up my alley because I came from a strong clerical/administrative background. So I had no problem doing all the paperwork and reports, crossing the t's and dotting the i's. But there wasn't much law enforcement, even though we were "law enforcement inspectors."

Eventually, I made chief. There were sixteen of us at our command that made chief, but I was the only female. I do remember asking and getting permission for my dad to come. He wasn't a chief. He had never made chief. But I wanted him there. If I had done it for anybody, I had done it for him. In one aspect, he was kind of continuing his career through me. So that the day I got selected for duty, I remember calling home, and my mom would answer the phone, and I'd ask, "What's Dad doing?" And I think she said, "He's taking a nap." I said, "Really. Well, wake his happy butt up, because I made chief!"

Patty Duwel faced sexism and homophobia in the navy, but she loved her job,
so she persevered. One of the highlights of Patty's twenty-year career in the navy
was the day that she made chief and, more important, made her father proud.
Photo courtesy of Patty Duwel.

I asked the command master chief and my other superiors if my dad could go to my initiation. They said yes, but they wanted to talk to him first. So he had to go talk to the master chief, and they said, "We don't want you to interfere with what we're going to do with your daughter." You know, dads can be kind of protective, but knowing my dad, he was probably like, "Oh, go ahead, do whatever you want." And he had fun because they let him participate. Nobody with me got hurt, and I only got mad one time during my initiation when a couple of the guys from the year before us were really starting to be stupid. Then, I thought that somebody could have gotten hurt. When I get mad, I cry. It's not a girl thing. It's just a Patty thing. So I was crying. My unofficial sponsor said, "Are you OK?" I said, "I'm fine. Get the hell out of my face! Let me get through this." It's how you handle stressful situations. It's how you handle the unknown.

I reported on board my first ship in '94 to be the chief master at arms. My philosophy is: I'm here to take care of the crew, to protect them from outside entities or from themselves, and to advise the command, and in some cases that's all you can do. When a ship gets under way, it's self-contained, and the CO is God. I'll be honest. I'm very lucky in my career. I was not ever sexually harassed. I really didn't hit the male testosterone brick wall in the military until I went on a ship, and then I just fell back on "It's a man's navy. You can manage to work with them, or you can work against them and make life miserable for yourself."

But I had fun because I enjoyed going to sea. I knew I would. I used to love being out there, walking out on the flight deck at night, having a smoke—nobody else around, a darkened ship, seeing the stars. I loved it. I loved the smell. I loved the ship. I loved everything about it. There was a part of me that said, "Man, I wish I could have done this twelve years ago." But it wasn't in the cards.

Despite her difficulties in getting certain assignments, Patty felt that as a woman she had better opportunities for advancement in the navy than she might have had in the private sector. But homophobia proved more difficult to deal with. In fact, she had a platonic marriage with a younger gay man so that she could live off base and be protected from witch hunts during the 1980s.

In the Marine Corps, I got this really bad crush on this girl, and I didn't know what to make of it. I knew it was wrong. I knew I could get into big trouble. But I finally got up the guts to write her a letter. So I leave it in her room, and she gets the letter, and she reads it. Actually, she handled it very well, said, "I'm really flattered." That was it.

In the navy, I went to Pearl Harbor. I'm working in this Com center, and I'm getting familiar with the people. My gaydar was in full force. I couldn't peg a guy for the life of me, but I was pretty certain I knew who was with the girls. I was doing my job, and one day a couple of people come up to me and say, "Hey, we get together, and we play spades, grab some beer, and have some wine. You want to do that?" So I would go over to this girl's apartment and play cards. One of the girls says, "You know, there's a group of people in the military. The military doesn't really like to admit that they're there but they are." And I said, "Oh my God! Yes!"

It was just like doors opened there, like all the weight came off, and I was in a group of friends that knew how I felt, and I didn't even have to say it. But you got to be careful. This was 1980 for crying out loud. The military was undergoing a great transition in the late 70s and early 80s. A few of my coworkers knew, because I finally got hooked up with a girl. She started seeing someone else, but I still cared for her a lot. That was my first. It's hard, breaking up. If it was all on the up and up and out in the open, or if this was a guy, I could go into work and say, "My boyfriend just broke up with me." Yeah, let me walk into my boss, my chief, and say, "Excuse me, but Renee and I just broke up." He'd be like: "What? Who?" So I had a lot of problems with my pet. My cat was sick a lot, had to go to the vet.

There could have been bad repercussions. I mean, this was the time of the *Gibson* Eight in San Diego, '82, where they kicked out like eight girls off the USS *Gibson*, and the XO had passed the word—"dyke departing"—when they kicked these girls out. I can remember going to a bar when some of them were there. There were witch hunts going on, and I was getting paranoid. A lot of softball games. Softball games and bars. But that wasn't anything fantastic.

I got sent to Hawaii. Well, I started seeing somebody right before I left. She was older than I was. And it opened my eyes to quite a few things. But long distance hurts relationships, especially gay ones in the military, because you don't have the support. There's no family support when you're gone. When you're in two separate locations, they just depart. To make a long story short, I wound up kind of being by myself for a while.

When "Don't Ask, Don't Tell" was passed, there was no change for me personally. I pretty much was in the closet the whole time. Don't ask, don't tell—I just don't know how that can be effective. The military's saying: "OK, you can be gay, sort of. We don't want to know about it. You can't tell us about it. We're not going to ask about it. But don't do anything that we find out about." What that tells young kids today is like, "OK, I'm gay. I'm going into the military, and I'm just not going to tell them." But they don't understand that they might do something that's going to get them caught, and even though the government can't ask, if it finds out for whatever reason, they're gone. There's no question. They're gone.

There was only one time when I truly felt that my career was in jeopardy. So I just went on the offensive. It was when I was at Pearl Harbor. I had just made chief, and I started hearing these rumors that my name was coming up in some investigations, so I grabbed the guy I was married with. He even put his boxers and jeans on. He wanted to look really butch. We tromped into the xo's office, and I said, "I hear I'm under investigation for being gay, and I'd like to find out if that's true." That was the only time. I was never, ever called in. Knock on wood. I was lucky.

At the time of this interview, Patty Duwel was working as a school administrator in Berkeley, California, and was active in Veterans for Peace.

THE GULF WAR

For gay men and lesbians in the military, the decade of the 1980s was an especially difficult time because of evolving Defense Department policies. In 1981 the department decreed that "homosexuality is incompatible with military service" and the presence of gay troops "adversely affects . . . the good order and morale" of the armed forces. Interviewed in 1982, Major General Norman Schwarzkopf explained that gay men and lesbians were simply "unsuited" for the military. Discharges of enlisted personnel, which had declined to fewer than a thousand per year during the Vietnam War, jumped back up to 1,976 in 1981 and 2,069 in 1982. Yet many more of these discharges in the 1980s were honorable, based on the excellent service records of the men and women accused of being gay, and signs of progressive changes were coming from some unlikely quarters by the end of the decade. In 1988 the Defense Personnel Security Research and Education Center, a nonpartisan military policy think tank, released a study finding that homosexuality "was unrelated to job performance in the same way as being left- or right-handed," and Dick Cheney, who became secretary of defense under George H. W. Bush, publicly opposed a ban on gay civilian employees in the Department of Defense.[1]

At the same time that the Department of Defense policy toward homosexuality was slowly evolving, the military itself was going through dramatic changes. With the elections of Presidents Ronald Reagan and George H. W. Bush, the 1980s witnessed a resurgence of patriotism and pride in America's armed forces. Military recruitment and the budget for the Department of Defense grew apace with renewed popular support for the armed forces. Eight years of Reagan administration defense budgets came in at a total price tag of over $1.6 trillion. Explaining this expansion of defense spending to his aides, the president said, "Defense is not a budget item; you spend what you need." Reagan argued that such increased military expenditures were necessary to win the global conflict with the Soviet Union. We now know that this was the twilight of the Cold War, but the interviews in this section remind us that for troops on the ground in Europe fear of military conflict with the Soviets or their Eastern European allies was very real.[2]

A witness to this history, Mark Landes served in West Germany in the late 1980s. Though oral history interviews by Steve Zeeland in the late 1980s and early 90s suggest that gay bashing and discrimination were problems on some u.s. bases in West Germany, Mark was not openly gay or even fully aware of his sexual orientation, and he faced no discrimination. His focus was on his job, defending Western Europe from invasion by communist forces. In the autumn of 1989, Mark trained for the day that the "balloon would go up," signaling that war with East Germany had begun. Instead, the Berlin Wall came down. November 9, 1989, marked the symbolic end of the Cold War. President George H. W. Bush hoped that this also represented the emergence of a "new world order," a world without the threat of global conflict between opposing superpowers. But as the conflict over political ideologies diminished, new tensions arose around nationalism, religion, and globalization.[3]

Less than nine months after the fall of the Berlin Wall, on August 2, 1990, Saddam Hussein's Iraqi forces invaded Kuwait. Saddam justified the attack by arguing that Kuwait was an ancient province of Iraq that had been severed from its mother country by British colonialists in the 1920s. Yet the Iraqi leader was also clearly interested in Kuwait's rich oil reserves and its access to the deep-water ports so necessary for exporting the region's most valuable commodity. The invasion brought a chorus of international outrage from the United States to the ussr, from Europe to the Middle East. When United Nations sanctions proved ineffective in dislodging Iraqi forces from Kuwait, the u.s. began sending troops to Saudi Arabia and the Bush administration began to lobby Congress and the un for support of military intervention.[4]

The 1991 debate in Congress over whether to support a military intervention in Kuwait was as intense as it was instructive. Proponents of intervention such as Representative Robert Michel from Illinois compared Saddam Hussein to Adolf Hitler, arguing that the Iraqi invaders should not be appeased as the Germans had been in the late 1930s. Paul Wellstone, a young, idealistic senator from Minnesota, countered that American military intervention in the Middle East would bring a new world disorder instead of the new order that President Bush envisioned. "What kind of victory will it be," Wellstone asked, "if we unleash forces of fanaticism in the Middle East and a chronically unstable region becomes even more unstable?" Though President Bush would later say that the Gulf War was not about oil, but about halting aggression, many of the hawks from both the House and Senate felt otherwise. Delaware senator William Roth argued that oil was "as basic to the economy as water is to life" and that Hussein's control of Kuwaiti reserves could cripple both developing and developed nations. Given that this was the largest oil-producing region in the world and that there had been an illegal invasion of a peaceful nation, Congress and the UN voted to support intervention by the American-led, multinational force amassing in Saudi Arabia.[5]

Greg Mooneyham, Mark Landes, and Lisa Michelle Fowler were three of the 540,000 American troops who had been deployed to the Middle East by January 1991. Mooneyham's part in the assault began in the middle of that month, when American planes started to bomb selected targets in Kuwait and Iraq. Mooneyham and other U.S. Air Force pilots flew between 2,000 and 3,000 sorties a day during the war, dropping a total of 142,000 tons of bombs to soften up Iraqi positions in anticipation of the ground assault. In February, Mark Landes joined the invasion into Kuwait and Iraq as a liaison officer between the armored division and brigade headquarters of the Third Army. He saw firsthand the devastation wrought by the aerial bombardment and heard stories from Iraqi prisoners of war who had withstood these attacks. At Camp Jill in Saudi Arabia, Fowler endured Scud missile attacks aimed at shaking American morale.[6]

In fact, Lisa Michelle Fowler's experiences in Saudi Arabia during the Gulf War are indicative of another important trend in the military during this period, the increasing presence of women soldiers at or near the front lines and the evolution of their roles in the armed forces. In the 1980s Pentagon officials had recognized that the lines between the support positions open to women and combat positions that excluded them were beginning to blur. "Women may be found in every battlefield sector," a 1982 army report explained, acknowledging that they could often be found "interspersed with direct combat units."[7] Fowler was one of approximately 40,000 American women serving in the Gulf, two of whom became prisoners of war and eleven of whom were killed in action. Fowler began the war in a clerical position of the type that women had filled for the military since World War II, but as combat forces were pulled into the ground war, she went from a secretary to a sentry. Fowler's new duties represented the changing attitude toward female troops in the armed forces. In the wake of the Gulf War, the 1990s would see barriers to different types of women's service begin to fall. For example, less than a year after the war ended, the law prohibiting women from flying combat missions for the air force was repealed.

One reason why all three of these interviews are so important is that American media coverage of the Gulf War was often spotty and heavily spun. Learning from the negative impact of media coverage during the Vietnam War, military escorts guided reporters through carefully selected and restricted areas, avoiding the worst of the bloodshed and devastation. Early on in the conflict, Walter Cronkite and other leading journalists argued that the military was "trampling on the American people's right to know" as a result of the "generally discredited Pentagon myth that the Vietnam War was lost because of uncensored press coverage." Military leaders responded during and after the conflict by saying that national security required discretion by the press that few Pentagon officials believed would be exercised voluntarily. "There were accusations of secrecy," Lieutenant General Thomas Kelley (Retired) acknowledged, "yet secrecy in military operations is valid and vital." Few images of the nearly 100,000 Iraqi casualties and the 184 American deaths reached the u.s. home front as the Pentagon closely monitored the release of footage from the battlefields of Kuwait and Iraq. Some scholars and journalists dubbed this a "Nintendo war" because the focus on weapons technology in American news reports made the conflict resemble a video game more than a bloody military campaign. Thus, the firsthand accounts in this chapter are a crucial part of the historical record in that they offer an unvarnished look at the reality of death and destruction in the Gulf War.[8]

Of course, the primary purpose of this chapter is to explore the experiences of gay and lesbian troops serving in both combat and support positions during the Gulf War. In contrast to the stereotype of gay troops as either unfit for or unwilling to engage in combat, two of these three interviewees volunteered for such duty during the war, placing themselves in harm's way when most of the other soldiers and airmen in their units decided to stay at home. Recognizing the potential problems of a volunteer force during wartime, the military instituted a stop-loss policy, halting most discharges, transfers, and retirements in units that had been or were about to be deployed to a war zone. Though it was not an official part of the stop-loss policy, the reduction in discharges for homosexuality during the Gulf War repeated what has happened during every modern American military conflict. Greg Mooneyham argues that this reduction in gay discharges during wartime exposes the hypocrisy of the military rationale for banning gay troops. If, as military policymakers posit, the primary argument for the ban is to protect unit cohesion and morale, Mooney-ham wonders why discharges of gay troops decline at the very point when good morale and unit cohesion are most necessary, times of war.[9]

Tragically, Landes, a West Point alumnus who volunteered to serve in the Gulf War, was one of the gay soldiers kicked out immediately after hostilities ended. His battlefield admission about his sexuality to a comrade during the conflict was used as evidence against him in interrogations afterward. Despite support for an honorable discharge by his immediate superiors who were impressed with his work as a liaison officer during the war, Landes would leave the Middle East with a dishonorable discharge as a reward for his volun-tary and valorous service.

Fowler and Mooneyham would ultimately volunteer to leave the services as well because even the "Don't Ask, Don't Tell" policy that was passed after they returned from serving in the Gulf provided little protection for them. Nor did it afford them the ability to lead the honest, upstanding, and honorable lives that the military had taught them to value. If not for the ban, all three of these interviewees would, in all likelihood, have joined other veterans of the first Gulf War who went on to fight in the Iraq War.

WINGMAN

An Interview with Greg Mooneyham

Greg Mooneyham could have stood in for Tom Cruise in the movie Top Gun. *He's that kind of fighter pilot. During the first Gulf War, he flew more than forty combat missions over Kuwait and Iraq. Mooneyham's memory of his missions was photographic. Even though he could not reveal the specifics of these missions, as he described them in general terms, there were times when I felt like I was there in the cockpit of his A-10.*

I'm Gregory Scott Mooneyham, and I was born in Jacksonville, Florida on June 26, 1965. My father was an insurance agent for Allstate Insurance Com-pany. My mother was a nurse, but she quit nursing in order to raise me and my brothers. I actually grew up in Spartanburg, South Carolina. We lived out in the country most of the time. We were lower middle class initially and then upper middle class later as my dad became more successful. Me and my brothers were all involved with football, some baseball. My dad played football in college, so we were all very involved with sports.

I took my first flight on an airplane when I was in the eighth grade. We'd flown up to Washington, D.C. I got hooked on flying at that point. I wanted to fly, and I made the decision probably about the ninth grade that I wanted to fly the best airplanes in the world—that was in the United States Air Force. So I decided that I wanted to go to the Air Force Academy, and basically focused on doing that through high school. I was pretty much a straight-A student. I think I ended up with a 3.96 GPA out of high school, and I was doing all of the things that the service academies tell you to do to get in. I was president of the student body my senior year, played sports, had good grades, focused on the SATs and that kind of stuff. In the South, everybody is very patriotic, and, of course, I was very patriotic. That maybe had a little bit to do with why I went, but I think that really my motivation was that I wanted to fly. Going to a great university and not having to worry about the cost of it, that was all part of it.

That first year at the academy, I did very well. Academically, I think I had a 3.6 GPA, which is pretty good. Militarily, I was always ranked pretty highly. I was not a rebel. I was going to do it by the book and work as hard as I could to do it the right way. Your days are so filled with everything that you just focus on what you have to do. And you're still being trained. You're still a plebe, a freshman. We call 'em doolies. You're still getting yelled at. You're still up against the wall. Some juniors and seniors also have to train the new classes coming in during the summers, and I actually did that twice. I enjoyed that program, bringing in the freshman and working with them. It's probably one of the most rewarding things I've ever done. You take kids right off the bus, and three weeks later they are walking, talking military machines, by the time you are done with them.

Graduation was the greatest day of my life! As we used to say, "The best thing in the world is the Air Force Academy . . . in your rearview mirror." Graduation week out there is a lot of fun. You spend it with family and friends and whoever comes out. There are different dinners and activities. And, of course, it culminates in the last day of the actual graduation. They have a speaker, and it's usually someone pretty significant. When I was there Reagan spoke one year and George Bush spoke one year. My year we got the secretary of the air force, Vern Orr. Then you've got this tremendous sense that it's over and you've done it.

My start time for pilot training was about sixty days after graduation, and pilot training was tough. I thought the Air Force Academy was tough. Pilot training turned out to be a little tougher for me. I had a really difficult time with airsickness. Everybody does. When you start out flying in jets everybody gets sick once or twice. Most people acclimate, but it took me a little bit longer than that. It worried me because I had been pointing at this since the ninth grade, and now, all of a sudden, I'm in a situation that I can't control. No matter how hard I work, I might not make it. That was very, very difficult for me to deal with. As it turned out, if I had got sick one more time, I'd have been thrown out of pilot training. I told my commander, "Well, you'll drag me out of here and I'll be leaving scratch marks on the wall." Just about when I was getting right down near the end, I got better, and I didn't really have any problems after that.

I was trying to figure out what I wanted to fly in, and the a-10 really was my first choice. The a-10 was the last real stick and rudder airplane, where you're down low and you're really flying the airplane, rather than managing computer systems. That kind of turned me off with the f-15 and f-16. To me, the fun part was the flying and the managing of weapons systems, and the a-10s got more weapons systems than just about anybody. Also, doing close support for the army appealed to me because I knew that's where the action was going to be. We have forced air supremacy on the rest of the world. In Desert Storm, after day two, the f-15 didn't have anything to do.

Greg continued his training as a fighter pilot over the New Mexico desert, and then he was stationed at various bases in the years leading up to the Gulf War.

My squadron was actually deployed to Germany when Saddam Hussein invaded Kuwait. We had people in Germany and part of the squadron back in Louisiana. I remember calling my mom from Germany just to say hello, and she was in tears because she figured that we were halfway to Kuwait or Saudi Arabia. Actually, we were recalled back to Louisiana, and they sent the other two squadrons. I sat around for two or three months waiting for a chance to go. They asked for volunteers at the end of November in 1990. My best friend and I immediately signed up because we were excited to go. After the sign-up period was over, we only had eleven names of volunteers out of my squadron of forty-something people, which I found to be very disappointing. Christmas was coming. Lots of people had families, and they didn't want to leave. But, still, I mean that's what we were there for. So as it turned out, when the list came out, my name was number one on the list to go, and my best friend was number two.

I went to the Middle East in December of '90. We landed in Saudi Arabia at Dhahran Airport. I remember it being very windy and hot, almost like a convection oven. It was funny. We got into a car and we started driving out to King Fahd, which was an airport that was under construction northwest of Dhahran by twenty or thirty miles. But on the way out, we passed a Kentucky Fried Chicken, a Hardee's, and a Baskin-Robbins, which really surprised me. At that time, we didn't really have any interaction with the locals or anybody.

Everybody I was seeing was essentially u.s. military. I think we actually stopped at the Baskin-Robbins to get some ice cream, and then went straight to the base.

We had a gate, and when I first got there, you could go outside the gate and wander around. We'd walk out into the desert and there'd be wild camels out there, and by wild I mean they'd just be wandering around. They were friendly. You could walk up to 'em. We'd go out and feed them Twinkies and stuff. They were like big cows. They'd come up and just rub up against you, and want you to pet 'em and stuff. There was also a really smart Saudi entrepreneur, who set up this grill right outside the gate, and you would smell him cooking hamburgers or camelburgers or whatever he was cooking. It smelled so good. Guys—especially 101st Airborne guys—you would just see them lined up to buy stuff from this guy. It always scared me. I was like, "There ain't no telling what he's cookin'!" But he was smart, because the smell would just waft over the base, and guys would just line up. As it got closer to the ground war, we were restricted, and you really couldn't go out anymore because they were concerned about terrorist attacks.

We knew very little about the ground war, until about three days prior. It was kept very, very secret, but we were going out on training missions every day, and we would fly over ground troops. It was very obvious that there was this humongous buildup on the ground close to the border. You were starting to see troops move west just a few days before the ground war started, but there was nothing at all official until about three days prior, when they divulged the plan to us. What they said was, "This will be happening any day, and here's what the army is going to do so expect to be ready."

I was reading my diary, because I kept a log of what I did, and I only counted up like forty missions. But the official record that DOD [Department of Defense] has is forty-four, so maybe I left out a couple here and there. I'm not sure. Typically, if you were going to fly a combat mission that day, you would fly at least two and maybe three. The idea is that you fly up and do your combat mission, come back and land at the forward operating location, which was King Khalid Military City (KKMC), which was just across the border. You'd refuel, rearm. You don't even get out. A crew chief would throw you up something to eat or drink, then you'd take off and do it all again, go back up, do a combat mission, come back to land at King Fahd to end your day. That's a ten-to-twelve-hour day. Then you'd have the next day off typically, because you'd just be wiped.

I flew in a day squadron, which meant that you flew day missions. You'd typically show up before the sun came up, and the first thing that you'd do was

After graduating from the U.S. Air Force Academy, Greg Mooneyham flew more than forty combat missions in his A-10 during the Gulf War.
Photo courtesy of Greg Mooneyham.

go in and get an intelligence briefing from your intel officer. This would be where the Iraqis are, where we are, where the air war's going, everything you missed while you were asleep. And the parts that you were interested in were the threats—who's shooting what and where are they. Then you would go in and update your maps. Then you'd go find out specifically where your target area would be or what your assignment was going to be. You'd go into a briefing where you'd brief your wingman. I was a two-ship flight leader at the time, which means if it was a two-ship, I would lead. If it was a four-ship, I might be number three. So whoever was leading the mission would then brief the mission of how we were going to go out and go at it.

Then you'd suit up, put on your G-suit and get your survival gear. You had a gun that would be issued to you, and you'd put it in your survival vest. There were some signaling devices that you would take in case you were shot down. There was what we called blood chit. It was basically a piece of paper with a number and an American flag on it. It had writing on it in four languages, like Farsi, Arabic, English, and probably French. It would say: "I'm an American fighter pilot. I've been shot down. If you help me, you will be rewarded by the American government"—monetarily, essentially. You would keep that with you, and if you got shot down and somebody helped you, you'd clip off a corner, which had a number on it, and you'd give it to 'em. You'd also usually keep some cash with you, as much as you felt like you could carry, because in that part of the world, cash is king. Then you'd take off your patches, except for your name.

You head out the door, meet with your crew chief and go over your airplane. Now, you're loaded with all live weapons, so you've got to check those out and make sure they're all configured properly. Then you'd get in the airplane, crank up, meet up with the rest of your flight, go out to the end of the runway, where then you have an arming crew that goes over your airplane and arms it up. It was also called "Last Chance," which means it was the last chance for somebody to look over everything on the airplane and make sure that it's ready to go. After they get you armed up and ready to go, you take the runway and take off.

It was about a thirty-minute flight to get into Kuwait or Iraq, depending on where your particular target was that day. We would typically be over target area for a good forty-five minutes, maybe an hour sometimes, depending on how much fuel you had. Then you'd head back over to the forward operating location and land. Immediately, you'd have a guy come up to your airplane and debrief you, an intelligence person, who'd ask you a certain amount of questions like: "What threats did you see? What targets did you hit? What was your

BDA—Battle Damage Assessment? What did you kill? What did you not kill?" And he would take that report while they were de-arming your airplane, assuming you still had any live ordnance left. Then you would taxi out of there, go over and refuel, and go to what was called a flow-through. You'd pull in between two revetments and they would rearm your airplane for whatever your next mission was—more bombs, more bullets, more chaff and flare, an air-to-air missile if you had expended one, which we really didn't do because we never had any air-to-air threats. But whatever you needed to completely rearm the airplane. And then as soon as your flight preparation was done, you'd taxi out, take off, and do it all over again.

In the first few days of the war, they wanted us to focus on artillery, because that's what the army was scared of, Iraqi artillery. You'd find a site, and you'd just drop your six bombs right across that site in one pass. Then, all of a sudden, the airplane is much lighter, much more maneuverable. Now, you've got two Maverick missiles, which are precision-guided, air-to-ground missiles on the airplane. And, of course, you had the gun; the gun was our primary weapon. The gun on the A-10 is a 30-millimeter cannon that will rip the top off a tank. We'd carry 1,100 rounds and that's twenty bursts out of that cannon, so you could do some serious damage.

The release point for dropping our bombs would be 7 to 8,000 feet, which is still pretty high up. But when you're dropping six of 'em, it's hard to miss. So what you do is these hiyakas straight down—we used to call 'em SFDs—straight freakin' down deliveries. [He laughs.] I thought this might be a family recording. So we'd just get real steep and drive straight down and ripple the bombs right across the target. At 7 or 8,000 feet, we were pretty accurate. The bad thing is that at 7 to 8,000 feet you're in prime threat from their anti-aircraft artillery, their hand-held, the flack that's coming up. If you were above 12,000 feet, you were pretty safe. At least, that's the way we felt about it. So for thirty to forty seconds, you're right in their prime threat area. You had to get in and get out quickly.

I mean they shot at you on every mission. You would always expect to be shot at. Luckily, they weren't very good shots as long as you continued to maneuver your airplane. Remember, once a bullet comes out of a gun, it's going to go in a straight trajectory, and if you're doing 3 or 400 miles an hour and they're not leading you properly, they're never going to hit you. If you don't fly in a straight line, they're never going to hit you, unless they just get lucky. So you just had to continue to maneuver the airplane. Every two to three seconds you needed to be changing something—altitude, heading, something —to make it very difficult for them to hit you. But, yeah, they shot at you all the time. They would shoot a lot of missiles in the air, but after about day two, they were scared to turn their radar on. So you'd see these missiles just go ballistic. If we were up at 15 to 18,000 feet, they would come up to that altitude and explode because they were just setting an altitude with a timer on the missile. Typically, they were so far away that it wasn't a huge issue.

Greg's most harrowing mission was a search and rescue operation to find a couple of American pilots who had been shot down over Iraq.

I was trained as a SANDY-2.[10] SANDIES were, even going back to Vietnam, the search and rescue guys. I was still relatively young, so I had training as SANDY-2, but not yet as SANDY-1. SANDY-1 would lead the mission; SANDY-2 would be the wingman. We were sitting on what's called SAR Alert (search and rescue alert) at KKMC. That put you close to the border where you could get across very quickly. My SANDY-1 was a guy named Joe Rikowski. We had that assignment for a week, Monday through Friday, and then somebody would come and relieve us. We sat there all the way through Friday. It was Friday afternoon, and we were going to go out and just patrol the border for about twenty minutes until the new SANDIES had landed.

That week, we had just started attacking the Hammurabi Republican Guard Unit, and they were serious. This was the first Republican Guard Unit that really fought back hard, and we had guys coming back through KKMC talking about how it was pretty hairy. But nothing had happened, so we're feeling pretty good about it. Well, we got to the airplanes, had just cranked our APUs [auxiliary power units] when we got a call saying, "Go ahead and crank, but don't go anywhere." So we looked at each other like, "OK, wonder what's going on."

Well, we got cranked, and they told us that two A-10s had been shot down. We were launched to go find them. They were just north of Kuwait, so once we got on the north side of Kuwait, we started our search and rescue. The way that works is that SANDY-1 sticks his nose deep in there, attempting to contact anyone who might be on the ground. And SANDY-2, which was my job, is above him, watching him, trying to protect him, and also coordinating all of the search and rescue forces. It was getting late in the day when we showed up over the target area, and you could tell they were shooting. They had shot down a couple of airplanes and they wanted a couple more. So we were working hard just to keep ourselves safe. And Joe was out there calling out there calling out, calling out, calling out, just to see if he could get anybody on the radio. We did that for about an hour until it got dark and never got anybody on the radio. Funny thing was, after it got dark, you really started to see how much was getting shot at you. During the day, you miss a lot. [He laughs.] There *is* stuff, but you don't see it. At night, you see it all! And then it really got scary. But once it gets dark, you can't really do search and rescue anyway—at least, not the way we did it at the time. Plus, your lights are off on your airplane so you can't even see your wingman anymore.

Once it got dark, we were getting low on fuel—very low, actually, much lower than we should have been. I was talking to Joe, and we decided that we needed to get out and get gas. There wasn't much else we could do. I had called the AWACS [airborne warning and control planes] and said, "We need a tanker, or else we're not even going to get home." They coordinated with a KC-135 [a refueling plane] that called us up and said, "Meet us at a certain point on the map." I said, "OK." And I started looking at my map to see where this point was, and it turned out it was well inside Iraq. I was like, "This KC-135 is going to meet us in Iraq," and I thought, "These guys are ballsy."

Well, to make a long story short, what had happened was that this guy named Rob Sweet had been shot down. But when he got shot down, his wingman, a guy named Steve Philis—a real fighter pilot's fighter pilot, who was very, very good—went down to try to help him, to try to protect him. He saw Rob get out, and he knew that he was under parachute and alive. At least, that's what we think happened. When he went down to protect Rob, Steve got hit very shortly thereafter. He never got out of his airplane. We'll never know why. He was killed in the crash. It turns out Rob was picked up immediately within a few seconds of hitting the ground, and was in a truck on his way to Baghdad. He was probably halfway there by the time we got over the area. So there was nothing we could do. Rob was gone and Steve was dead.

Once the prisoners of war were released after the war, Rob came back to the States. I was now in Baltimore, and I had flown down to Pope Air Force Base for some reason. I was at the officers' club that evening and I saw Rob. I walked up and I said, "Rob Sweet, how are you doing?" He goes, "Hey, I know you." And I go, "No you don't." He goes, "Yeah, haven't we met?" And I go, "No." He goes, "Well how do you know me?" And I said, "'Cause I was SANDY-2 on your search and rescue in Iraq." He was like, "Oh my God!" So he was buying me drinks the rest of the night.

I knew that Greg had attacked many targets and may have killed dozens of enemy soldiers during his Gulf War missions, so I sheepishly asked him if he felt any remorse for killing Iraqis.

I can't say that I did. For one thing it's a lot easier for fighter pilots than for ground attack guys, because you really don't see guys getting blown up. You don't see the enemy, and you don't have that image in your mind. I only actually saw guys on the ground one time. I was out west, Scud hunting with a colonel. He was the wing commander. The Iraqis were launching Scud [missiles] from out in the desert and we were there to keep them from launching 'em. Because if they knew we were out there, they weren't going to launch; they'd try to keep them hidden. So we were out there flying around with nothing to do. They sent the colonel out there because they don't want him to get shot down, and they know it's pretty low risk. They send somebody with him to keep him out of trouble. So we're out there looking around, with nothing to do.

All of a sudden, I see this truck, and it's on the Amman-Baghdad Highway. It's just this long straight road that runs from Amman, Jordan, to Baghdad, Iraq. The rules of engagement were nobody goes on that road, and if they do, they're going to get killed. I called the colonel, and said, "Hey, you've got a mover on the highway." We weren't really in a hurry, because there's a hundred miles of desert in front of him, so he's not going anywhere. So the colonel arms up his gun, and he says, "One's in." He takes a shot at the truck, and, to his credit, he actually led the truck. He didn't shoot directly at it. He led it just a little too much and shot right out in front of it. But when his bullets impacted the road, the truck just comes to a screeching halt. When he pulls off and gets into a position to cover me, I rolled in. I said, "Two's in." The truck was now sitting still, and as I'm rolling in on it, I can see soldiers piling out of the back of it with weapons in their hands—AK-47s, that kind of stuff. I basically destroyed the target with the gun. I killed the guys and the truck and everything around there. That's the only time I actually saw guys on the ground.

The way I looked at it was—this was a country that invaded another country, one of our allies. Anybody that's left on the ground alive is somebody that's going to attempt to kill our army guys, American troops on the ground. So it was our job to soften up the enemy as much as we could. I never really felt any remorse about it at all.

After we discussed the war, I asked Greg to talk about how his sexuality affected his experience in the military.

Very little. I knew I was gay from the time I was twelve years old, by the time the first hormones start raging in your body. But I was so focused on what I wanted to do, it really wasn't an issue. There was only one incident that kind of scared me when I was in the military and that was when I was in Louisiana there was another officer there who was caught and court-martialed and sent to jail. He was sentenced to two years in jail, but I don't know how long he actually spent in jail. About three months prior to that, he had found out that I was gay. Then I was scared. Here's this guy caught and going to jail. What's he going to do to save his tail? The really scary part was that word got out that he knew other gay people there on the base. But he never gave up any names. That affected me a whole lot. It made me paranoid. But that was really it as far as my sexuality goes; it never really had any effect at all.

Homosexuality was almost never talked about. Most people didn't care or even think about it as far as I knew. There was one incident where I remember there was a guy taken away in the middle of the night by OSI [Office of Special Investigations]. He disappeared, but apparently he had made a pass at somebody or done something, and it came to light that he was probably gay. One of his friends told me that he went to bed that night, and the next day he was gone. They woke him up, talked to him, and took him away. He never showed up again. Other than that, I don't remember hardly ever discussing it. I had never really been in gay culture at all. Much later, as I got involved in that and developed a little bit of gaydar, I look back on it and think, "Yeah, I knew a few guys who were probably gay." I just never knew it at the time.

I do know that there was one other fighter pilot there in Louisiana, and I thought, "He's gay." I never asked him, but I knew he was gay. And it's funny, because I think everybody else kind of knew he was gay too, but nobody really cared. As long as he just didn't say anything, and this was before "Don't Ask, Don't Tell," I don't think anybody really cared. The military was starting to get to the point where instead of throwing people in jail, which is what they did for a long time, they were just kicking people out. And it went from dishonorably discharging people to honorably discharging people based on their service. In that sense, I think it's gotten a little better. Under "Don't Ask, Don't Tell" it's pretty much always an honorable discharge, assuming you have good service. But in terms of how many people they're catching and kicking out, it didn't change anything at all. In fact, it's gone up recently.

If you look at the military regulations, essentially, they say that homosexuality is "incompatible with military service" and "detrimental to the good order of morale in military service." So when is the good order of morale most important? During a war, one would think. When is the one time they do stop-loss and force gay people to serve? During a war. So they're saying that it's detrimental to good order and morale and incompatible, but during a war they say, "No, you're completely compatible and you're fine." It's just so unbelievably hypocritical and so weak of an argument on the DOD's part; it just astounds me that they get away with it.

At the point that "Don't Ask, Don't Tell" was being debated, I was in Baltimore attached to the Air National Guard unit. I found that among the pilots nobody cared. Interestingly, in an Air National Guard unit, most of the pilots are airline pilots by trade. Airline pilots deal with flight attendants, and most male flight attendants are gay. They deal with gay people all the time, and most of them could care less. In fact, there was one guy at the unit, an officer, who everybody assumed was gay. He was a pilot, and nobody cared. Nobody really thought twice about it.

Among enlisted people, there was a very different attitude. They tended to be very much against gay people in the military for whatever reason. I used to argue with them. I was a straight guy defending gay rights as far as they were concerned. It's funny; nobody ever suspected that I was gay, as far as I knew. So, yeah, there were discussions that were pretty heavy, and typically, it broke down along those lines. I found that most officers could care less. Most enlisted people were against gays in the military.

I think there's two reasons. One is that most enlisted people have been in situations where they may be in much closer living quarters, in a dorm or in communal showers. They see that as a problem. Whereas most officers live in a house with their wife and a family, and they're not exposed to that so much. So, to them, it's not as big a deal. The second thing, I think, is that a good part of homophobia is just plain old lack of education. If you look at the officer corps, they're all college graduates. They have to be. And if you look at the enlisted corps, they are typically high school graduates at best. Even though in the air force that has changed a lot. You're getting a lot more college graduates in the enlisted corps, but typically, they've graduated from college after they've enlisted. So I think it's to a large extent lack of education. The number one way to overcome homophobia is to get to know someone who's gay and become educated on the thing. So I think that's a big part of it.

Playing devil's advocate, I suggested that some of the strongest opposition to "Don't Ask, Don't Tell" came from the Joint Chiefs, the most educated and highly decorated officers in the armed forces. So I asked Greg to think about why they would oppose the ban.

Well, that's a great question, and I have thought about that a bit. Again, I think it's a couple of things. One is they're from a different generation, much older. Typically, the people I was dealing with were forty and younger. Most of them were a lot younger, in their twenties and thirties, which is a whole different generation of people. When you get into the Joint Chiefs, they're in their fifties, maybe sixties, so they're coming from a much different time period, number one. And, number two, I think a part of it was they were looking at a lot of their core people who were against it, and I hate to say this, but the Joint Chiefs are really political and they want to come across having the "right" position. They're just political in nature, conservative in nature, and from a different generation.

Near the close of the interview we talked about the end of the Gulf War and Greg's return to the States.

The morning that they called the cease-fire, I was actually taxiing out for another mission. I remember they called us up and said, "Taxi back. War's over." That was the radio call we got. I remember a great feeling of relief at that point, going, "Wow, we did it. It's over." I taxied back, and obviously everybody was very excited, but we thought that this could flare up at any minute. We still had to fly protection missions, because we were the close air support guys. We would fly over the top of the army and let them know that we were there if anything happened. We were ready to support them. But after that there was no enemy fire. We never got shot at again. Still, the army could be attacked at any time, so we had to be there. I stayed until April and then came back to the States.

We landed back at Dover, had a great welcome, went back to Louisiana, had a great welcome. Actually, it was pretty cool. Everybody treated us like heroes for the longest time. I don't think I bought a drink at a bar for six months after the war. I've got a license plate that says, "Proudly Served: Veteran of Desert Storm," from the state of Georgia, and I put an HRC [Human Rights Campaign] sticker right next to it.

I loved the air force, and I would have stayed in if I had not been gay or if they had lifted the ban. I wasn't willing to live in the closet anymore and continue to serve. But I absolutely loved it. I absolutely think everything that I did was good. Just graduating from the Air Force Academy alone opens up more doors than you can imagine. Then, being a fighter pilot, the discipline you learn, the skills you learn—everything you learn is valuable in the outside world. The honor and integrity that they teach you will keep you in good stead for the rest of your life. Life lessons abound when you serve in the military, and I'm very thankful that I did. I'm very grateful that I had the opportunity. And a little ticked that I had to leave.

At the time of this interview, Gregory Scott Mooneyham was a business consultant in Atlanta, Georgia.

STOP-LOSS

An interview with Mark Landes

Mark Landes is an alumnus of West Point. He was serving in Germany when the Berlin Wall came down, and then he volunteered to serve in the first Gulf War even though the rest of his unit was never sent to the Middle East. During the war, he was a liaison officer, communicating between the Third Armored Division and Brigade Command. It was not until after the war that his homosexuality became a problem in the eyes of the u.s. military.

I'm Kenneth Mark Landes, and I was born in Montevista, Colorado, November 5, 1964. Montevista is not close to anything. [He laughs.] It took until my senior year of high school, 1983, for us to even get a McDonald's in a town that was seventeen miles away from us. My father was a farmer, and my mother worked at various accounting jobs. I grew up on a small farm. My family is farmers. I just recently found my sixth great-grandfather's grave here in Bucks County, Pennsylvania. He died in 1791, and he came over from Germany and he was a farmer. So my family has been farmers here in the United States since 1791.

I was definitely breaking the mold. I was the first generation to ever graduate from college. Because my parents were in the lower middle class and didn't save any money, and when I was trying to figure out how I was going to go to college, my mother reminded me of that. Being a good Republican kid, I decided that I would apply to the service academies, and I actually applied to all three of them. I was selected by Senator Gary Hart to go to West Point. I decided to go visit for a weekend and fell in love with the place and decided that's where I wanted to go.

They don't call that first summer Beast Barracks for nothing. It was very difficult, but I had ten varsity letters in high school. I played football, basketball, and ran track. I was also the editor and chief of the school newspaper and the yearbook. I was the valedictorian of my class. We've only got twenty-one people in the graduating class. Someone has to be that person. As far as the physical stuff went, that was not a problem. I had thrown my shoulder out during plebe boxing, so I had to take it again as a sophomore. And, unfortunately, I was there with all of the football players who couldn't take it the year prior, so I was actually the smallest guy there. Every time that I got matched up, I faced these guys that were bigger than I was, and I got pounded. My final matchup, I actually had my nose broken. And after that happened, I got so pissed that I started wailing on the guy. I had apparently crossed the line as I was beating on this guy.

I didn't have a problem with the disciplinary stuff at West Point because I was trying to make sure that I fit in. I looked at it as an opportunity to find out about other leadership styles as a follower, to find out what type of leadership style I wanted to build for myself. I tried to build a leadership style that was not based on authoritarian scare tactics as much as trying to build a relationship with people who worked underneath me in such a way that we were a team working together to accomplish a goal, rather than me sitting up at the top, dictating what they were going to do. So I was trying to take input from other people to come up with a goal that we would be shooting for, and actually try to attain that. Even though my grades and my military rank didn't allow me some of the higher positions, I did my best whenever I got into a leadership position to try to lead the people that were underneath me. I was assistant squad leader, squad leader, and then became a platoon leader my senior year.

I graduated in 1987, and after finishing the Armor Officer Basic course in Fort Knox, Kentucky, I was stationed in Germany with the Third Squadron, Seventh Cavalry Regiment. I was happy to get cavalry. I kind of liked the romance of it, and because I grew up on a farm, I had my own horse until I was ten years old. So I liked the idea of that. But also, it was a very forward unit. If the balloon had gone up and the Soviet Union had actually invaded Germany, we were going to be right on the border between East and West Germany. At the time, that was *the* place to be. And, also, cavalry is different from just a regular tank company, because it's a mix of infantry and armor at the same time. So my first position was actually as a scout platoon leader in Alpha Troop. It was interesting because, normally, second lieutenants just out of the basic course go to a tank platoon first, and then become a scout platoon leader, but because the position was available at the time, they put me right in as a scout platoon leader.

In 1988 there was no thought of the Cold War ending. That year, I had actually served as a camp commander for a forward camp that was on the East German–West German border. You still saw signs of where people had been shot and killed trying to escape. They basically told me that as soon as I took over the command, the East Germans knew my name. I should expect that if they invaded, I would be the first person to be shot. So, at that point in time, the Cold War was not anywhere near being over. Later that year, I actually went to Berlin and went through Checkpoint Charlie, and I had to wear my full dress uniform to go into East Berlin. At that point in time, the only way that I thought East Germany and West Germany were going to be reunited was if the Soviet Union invaded. There were no chinks in the wall in 1988. There were no indications.

But I have gotten a chance to see a lot of history happen, fairly up close. It was a year almost to a day after I went to Berlin that the Berlin Wall came down. It was so amazing because we were actually on a training site going through tank gunnery at the time that it happened. We were just blown away. We didn't know what to think about anything at that time because everything that we had trained for was gone. People were extremely happy. But there was also the uncertainty involved. What happens now that the Berlin Wall comes down and East Germany is collapsing? Does West Germany absorb East Germany? Do they get reunited, and how exactly would that work? And what effect would that have on the military? I went back to Berlin almost a year after it came down too, so I got to see some of the changes that were going on. The Soviet Union hadn't really collapsed yet, so for the military, the threat changed to "OK, if the Soviet Union tries to come back and take over these breakaway countries, what exactly do we do? And where is the next threat going to come from?"

The next threat came from the Middle East when Saddam Hussein invaded Kuwait. I asked Mark how he felt about that war and why he volunteered to go. Though he didn't say it, I could tell that he thought that last question was unnecessary.

Well, I didn't get sent to the Persian Gulf until after Saddam Hussein invaded Kuwait. It was real interesting, because my mother was visiting me from the United States at that time, and we were actually in London, I believe, when we started seeing the reports that he had invaded Kuwait. My mom was constantly asking me, "Well, how does this affect you?" And I'm like, "I don't know yet." Because I didn't know what the response was going to be, but I also believed wholeheartedly that if the United States did not step in, he was going to invade Saudi Arabia.

I supported the first Gulf War, because we had a request from Saudi Arabia to help defend them. We had a request from the rightful leaders of Kuwait to help them bring back the country that was invaded by this person, much the same way that the French asked us for help when they were invaded in the First World War and Second World War. So I had no problem with that. We had full support from the UN. We had an Arab and Western alliance going into it.

I volunteered to go. I'm a West Point graduate. My country is about to go to war, and I get asked if I want to volunteer to go and serve my country. Well, I volunteered to serve my country when I chose West Point. It just seemed to be the logical thing. I couldn't stand by safely in Germany and know that other people had the possibility to give up their lives. Part of it is pride. Part of it is the desire to serve my country, because that's what I was trained to do. The

$150,000 education that I got was supposed to be paid off by me serving my country during a time of war.

We landed in Saudi Arabia at night, and it was all of a sudden the realization of how cold the desert can be. [He laughs.] Because we had to sit on the tarmac and it was freezing. But during the day, it would get to be 100 degrees. So that was the first impression. Also, everywhere that I've lived, I've tried to understand the culture. As much as I could, I tried to understand and experience the culture of Saudi Arabia, really expand my knowledge of the region. So every opportunity that I could, I would actually talk to someone that could speak English, because I didn't speak Arabic. But I tried to get an understanding of how they thought and what the thought process was for a culture that's radically different than mine.

Some Arabs were thankful that we were there, and the only reason we were there was because we were asked by their government to be there. There was no idea that I wanted to push any of the Judeo-Christian things that I grew up with on anybody, and I certainly didn't want anybody pushing anything on me. At that point in time, I was a born-again Christian. One of the things that I did realize real quickly was that the similarity between the three religious factions that fight over the Middle East—Judaism, Christianity, and Islam—is that they all worship the same god. It's interesting that they all worship the same god, but they can't see beyond the differences in that, because they all think that their religion is the only true way to understand God. That was the start of the process of me trying to understand how these religions could coexist.

My assignment once the war started was to be the division liaison officer between the Third Brigade and the Third Armored Division. I would attend the same meetings that the Third Armored Division commander would attend and take that information back to the brigade commander and to other people who needed it within the brigade. So I knew an awful lot of stuff that was going on that civilians didn't know was going on. Even today, people don't know exactly what happened. I got to listen to interviews that were done with Iraqis who had actually surrendered to u.s. forces, and I learned what led them to surrender. Some of the people were actually pulled off the streets of Baghdad, given a rifle, and told, "Here, go fight the Americans." After all the bombing that we did to prep before the actual ground assault, they couldn't stand it anymore. Some of them hadn't eaten for weeks, because we were bombing their supply routes to such an extent that they couldn't get any food. And they were being threatened by the Republican Guard: "If you defect, we'll shoot you in the back." So these people had lived in fear. Something finally snapped with them that said, "I'm going to go over and surrender."

Knowing that Mark had served in southern Iraq during the war, I asked him if he was ever afraid for his life.

The two things that really stick out in my mind of when I was really afraid were the night the war started and the following day. I was actually the acting brigade commander at the time that the war started. As a junior military officer, you got officer of the day duty, and your worst fear is that the war starts when you're in command. Even though it's a temporary command, all of a sudden the balloon goes up, and I'm in charge. I have to make these decisions; I have to alert these people. I got a call from our division commanders that the balloon was about to go up, which is a euphemism that the war is about to start. So I had to wake up my full-bird colonel (commander) and lieutenant colonel (deputy commander) and say, "OK, guys, this is it. The war is about to start. The air campaign is about to start. We need to start preparing for what might come our way, once the air war started." I didn't get any sleep that night, obviously.

I then had to go and warn some of the other units, and as I'm going over to these other apartment buildings, all of a sudden, the air-raid siren goes off. Everybody was afraid of the Scud missiles and potential chemical weapons that were involved. I had to put on my chemical protective suit. For some reason, our walkie-talkies weren't working through the concrete buildings, so I had to go over and tell other commanders that the war was about to start. Then, as I'm going down the stairs, all of a sudden, the air-raid siren goes off again. We were told that the safest place to be would be in the stairwell of the bottom two floors in case a Scud missile landed on top of the building, because that's the most structurally sound place to be.

I'm huddled there with all of these people I don't know, because it was a National Guard unit. And I had this private standing next to me, who looked terrified as he was trying to put on his chemical protective suit. I ended up having to help him get his chemical protective suit on, because he was so scared about what was going to happen. So that was the first time that I really experienced the possibility that something would happen.

Then, the next night, I can't go to sleep again. I'm lying there awake in my sleeping bag listening to Armed Forces Network Radio, and listening to an ABC reporter describe an event that was happening. Well, it was happening to me at the same time, because I heard this woosh and this KABOOM. At first, I thought that it was one of our planes that had actually blown up on takeoff, because we weren't that far from the air base. But I remembered a conversation that I had had with one of the air defense guys, and he said that we wouldn't have a real good warning if a Scud missile was in-bound. The first good notification that we would actually have would be to hear the Patriot missile batteries firing. So as this ABC reporter was describing hearing a Patriot missile shooting down a Scud, I realized that that had happened over my head. Everybody starts running around. We have to get in chemical protection suits. It was actually our brigade's chemical officer who went to find out if there were any chemical weapons in that Scud missile, because it landed not far from the apartment complex that we were in. So that was the first time that I realized, "Hey, dummy, you're in a war."

About a week later, I was with the vehicles. Our vehicles had gotten off-loaded from the boats, and we were actually getting ready to go out into the desert in preparation for the actual ground invasion. So we were going to be going out into Saudi Arabia. I was the convoy commander taking our vehicles out there, and as I'm riding in the truck with this Arab driver from Saudi Arabia, we're driving out, and all of a sudden I see this rocket in the sky and an explosion. We're just pulling out of Dhahran, and a Scud missile attack is happening. The Arab driver looked at me like, "What the hell are we supposed to do?" And I'm just like, "Go! Go! The further we are away, the better off we're going to be. Just keep going." That was the second time I was attacked.

I was still working as a liaison during the offensive. But we were moving so fast, I actually got stuck most of the time with the division headquarters. I couldn't actually catch up with my unit, because they would be moving as we would be setting up to find out what they were doing. I ended up being the lead vehicle in the division headquarters right up to the time we started going through unexploded bombs. At that point in time, we decided that my Humvee was not the best protection in case I ran over unexploded munitions. We were going into the places where the Republican Guard had been, so there were burning tanks, burning vehicles. There were still unexploded American bombs that we were driving through.

I saw mainly Iraqi casualties, because they had been abandoned on the battlefield. [He sighs.] I didn't like to think that there was someone in the vehicles that I saw burning, but there were. Some people actually took pictures of it, and that disturbed me. These are human beings. Some of them didn't even want to be fighting. As much as you think that West Point and time in the military can prepare you for something like that, you don't know what you're going to do until you actually get there. It was disturbing, and fortunately, shortly after that, we got the word that the 100 hours was almost up and the ground war was coming to a halt. So we were pretty happy about that.

But we didn't have any celebrations because we still had a job to do. Even though it appeared that the cease-fire was going to hold, there was always the possibility that something could happen. I actually caught up with my unit and found out that we had had no casualties. I was happy about that. Even though the brigade had been in the battle, nobody was killed or seriously injured at that point.

Knowing that Mark's trouble with the military because of his sexuality began after the end of hostilities in Iraq, I asked him to give a little background about his sexuality.

I didn't even come out to myself until my junior year of West Point. I didn't realize that the feelings that I had could be termed being homosexual. I am a very late bloomer at that point in time. In my senior year, I find out that being homosexual is grounds for dismissal, could even potentially lead to jail time. So you pretty much have to hide that, and, being a born-again Christian, I felt that I was supposed to heal myself and no longer be gay. Those are the things I was struggling with all through the time I was in Germany, all through the actual war itself. I was trying to understand why I felt the way I did, what that really meant, and how am I supposed to relate to other people. Especially growing up where I did, I had no guidelines; I had no role models to identify with in how to be a gay man.

When the war ended, we were actually in southern Iraq. We were in an oil refinery that had been blown up. I had met a guy, and he was enlisted and I was an officer. He was a driver for the air force, a guy that was attached to the brigade. We started talking and started sharing a bunch of things. We started talking about everything. They call it becoming foxhole buddies when the threat on your life is such that if you're with someone, you're going to tell them everything. At that point in time, I had never told anybody what was going on other than my parents and my sister. That was before the war. But those were the only people I had ever told. I actually told the air force guy that not only was I gay, I was attracted to him and knew that nothing could happen, but I just had to talk to somebody. He told me, "No problem. Understood." We continued to talk. It didn't seem to be a problem. I think it was a month later, and we had moved to a new location. All of a sudden, Criminal Investigation Division (CID) starts interviewing people, and I had no idea why at that point, until the deputy brigade commander called me in and let me know that they were investigating me. I was just continuing to do my job.

Then CID pulls you into a room where you're by yourself. They tell you that you can have someone represent you, but at this point in time I was tired of it all. I was tired of having to live this double life of trying to understand who I was as a person and as a gay man and what that meant for me. I had actually decided that I was going to get out of the military after my five-year commitment was up because I couldn't deal with this double life. I told CID everything simply because I was tired of it.

They ask you all kinds of things. They ask you to name names of people that you've had relationships with, other military people, and it becomes a witch hunt. It's real interesting, because they'll actually stop—and they did this with the recent Persian Gulf War. They'll actually stop the process of getting a gay man out of the military if a war happens, because they still need you to serve your country, and they're happy for you to serve your country during a time of war whenever something is needed, but as soon as that threat goes away, they kick you out.

After it all came out, my brigade commander and the deputy brigade commander both wrote letters supporting me and asking that I be put out of the army with an honorable discharge. They wrote that we had talked and that I had said, "I just want to get out right now." They were supporting me with that, and then the division commander said, "No, I'm going to give you an other than honorable discharge." That really hurt a lot, and I ended up going to the brigade chaplain and telling him that I was thinking about ending my life. That set off whole new shockwaves, because at that point I became a mental patient. They took away my gun, my bayonet, everything that I could possibly use to kill myself. They put me in the medical facility.

The very next day, I'm being flown out of my unit without anybody knowing what's going on. I didn't get to talk to anybody. All of a sudden, I'm being sent back to a rear echelon place to await my transportation as a patient back to Germany. It's the most humiliating thing in the world, because I'm going back with people who were actually injured. Most of them weren't shot, but they had been injured, and I'm going back because I'm a basket case. No one, other than Criminal Investigation Division, really knew why.

Most of the people in the military who did know were actually fine with it because of my performance. I had never received a bad performance rating. I had succeeded beyond some people's ideas of what a second lieutenant should do, because after I was a scout platoon leader, I was a support platoon leader, which was one of the premier positions, because you were actually in charge of the food, fuel, and ammunition for the entire squadron. That was a tremendous responsibility. Normally that goes to a very senior first lieutenant, and I actually got it as a second lieutenant and did extremely well. My military performance, my military leadership, everything like that was fine.

Well, most people did not know why I came back. The only person who knew was the squadron commander. I had been the support platoon leader for most of the time he had been squadron commander, and he also wrote a letter of recommendation saying that I should get an honorable discharge. This was actually after I got released from the hospital, because I had to be released before I could go back to my original unit. Almost everybody involved felt that I had done a good job, and that's the hardest part. Even though all of the people I served with felt like I did a really good job, the United States government and the army see my service to my country as other than honorable, that it was less than what it should have been. And the only reason for that was that I admitted that I was gay.

The problem is the policy. I volunteered to potentially give up my life to serve my country when they asked me to. They responded to that by saying that my service was less than what it should have been. I have no military benefits at this point in time. Being other than honorable, I don't even have VA benefits. At a certain point in time, I actually stopped worrying about that. At first, I was trying to figure out how to get it overturned, but then the realization was that that's not how I see myself. That's not how people see me—as a veteran. In reality, that's nobody's business, and I don't see how that little stigma affects anything about who I am. I've been able to get beyond that, but that was not easy.

My goal after graduating from West Point was to have a military career. Going to West Point, serving in the military, it made me who I am—made me a person who is more well rounded, more accepting of other ideas. I'm someone who has a sense of discipline and an idea of what's right and wrong. Even though I don't agree with everything the government and the military stand for, I still have strong patriotism. It s just that I d like to see the country go a different way.

At the time of this interview, Mark Landes was a computer consultant, living in Exton, Pennsylvania.

FROM SECRETARY TO SENTINEL

An Interview with Lisa Michelle Fowler

Lisa Michelle Fowler was raised in the South. You can hear this in the cadence of her storytelling. She has a wonderful sense of humor that makes even the most mundane stories of life on base and in the barracks crackle, but there's also a sense of sadness here that captures the pain and anger she endured as she came to understand who she really was. Many of the people in this book "found themselves" during their time in the military or in combat, but none more so than

Michelle. That she did this during an era when the American military was coming to terms with new roles for women at war was even more impressive.

I'm Lisa Michelle Fowler, and I was born in Stuart, Florida, in 1970. My mom was really young, like sixteen, when I was born. My dad did drywall with my grandfather, and he still does that today. Actually, I grew up mostly in North Florida, in the panhandle. Kind of a hick town—rednecks, hicks, country, you know; people have wooden teeth. It's just not my kind of town. I was pretty much a loner. I joined the army to get away from my hometown and go somewhere. I never wanted to go back!

When I went to boot camp, I thought that I hated my family, but I found that I was homesick very quickly. I did a lot of crying, which is something I would never tell anybody right now. I'd be like, "I never cried." It actually meant a lot to me in basic training when Drill Sergeant Hicks said, "Private Fowler, that was out-fucking-standing!" When she said something was "out-fucking-standing," let me tell you something, you did something good.

At the beginning of this interview, I referred to Fowler as "Lisa," but at this point she gently corrected me and explained why she didn't go by that name anymore.

Actually, I chose to change my name when I went into basic. Well, my name's "Lisa." But a friend of mine in Florida, who I went to church with, told me, "This is pretty cool, Lisa. You get to go somewhere where you've never been before. You can change anything about yourself and nobody would ever know the difference." I thought about that for a while, so when I got on the bus, there was this girl by the name of Tammy Rapley, who was sitting beside me. She was an African American girl, and she asked me my name. For some reason, I just blurted out "Michelle" instead of "Lisa." So ever since then I've been "Michelle" or "Shelly." A lot of people ask me if that symbolizes something. I was a really confused teenager. I was having crushes on my girlfriends —secret, of course. And I was raised Southern Baptist. You know how that is. I was just trying to be a good Christian, and I would pray to God, "Please, please, blah, blah, blah." I thought maybe if I changed my name that my confusion would go away. I think I was also just tired of being the person I was in high school: Lisa the loner, Lisa who had no friends. I wasn't a popular person; my parents were poor. Yeah, I guess it is kind of symbolic. Lisa was lost, you know. Michelle was found.

But anyway, in basic, I got good at doing push-ups, very, very good. I could even do the triangle push-ups, and I ran a lot. Oh, and I remember this spider incident that was pretty funny. I'm extremely arachnophobic, extremely. One time, we were marching out in the woods with our backpacks and our weapons, and I ran right smack into one of them big ol' huge spiders on those big huge spider webs. [She whispers.] I peed. Everybody started laughing at me, so the drill sergeant made everybody do push-ups until they stopped laughing. I already peed myself, and now everybody is mad at me because they're doing push-ups. That was pretty funny.

Well, AIT [advanced infantry training] was in the same place, in Fort Jackson, South Carolina. And it was typing school. That's all the recruiter would let me do was typing, which didn't thrill me none, but, hey, I was in the army. Some of my friends from basic were in AIT with me. There was Tammy, who ended up coming to all the places with me. And there was Candice. I had a little crush on her. She was real nice. She was a buddy of mine. We kept in touch for the longest time, but we lost touch eventually. I think those were the two of my closest friends.

It was a little unusual for me to have black friends, because my daddy wouldn't let me when I was growing up. Or it ain't that he wouldn't let me. Maybe I thought that he wouldn't let me. It's always been in Southern Baptist religion, when people get married, the yolks be with the yolks type of thing. In the Florida panhandle, you know, stuff like that don't happen, but when I joined the army, it's like my whole world opened up, and people were just beautiful to me.

I finished AIT in—I think it might be 1990, and then I went to Fort Hood, Texas. It was nice there. I learned how to country western two-step at Cody's. And I met a whole lot of friends, and they were all straight. Since I'm not mentioning names I guess I can say it—they were all very promiscuous. So me, still being confused about what's going on with myself, I watched them be promiscuous, and I was thinking, "I'm supposed to be acting like these girls. I'm supposed to be doing what they're doing, 'cause I'm a girl." So, unfortunately, I did try to do what they did. That's not something I'm too proud of—trying to be something that I'm not.

At work, I was making ID cards and dog tags, nothing exciting to talk about there. I was in Texas about six or seven months, before I found out I was going to the Middle East. I remember that day. Well, first of all, my sergeant, Sergeant Emerson, told us, "Ain't no way that we're gonna go over there. We're personnel." She's like fifty-something years old. She's never been anywhere in the military, as far as tours, so she just assumes, 'cause she's personnel, that personnel people don't go. We're all really relieved, but then we get into formation one day, and they're telling us, "Okay, we have orders. We're going." Needless to say, we were all a little freaked out. I was shaky. Me and Sergeant Emerson cried. We couldn't believe it.

I don't know if you watch movies on TV, war movies. You see all that blood and *Hamburger Hill,* and they kinda make wars look scary. That's what you think about. That's what I was thinking about. That's where I'm going. That's what I have to put up with. But it was nothing like that.

They gave us handbooks about Saudi Arabia before we went, to tell us about the rules and regulations. About how you ain't supposed to put your right foot on your knee. Like suppose you cross your knee, you ain't supposed to show the bottom of your feet. And like if you do the peace symbol that's like flipping the bird. And then they tell you, "If a Saudi man sees your body and you're naked, you pretty much blasphemed him."

All I remember when we got there was seeing dirt. And I remember them handing us two bottles of water and telling us to drink up, because we wouldn't know when we'd get our next water, which didn't make no sense to me. I was thinking if you didn't know when you'd get your water again, you'd wanna take your time with the water you have. They told us to drink it up, so we did. I ended up taking a four-hour bus ride, and I had to pee so bad I couldn't stand up.

For the most part the Saudis were nice. I never had a problem or a quarrel with any Saudi civilian. In fact, I met a very good friend—and I'll send you a picture of him. His name was Mohammad. He actually wrote me here in the States for a couple years after I got back. Very nice guy, young, he was in the Saudi army. Honestly I don't remember how I met him. I just know he was a real nice guy, and me and my friends kind of hung out with him. He showed us around sometimes.

It was "Desert Shield" at the time we got there, and then it turned over to "Storm" while I was there. During Desert Shield, my main job was clerical, personnel. If people lost their ID cards, I'd make those. People lost dog tags; I made those. When people get shipped in, we get their records. And when they get shipped back to the States, we sent their records to their personnel company. Stuff like that.

When Desert Storm started, I did mostly security duty at Camp Jill. There was a big huge camp area, bunch of trailers. There were these little trailers. They were probably about thirty feet by fifteen feet wide. And there was three of us in each trailer. They also had shower trailers. I bet there was at least 300 trailers with over a thousand people, all different units.

On guard duty, I'd just play solitaire. It was just the opening and closing of a gate, just stay up all night, because I had the night shift. And they were twelve-hour shifts. I had a weapon, but they never gave us any real bullets. I never understood that. I had to assume that maybe they didn't think we was in that much danger, seeing as I got a weapon, with no bullets in it. I mean, I was young. So I guess I could just point it at you and scare you to death. [She laughs.]

On our days off, with permission, we went to downtown Dhahran, and went to a couple of restaurants. My first sergeant, who was Muslim, wanted us to understand that women Muslims ain't unhappy in their life. Like we'd think, "That'd be miserable." But he wanted us to understand that they're not unhappy with their life, the way they'd be covered up and be six feet behind the husband. You still can't tell me they ain't unhappy.

There was actually a lot of women in my personnel service company. The guys there were just personnel service guys. I did not have any issues with sexual harassment from them. If I was in a grunt unit or trying to be a ranger or trying to do something that men like to do, then maybe I'd suffer some sexual harassment or be told that I can't do something when I can. But I think because I was in that kind of company, that's why I just didn't see it. No one said: "Okay, I'm gonna file more records than you because I'm a man."

When I joined, they didn't have the "Don't Ask, Don't Tell, Don't Pursue." They came right out and asked you, and at the time I told the truth. I was confused, but I never acted. So I didn't lie. Where I'm from, people don't talk about stuff like that. I knew there was something different about me, but I didn't know what it was. So when I joined I didn't lie. I had a couple of boyfriends—one, in particular. He really, really liked me, and it seems to me that whenever I had a boyfriend, everything was fine until we had sex. And then I never wanted to see him again. Never. I didn't even want to have to look at him. So I told this fella, because I was raised Southern Baptist, I think you should wait until you get married to have sex. As long as me and him were just not having sex, we could hang out.

I was seeing that guy. Okay, and I was really struggling and praying to God to take this away from me. It was a big struggle for me. I fought it tooth and nail. I fought it, I swear to God I did. You can't fight what's there, though. But, anyway, I remember that I went to a party with him. In my mind, I was just like struggling. I had a little Ford Ranger at the time, so I left the party. I drove to a parking lot, and there I prayed. Actually, I screamed at God. I was like so angry at him for not taking this away from me and not answering my prayer to why am I feeling this way. As I was growing up and even when I was in the military, I could never say the word "lesbian." Especially say I was one, because that was a sin. I'd be like, "I'm a l-l-l . . ." I couldn't let it come out. So I just sat in my truck and I just screamed to the top of my lungs, "Okay! Fine! I'm a lesbian!" And then, the next day, I had a whole new world waiting for me. I thought I was the only lesbian on this earth, but I found out different soon.

I didn't tell nobody about what I had done. But I did have a very good friend by the name of Belinda. She was like my best friend. She was married and had a husband. She was like my very best friend—I had the hugest crush on her—but she was like my very best friend. She never knew. Soon after I came out to myself, I did come out to her. She didn't believe me at first, because I'd been playing this straight role. Soon after that, she believed me, and she loved me even more for it.

Well, I felt opened up. Now, I know why I'm having these feelings, and now I can stop acting like someone else. When I'm off post, I can act like me. And when I'm on post, I just go back to being a soldier. See, that's what I was, I was a soldier. So when I wasn't being a soldier, I was being me. I think that's the problem. People think that just because you're gay means you gotta have sex 24-7. That's not a fact, Jack. I work for a living. I pay taxes. I ain't had sex since November.

I remember the marches when Clinton came into office. I remember *hoping* that it would turn out to be something a little more than "Don't Ask, Don't Tell, Don't Pursue." I was hoping it would give everybody our freedom to serve, which it didn't, you know, openly. It seemed to me in the service that there was more of a problem with men than it would be women. I think if you were a lesbian in the military, it was fine in most cases. But you know, guys say, "Oh, I hope I have a lesbian friend, maybe we'll have a threesome. But guys?! Screw that!" That's how they are. Maybe that's the reason why we have such a problem having equal rights in the military. Even though I did know some gay guy friends in the military, and they were excellent soldiers—make sure you put that in capital letters. EXCELLENT, decent soldiers, and they loved America as much as everyone else did, and they served right along beside me. I just want to say that. So I don't think it has anything to do with men or women, but I think that's how they perceive it, the heterosexuals.

When Michelle was at Camp Jill, she had to endure Scud missile attacks, so I asked her to talk about what that was like.

I remember when the war started I didn't know nothing about Scuds or Patriot missiles. I'd heard about it, but didn't know nothing, because I'm a little secretary. But I remember that at the time I was pulling guard duty on days, or maybe I was still working in the office. But I remember being by myself at nighttime, because my roommate was working nights for some reason. I was listening to the army radio station, and I was reading a Sidney Sheldon book. All of a sudden, I heard these alarms go off—kinda like a tornado alarm—and it kind of scared me a little because they told us in training that once you open your chemical suit it only has about six hours of life. So I'm debating, "Well, if I open it now, and it's a false alarm, then that's time off my chemical suit." So I don't know what to do. But it ended up being a real Scud. Our first sergeant came up and knocked on everybody's door. Of course I ain't in full MOPP gear.[11] That's your whole chemical suit—your boots, your charcoal suit, your mask, and your gloves. I was shaking so badly that I couldn't even put my pants on. My first sergeant had to help me put my MOPP gear on. It was pretty scary. I didn't know, but there was Patriot missiles out there. And these Patriot missiles actually hit the Scuds before they hit down here. The "boom" was the Patriot missile hitting the Scud. It wasn't a chemical bomb, thank God, but you could actually smell whatever they put in the bomb.

When you put on your chemical mask, you put it on your face. In order to clear it and seal it, you hold your hands on the sides of the thing and you blow out. If there's any chemicals, you're supposed to hold your breath while you put your mask on. So then you blow out to get the chemicals out of your mask and then put your hand in front of your face and suck in to make sure you get a good seal. So it's like [blows out breath] that. We had so many Scuds or so many incidents that we kind of got used to them after a while. It was kind of like, "Oh, here we go again. Put the MOPP gear on, blah, blah, blah."

One time, I remember that it was me and my friend Sherry and a bunch of reservists. Well, there were three reservist guys, older gentlemen. They were funny as hell, real southern, real funny. We were sitting there hanging with these guys, and the alarm came on. We were all having fun, but we got serious quick and put our masks on. So we [blows out breath] got our suction. We all get done putting our mask on, and we all look at Johnny over here; he ain't got his mask on. I said, "Johnny! Put your mask on!" And he said, "I ain't putting my mask on 'til I smell gas." And we're like, "This ain't funny. Put your mask on." Our masks are on, and he's like, "I ain't putting my mask on 'til I smell gas." So we all stared at the guy. We're waiting for him to do something, like go into convulsions. And sure enough, he starts shaking. I had a commode ring around my face I had that mask on so tight. But he was just joking. I tell you, we were like [blowing breath really fast] I was a-clearing and a-sucking, a-clearing and a-sucking. [She laughs.] It was funny.

Then, I remember one time a Scud hit, and it was like two o'clock in the morning. And we were sleeping. Yes, we've slept in those masks before. I remember another Scud attack, when Sherry—she was a very good friend of mine, heterosexual. She couldn't get a seal on her mask, and she could have sworn she was smelling something. So me, being the stupid but nice person that I am, I trade masks with her. We don't know if there's chemicals out there or not. So I'm gonna try to trade masks with her. I said, "Sherry, take yourself a deep breath and then take off your mask, and I'm gonna do the same thing. I'm gonna hand you my mask, and you give me yours. Let's see if you can get a better seal with my mask." So we did all that. "No, Michelle, Michelle, I can still smell it!" I said, "Well, hold your breath." I ended up running out, and I was like screaming, "My friend needs help! She can't get her mask to seal!" Oh, sure it was stressful, but eventually, I just remember that it was like, "Okay, here we go again."

At the end of the interview, Michelle talked about missing her family and coming home from the Gulf.

We flew in, and my grandma and my mother, my grandpa and my dad were at Fort Hood, Texas, waiting for me. The military had gotten us all brand-new desert uniforms to wear on our way home, so that was kind of cool. I remember it being a long flight. Coming home, it's a really long flight. It was a lot of hugs and tears. Of course, I was ready to party hardy. Even though I missed my family, I think I was with them for 'bout two hours, and then I was at the bar with my friends.

I went and got a tattoo. It didn't say nothing. I have a rose bracelet, and it had a yellow ribbon on it. But the yellow didn't take very well to my skin, so I had the color changed to blue. I told myself before I went into Saudi Arabia that if I lived, I wanted a tattoo. I'm gonna get one, whether my mom likes it or not. My dad didn't believe it was real. He took his thumb and licked his finger and was trying to rub it off. He said, that's a real one, isn't it? I said, yeah, it's real.

My daddy don't cry. He's like a box of nails; he just don't cry. I remember something my mom told me after I got home. The USO [United Service Organization] has a setup where we could actually send videos to our families, and I guess the first videotape that I sent home, I looked pretty bad. My eyes were black underneath, really bad. I guess I was dirty and disgusting, and I looked like I was just about to die—pale, probably. And I guess my dad cried. He didn't let nobody know that, but momma said she saw him crying. I kinda leapt in my heart a little bit when I heard that.

At the time of this interview, Lisa Michelle Fowler lived in Joliet, Illinois. A proud union member, she worked as a construction foreman on the night shift.

THE BAN

Behind the official ban on open gay and lesbian military service lies a policy that has been continually reconsidered and revised. The passage of "Don't Ask, Don't Tell" was simply the most public stage of this evolution. In fact, men and women within the military, the courts, and the federal government have long debated the ban. Public challenges began in earnest during the 1970s.

The years during and immediately after the Vietnam War were in some sense, a high tide for gay liberation, before the ebb that came with the AIDS epidemic and the conservative backlash to the social movements of the 1960s and 70s. This was an era of possibility, following on the heels of the African American civil rights struggle and the women's movement, when it appeared that gay rights might also be acknowledged. As gay and lesbian veterans understood, honorable and open service in the military could serve as a foundation for other civil rights. These men and women began to speak out. One of the first to do so was an air force sergeant named Leonard Matlovich.

Leonard Matlovich was the son of a soldier. He volunteered for the air force and served three tours of duty in Vietnam. As he explained years later, "I had to prove that I was just as masculine as the next man. I felt Vietnam would do this for me."[1] During his first tour in 1966, Matlovich received the first of two Air Force Commendation Medals for bravery in the face of a mortar attack. During the attack, he went out to positions on his base's perimeter to improve the defenses and check for casualties among his comrades. He eventually won a Bronze Star and a Purple Heart.

When Matlovich returned to the States in the early 1970s, he became an instructor in a new program set up by the air force to improve race relations.

Though Matlovich had been born in the South and grew up as a self-avowed racist, he had come to know black troops in Vietnam and had been greatly moved by the civil rights movement and Martin Luther King Jr. Consistently awarded the highest marks when up for promotion, Tech Sergeant Matlovich was praised in an evaluation of the race relations program in 1974 for being "dedicated, sincere, and responsible," an "absolutely superior NCO in every respect." That was before Matlovich told the air force that he was gay.[2]

"What does this mean?" Matlovich's superior officer asked when handed the letter announcing the sergeant's intention to challenge the ban on gays in the military in 1975. "It means *Brown v. Board of Education*," Matlovich told the African American captain. In fact, it meant *Matlovich v. Secretary of the Air Force*. It also landed Matlovich on the cover of *Time Magazine* and put him at the forefront of the movement for gay rights.[3]

When his case made it to the U.S. District Court in Washington, D.C., in 1976, Matlovich's lawyers argued that the air force policy was a denial of their client's privacy and liberty, that it was arbitrary and capricious, and, finally, that it was a denial of due process and equal protection—the same arguments used to win civil rights cases for African Americans and women. Judge Gerhard A. Gesell acknowledged the power of these arguments: "No one . . . who has studied the civil rights movement and the striving of blacks for opportunity will ever fail to recognize that the Armed Forces, more than any branch of government and far ahead of the private sector in this country, led to erasing the stigma of race discrimination. . . . Here, another opportunity is presented." But it would not be presented by the court. While Judge Gesell strongly urged the air force to reconsider its ban on gays, he deferred to the Pentagon decision makers. After five years of fighting for his rights, Matlovich accepted a settlement and an honorable discharge in 1980.[4]

As a result of the Matlovich case, the federal government clarified and hardened its opposition to gays in the military, at the same time that more gays in uniform began coming out to challenge this discrimination in court. Before the members of Jimmy Carter's administration left office early in 1981, they began to revise the wording of the ban. The new policy began bluntly: "Homosexuality is incompatible with military service." Though the new policy was a slight improvement over the old in that it offered an honorable discharge to most gays drummed out of the military, it codified the reasons why homosexuals (regardless of whether or not they broke the law against sodomy) should be banned from service. The DOD explained that the primary reasons for retaining the ban were to "maintain discipline, good order, and morale," to "prevent breaches of security," and to ensure the successful recruitment and retention of heterosexual soldiers. As many activists and scholars have pointed out, this rationale was strikingly similar to the defense of racial segregation in the armed forces during the 1940s, when federal officials feared that integration "would produce situations destructive to morale and detrimental to the preparations of national defense."[5]

Despite the new policy, gays and lesbians continued to serve their country and a courageous cadre of activists followed Matlovich to challenge the ban in court. Vernon Berg, Miriam Ben-Shalom, Perry Watkins, Dusty Pruitt, Joe Steffan, Keith Meinhold, and a handful of other active-duty servicemen and servicewomen risked their careers to defend their principles. In this chapter, Miriam Ben-Shalom and Dusty Pruitt describe their time in the service and their challenges to the ban in the 1970s and 80s. Like Len Matlovich, Miriam and Dusty found sympathetic judges, but their individual decisions did not set legal precedents that would have licensed the lifting of the ban. Still, both of these women persevered. Deeply held religious views sustained them.

Religion and morality have been at the heart of the discussion of homosexuality and military service, so it is not surprising that military chaplains have often found themselves on the front lines of the conflict. In World War II, chaplains wrote to their superiors requesting advice on how to handle confessions of gay soldiers. In reply to one such letter in 1943, Chaplain Frederick W. Hagan wrote, "There is an old saying that 'there's one in every hundred.' This may not be an accurate statement, but sooner or later every chaplain contacts such men and there is a need for a sympathetic and understanding approach." Taking a harder line, Major General William R. Arnold wrote in 1945 that a gay man who confided his sexuality to his chaplain should be given a dishonorable discharge immediately, because such a soldier was "a virulent danger to the Army. His immorality exerts a vicious influence." Military chaplains since the 1940s have had to chart their own paths between compassion and castigation of gays or lesbians facing spiritual and sexual dilemmas. Gay chaplains have faced these dilemmas as well.[6]

Paul Dodd was a Southern Baptist minister when he joined the army reserves as a chaplain during the Vietnam War.[7] He then spent twenty years in the regular army from the 1970s to the 1990s. When "Don't Ask, Don't Tell" was being debated and implemented, Paul was gradually coming to terms with his own homosexuality. Paul's experience as a chaplain ministering to gay and straight troops gives insight into the conflicting mandates of enforcing the ban. One of the ironies of the debate around lifting the ban was that Paul Dodd and others whom the new policy would affect directly had to be very careful if they decided to take part in the discussion. In effect, the policy insulated itself from internal critique.

The issue came to the fore in September 1992, when presidential candidate Bill Clinton was asked whether homosexuals should be allowed to serve. "Yes," he replied. "I support the repeal of the ban on gays and lesbians serving in the United States Armed Forces."[8] The next month, Clinton was elected president. He entered office in 1993 believing that after a meeting with the Joint Chiefs of Staff for the armed forces, he would lift the ban on gay service with an executive order, much the same way that Harry Truman had desegregated the armed forces.

But Clinton faced surprisingly stiff resistance from the Joint Chiefs and from Congress. His first meeting with the Joint Chiefs went badly, with unanimous resistance to lifting the ban, despite the president's argument that the military could have saved $500 million in the previous ten years if it hadn't investigated and discharged 17,000 gay service personnel. The Joint Chiefs, including their chairman, General Colin Powell, were unmoved. Powell argued that lifting the ban would be "prejudicial to good order and discipline."[9]

As the debate in Washington heated up, pressure began to build on u.s. bases and ships around the world. Three marines in North Carolina were arrested for beating up a man leaving a gay bar. As they beat the man, they reportedly shouted, "Clinton must pay!"[10] Yet this attack paled in comparison to one the previous October at a u.s. naval base in Japan. Though probably unrelated to Clinton's promise to lift the ban, the brutal murder of Allen Schindler in the fall of 1992, placed a spotlight on harassment of gay service personnel. Schindler had informed his superior officers that he was gay, and he was in the process of being discharged. According to another sailor on Schindler's ship, slurs and harassment made it a "living hell" for gays or those suspected of being gay. Not long before his discharge came through, Schindler was followed to a public park by two sailors and beaten so badly that the navy could only identify his remains by his tattoos. Initially unrepentant, the primary assailant, Terry Helvey, told investigators that he was "disgusted by homosexuals" and that he would "do it again" if faced with another gay shipmate. The navy gave Helvey a life sentence.[11]

For some in Washington, the message was clear: lift the ban and chaos would ensue in our armed forces. Congressional opposition to lifting the ban came from the president's own party, and it was led by Sam Nunn, the Georgia Democrat who chaired the Senate Armed Services Committee. Nunn had two primary arguments against lifting the ban. First, Nunn believed that lifting the ban would force heterosexual troops to share showers and bunks with openly gay personnel, infringing on their privacy rights. To prove this point, Nunn took members of the Senate Armed Services Committee and the media on a tour of the *Montpelier*, a submarine, where he interviewed sailors who slept within inches of one another in close quarters. Women had long been banned from submarine duties for this very reason, but as gay submarine commander Steve Hall notes in this volume, gays had always served on subs, shared bunkhouses, and even showered with straight troops. Would the open acknowledgment of these sailors and officers' sexuality really upset the applecart? Hall did not think so, but the sailors whom Nunn interviewed on the *Montpelier* disagreed.[12]

Nunn's second argument against lifting the ban was that hostility toward openly gay troops would destroy unit cohesion and the bonds between soldiers that were so crucial in combat. The Schindler murder seemed to underscore this point, yet the same arguments had been made in opposition to racial integration and the integration of women into the armed forces.[13]

The racial analogy was a hotly debated topic. Was homophobia a form of discrimination akin to racial bigotry? Was this debate really about civil rights or sexual morality? Ron Dellums, an African American veteran of the Marine Corps and the Democratic chairman of the House Armed Services Committee from California, saw this as a civil rights issue. Witnesses called before his committee disagreed. The "homosexual lifestyle has never been embraced as a value within the black community," one black navy veteran testified.[14] In fact, many socially conservative African Americans, who viewed homosexuality as a sin, were offended by the comparison between gay rights and civil rights.

The one soldier whom many looked to for leadership on this issue was Colin Powell, the first African American chairman of the Joint Chiefs of Staff. Many civil libertarians and gay rights advocates hoped that Powell would favor lifting the ban because, as one black scholar said, "If any people should understand another group's desire, drive, and thirst for full citizenship, it should be us."[15] But Powell found the comparison spurious. In a response to Representative Pat Schroeder, who had asked him to support lifting the ban, Powell wrote, "Skin color is a benign, nonbehavioral characteristic. Sexual orientation is perhaps the most profound of behavioral characteristics. Comparison of the two is a convenient but invalid argument." Powell went on to echo Nunn's arguments, saying that privacy rights of straight soldiers and potential negative effects on unit cohesion convinced him that the ban was necessary.[16]

Vince Patton, the final interviewee in this chapter, disagreed with Powell. Like the chairman of the Joint Chiefs, Patton had achieved an African American first, becoming the first black master chief of the u.s. Coast Guard. Assigned to research the parallels between Truman's executive order desegregating the armed forces and Clinton's proposal to lift the ban on gays in the military, Patton saw "no difference" between the two instances of discrimination. Patton could speak out about these issues, in part, because he was not gay.

President Clinton agreed with Patton's position on principle, but the consummate politician was swayed by congressional opposition, the Joint Chiefs, and most important, opinion polls. In 1993 about 48 percent of the American public opposed lifting the ban versus only 42 percent in favor of the president's position.[17] The young president, who had never served in the armed forces, deferred to Congress. Clinton ultimately supported a legislative compromise that would come to be known as "Don't Ask, Don't Tell." On the "Don't Ask" side of the compromise, the Department of Defense would no longer require recruits to discuss their sexuality before they entered the military, and superior officers were not supposed to question or investigate their subordinates' sexual lives. On the "Don't Tell" side, military personnel were expressly forbidden to perform homosexual acts or state that they were gay or lesbian. Still, investigations would continue; and if military personnel were caught committing a homosexual act or if they admitted to being homosexual, they were immediately discharged. "It's not a perfect solution," Clinton admitted at the time, and he later described it as a political defeat. But "Don't Ask, Don't Tell" became law in 1993.[18]

CHALLENGING THE BAN

Interviews with Miriam Ben-Shalom and Dusty Pruitt

After Leonard Matlovich challenged the ban on homosexuals in the air force in 1975, a cadre of courageous individuals stepped forward to join in the cause, publicly admitting that they were gay and in the military. Miriam Ben-Shalom and Dusty Pruitt were two of the women who joined in this legal challenge, refusing to go silently when the army decided that their sexuality was "incompatible with military service."

MIRIAM BEN-SHALOM: I was born in Waukesha, Wisconsin—May 3, 1948. My mother was probably a housewife. She was killed in an automobile accident when I was six. My father had different professions; but when I was born, he had his own business called "Johnny's Trading Post," a forerunner of the so-called convenience stores today. I grew up in Big Bend and East Troy. These are small, rural Wisconsin towns. I learned to swim before I could walk. My father took me hunting. I grew up appreciating nature.

My father was a World War II veteran. He served in the Pacific theater. I joined the army reserves near the end of the Vietnam era in 1974. I really didn't have the animosity towards the military that so many people my age had. I was going to be a rabbi and maybe a chaplain. My initial MOS [military occupation specialty] was that of chaplain's assistant. Later on, when I became a drill sergeant, people used to kid me and say, "You must be the drill sergeant for people who don't have a prayer."

DUSTY PRUITT: I was born July 19th, 1946, in Ballinger, Texas. In the beginning, my father was a grocer. He owned a grocery store, so the first six years of my life I grew up in this little, mom-and-pop grocery store that also had dry goods. That was in Bronte, Texas. We roamed all over rural Texas— waded through creeks and out through cotton fields and all kinds of things, and just really had a great time. Then, my dad became a Baptist minister. So we went from church to church, and I went to like ten different schools before I graduated from high school.

When I graduated from Stephen F. Austin College, it was 1970. I had run into some sex discrimination and the women's lib movement was just taking off. I found out, after trying to apply for various jobs, that my degree got me nowhere except into a secretarial pool. My male friends, they got management positions, but I got the questions: "Can you type?" and "How many words per minute?" So the army looked like a pretty good place to have a nontraditional career without too much of the sexist stuff. I wasn't so naive as to believe sexism didn't exist in this good ole boys' army, but it actually turned out to be a place that was not quite a sexist as the general population.

My dad was very supportive of me going in the army. He gave me one sentence of advice that I've carried with me all my life and that is, "Dig the first fox hole." [She laughs.] What he meant by that is, "Don't ask somebody to do something you wouldn't do yourself." I've always seen myself as somebody who's climbing a mountain, and if there are people behind me or beside me, at least I'm there. I'm not saying, "You go up there, and I'll stay down here."

MIRIAM BEN-SHALOM: In 1975 Leonard Matlovich was on the cover of *Time Magazine*, and I read the article and it didn't make any sense to me. I asked, "Why are they kicking him out?" "Well, he's a fag." I said, "Yeah, but he won a Bronze Star. Who cares? What difference does it make?" I guess I asked one too many questions, because I got called in my commander's office and it was, "Sergeant Ben-Shalom, are you a homosexual?" "Homosexual" is an adjective, and I'm a noun. But I knew what he meant, so that's what began the whole proceeding, because I refused to lie.

I received an honorable discharge because I never engaged in any misconduct and because there was a whole lot of press around. I think the army was forced to look at my service record and say, "Yeah, she didn't bother anybody." As a matter of fact, in the court transcript for *Ben-Shalom v. Secretary of Defense*, the army says, "She did not ogle, eye-up, or even stare at any female personnel." That's the actual words they used. They thought that homosexuals—which is such a lousy word because it implies that all we are is our sexuality—all we want to do is screw around. Okay? Nobody joins the military for a date. I think, in my case, it was really obvious that what I really wanted to do was soldier.

I understand my people's history, and I don't like injustice. It's not hard to explain, but it might be hard for somebody who doesn't know about Shoah, the Holocaust, to understand. When I was thinking should I fight this or should I just shut up, I thought about the fact that 6 million of my people didn't have a choice. When the world should've been paying attention, it ignored them because they were Jewish. So they ended up in Auschwitz and Treblinka and Dachau and Sobibor. I felt their presence very strongly as if they were saying, "We didn't have a choice; all we had was silence. You have a choice. How dare you engage in silence?!" I don't like injustice, and I don't like it that people are judged by whom they love. The rabbis have a saying, "If I am not for myself, then who is for me? If I am only for myself, what am I? If not now, when?" Honestly, as a Jew, I don't think that I have anything to be ashamed of, and, as a lesbian, I don't think I have anything to be ashamed of.

DUSTY PRUITT: Well, I'd already come to see that I was lesbian, but I was having a real struggle with the whole gay and God issue, even while I was in the military. There was a woman in my office. I was her supervisor, and she asked leave to go over to Atlanta for church. I looked at her, and I thought, "She certainly looks like a lesbian. I wonder where she's going to church?" I asked her to bring me a tape, so she brought me a tape back of the Reverend Troy Perry preaching. I put that in my little cassette player and I'm driving. Here's Troy preaching away about how you can be gay and a Christian, and I almost wrecked the car. [She laughs.] So the next day I came in, and I had this tape in my hand. I went over, and I'm waving it at Sergeant MacMillan, and I go, "Sergeant MacMillan, what kind of a church do you go to?!" She flat out said, "It's a Christian Church with a primary outlet to gay men and lesbians."

A deep religious faith inspired Dusty Pruitt
to fight her discharge, which was based solely on
the fact that she admitted she was a lesbian.
Photo courtesy of Dusty Pruitt.

Well, we had the IBM electric typewriters then, and everybody was typing away. There were thirteen women in my office. We were the Women's Army Corps, you know, and it got quiet as a mouse in there. [She laughs.] There was this big pause, and then I said, "Well, what about the Bible?" She said, "Let me bring you some stuff." She was very courageous, doing this right at work when she could have been tarred and feathered, kicked out of the service. She brought me a copy of Troy's book *The Lord Is My Shepherd, and He Knows I'm Gay.* I read this, and then I brought it back and laid it on her desk, and it just kind of surreptitiously went around the Women's Army Corps. [She laughs.] After about four, five, or six months, it came back on the desk where it started.

Eventually, I moved from Texas, where I was on recruiting duty. I actually spent a year in the reserves down there in Texas, and then my partner and I moved to Denver, and I spent three years at the Iliff School of Theology and I graduated with a master of divinity degree in 1980. In 1983 I gave an interview to a reporter at the *Los Angeles Times*, and it was about the Metropolitan Community Church and how people reconcile gay and God. She asked me what I'd done before, and I said, "Well, I was in the army, and I'm still in the reserves. I'm about to be promoted to major." Then I said, "Maybe you'd better not print that." In the article, this is the sentence: "She paused, frowned and said, 'Maybe you better not print that.'" [She laughs.]

Somebody cut that article out and sent it to my commander, and he felt like he had to do something about it because, between Carter and Reagan, they had put in the most draconian rules that you've ever seen where you couldn't even think homosexual thoughts or they'd throw you out. So when this information came to this commander, he started an investigation of me for moral dereliction. I'm telling you it had to cost the taxpayers a million dollars to investigate me for three years, to find out if I was a lesbian, like I said I was in the paper. Now is that army intelligence or what? [She laughs.] I thought to myself, "I'm taking this rule down. This is bull!"

MIRIAM BEN-SHALOM: The army offered to settle my case. They sent me a check, and I gave the check to my lawyer; I didn't cash it. The issue was not getting paid off. The issue was, "I want my job back." Finally, when we got back into court, I said, "I never wanted a payoff; I want my job back." After the court ruling in 1980, I had a writ of mandamus that ordered me immediately reinstated with all rank and privileges. The army just ignored it. The court had to threaten them with contempt and a big fine. So they took me back in with all ranks, privileges, and protection.

When I went back into the army, there was media all over the place. I went through the chow line, and they had these big round tables, seating perhaps eight people. I sat down and nobody would sit with me. I was prepared for that, you know what I mean? No white person came down and sat with me to eat, but black troops did, and I will always honor my African American brothers and sisters for that reason, because when nobody would sit down next to me, they did. I said, "Are you sure you want to do this? I don't want you guys to get in trouble." And one of them said, "Well, what else are they going do to us?" [She laughs.]

It's a hard thing to deal with when somebody gets dropped in your lap and there's media all over the place. So my job was to soldier, and to convince them that I was not interested in messing around. And that's precisely what I did. When anybody would do something, I'd turn to them and say, "Yeah. I'm gay, but . . . here's the deal." Then I'd try and educate them. It was interesting. Once they realized that what I was saying was the truth, once they realized that I was not what they thought I was and that what I really wanted to do was soldier and serve my country, there wasn't a problem anymore.

Do I say that every person I worked with was prejudice free? No, I don't. But a classic example of what I'm thinking about is that I lifted weights. When I was in the military, I could bench press 175 pounds and dead lift 400 pounds. So they made me weight control NCO because I was so strong. And there was this one sergeant, a female, who was a ne'er-do-well. She did not want me touching her, partly because she was overweight. She didn't want me to do a body mass/weight calculation for her. So she went to my first-line supervisor, also a woman, and said, "I don't want that woman touching me." My supervisor said to her, "You're not Sergeant Ben-Shalom's type of woman." [She laughs.]

In drill sergeant's school, I was deliberately assigned to some senior NCOs who were bitching (pardon, but the word fits, you know?) about the fact they couldn't wear their rank. The trainees, the drill sergeant candidates had to remove all rank. So I got all of these guys—and they were all guys coincidentally—who were just bitching, bitching, bitching. Didn't like this, didn't like that. I sat them all down took off my shirt. I don't mean I stood there in front of them in a bra—you have a t-shirt on underneath. Basically, I removed my rank, and I said to them, "I'm taking off my shirt. Now, what would you say here, stays here until I put my shirt back on."

I listened to them, and I said, "Okay, here's what I can do about some things; here's what I can do about others, but the fact is that you're drill sergeant candidates, you're my candidates, and I'm not going have it be said that I didn't train you correctly." I said, "I'll be right with you, and I'll do everything that I ask you to do right alongside you, but on the issue of rank you know you are going to have to take it off. I know some of this other stuff is bogus, but it's what you need to do in order to get the drill sergeant's badge." I put my shirt back on, and those guys did everything I asked and more.

We were out in the field, and we were setting up a perimeter. The brass came out in the field, and here I am with my squad. We had established our parameters. We had set up our guards, and it was one woman with all men. Well they were like, "Oh, we can't have one woman in the field." I said, "Major, I'm the squad leader. These are my men." They said, "Oh, we can't have this because there have been improprieties. So we're going to send you over here with the other women." I said, "I'm Sergeant Ben-Shalom, and I want to stay with my men." Well, they sent me over to be with the women anyhow, and the guys bitched and bitched. Soldiers will follow leaders. If leaders have courage, commitment, and candor, they will follow. And it doesn't matter whether they're gay or straight. Soldiers will follow those they trust, who they know they can rely on, and my guys knew they could rely on me.

DUSTY PRUITT: It was intimidating, even with the ACLU [American Civil Liberties Union] behind me. The original federal judge basically dismissed the case, saying, "When you go in the army, you drop your civil rights at the door. We're not going to hear any challenge to gay civil rights in the army." We were challenging them based on the fact that what I did was speak up and say I was gay, in a public forum, and that's political speech. So it was a First Amendment thing. And he dismissed it and said, "Civil rights are limited in the military."

That was a very discouraging time, but Lambda Legal and the ACLU appealed the decision. They took it to the Appeals Court, Ninth Circuit. And that court ruled that gay men and lesbians could sue the military. They said that we had a constitutional right to sue the military at the level of any other citizen that would sue for their constitutional rights. So they sent my case back to the district court. I apparently got assigned a really right-wing judge. [She laughs.] The legal strategists looked at that, and they said, "Let's just not do anything with this." That's when Greta Cammermeyer's case came to the forefront as well as Keith Meinhold, and a guy by the name of Mel Dahl. Ultimately, all of us were allowed to serve out our time, openly gay in the military, and retire. Thus putting the lie to their thing, how bad it is for morale and all that.

Clinton was elected and the whole brouhaha about "Don't Ask, Don't Tell" came up, and the whole thing changed. Bye-bye went the Reagan era rules. Now we have something that's probably even worse. [She laughs.] Clinton was trying to help us, but ultimately made it even worse. Congress got involved and actually passed a law, and in order to get it overturned, that means the judicial branch is going to have to go against both the legislative and executive branches.

MIRIAM BEN-SHALOM: When Clinton promised to lift the ban, I was filled with such enthusiasm, with such hope, with such a belief that perhaps things were going to change and the future would be filled with light. When he started backpedaling, and we ended up with "Don't Ask, Don't Tell, Don't Pursue," I realized that he had sold us out. I mean President Clinton was commander in chief. Military leaders will harrumpf and rattle their sabers and grouse. Soldiers always do these things. But, in the end, they will obey orders. And if they refuse to do so, what he needed to say was, "I want your resignation on my desk inside of twenty-four hours." That would have ended it all.

I was devastated with "Don't Ask, Don't Tell," because what is that? People talk. "What did you do this weekend? Where'd you go? We're having a party, do you want to come?" If you say nothing, it's like saying something. It's a no-win situation, and you still have discharges.

From 1991 until 1994, I traveled in excess of 350,000 miles trying to organize people in protesting. I protested in front of military bases. I was arrested in front of the White House for nonviolent civil disobedience, and I was wearing my uniform.

At the time of these interviews, Miriam Ben-Shalom was teaching English composition at Milwaukee Area Technical College. Dusty Pruitt was working as minister of outreach for the United Church of Christ in Aurora, Colorado. Both women continued to advocate for gays and lesbians in the military.

FAITH

An Interview with Paul Dodd

Paul Dodd was the son of a Southern Baptist preacher whose ministry took him all over the South. Paul felt called as well, both by a devout Christian faith and a strong sense of patriotism. He served as an army chaplain from 1967 to 1998. He tried to be a sympathetic sounding board for all of the troops with whom he served, both heterosexual and homosexual. This was especially difficult in the 1980s because the AIDS epidemic hit the ranks of the army just as it was sweeping through most of American society. Paul responded by studying the role of spirituality in helping soldiers face the deadly disease. Just as the military began to reckon with a new policy concerning gay and lesbian service members in the 1990s, Paul was beginning to wrestle with his own sexual identity.

My name is Paul Dodd. I was born in Crowley, Louisiana, in Acadia Parish, and that was February the 25th, 1942. My father was a Baptist preacher who was pastor of the First Baptist Church in Crowley, Louisiana, when I was born, and my mother was a homemaker. There were times when Dad was gone a lot, caring for other people. But I believe that he was a very good father.

My childhood was spent going to Sunday school every Sunday morning, and then going to church. Then we did it again on Wednesday night. So my life was really spent growing up in the church. Living in a parsonage, just next door to a church, had a few challenges. I didn't realize until I got to college that Dad was really a very fundamentalist preacher. He was very articulate, widely read, but he was really a fundamentalist Baptist preacher, and growing up I just thought that's how the whole world was.

I was a student at Little Rock Central High School during the integration crisis. I was in the tenth grade in 1957. As I think back on that experience, I'm still kind of amazed at the rage and the hatred that I saw. Even growing up in the South, I never knew the extent of the hatred and racism. But I recall there were armored personnel carriers, military vehicles all around Little Rock Central High School—soldiers standing all around the school with their weapons and fixed bayonets. The students, we had ID cards to get through those lines in order to go to school. Every morning there were hundreds of people across the street from the school, yelling racial epithets and throwing rocks and shouting all kinds of obscenities. The next year, when I was in the eleventh grade, Governor Orval Faubus, who was a racist governor of Arkansas, literally locked the schoolhouse doors and wouldn't let the students and teachers go to school.

Consequently, I never graduated from high school, and Dad arranged for me to go to college at Ouachita Baptist University in Arkadelphia, Arkansas, without graduating from Central High.[19] Ouachita is a small college, about 1,500, and it has always been about that size. There, I began to meet people from other parts of the country. I was in the ROTC [Reserve Officers' Training Corps] program for the first two years, and so that was my introduction to the military.

One of my great-grandfathers was a chaplain of the Confederate army. I had a brother who was in the ministry for quite a long time. My sister married a minister of religious education, and I had nieces and nephews involved in ministry, so we're really a family that's been involved in church leadership and ministry. But I truly believe God was calling me to some form of ministry. I wasn't always sure what form that would take, but I've never really doubted that call.

After graduating from Ouachita, Paul married his college sweetheart and at-
tended Southwestern Baptist Theological Seminary in Fort Worth. He eventually
returned to rural Arkansas to begin his own ministry. He learned how to preach
from his dad, but his sermons tended to be "more liberal and progressive"—
something he attributes, in part, to his experiences at Little Rock Central High.
In 1967 Paul joined the army reserves. He went on active duty in 1977.

I actually was commissioned as a second lieutenant in May of 1967. And
then I was promoted to first lieutenant, became a chaplain on the 5th of
August, in 1968. My first assignment on active duty was at Fort Campbell,
Kentucky, with the 101st Airborne Division (Air Assault). I became the division support command chaplain. In some ways, that continued what I was
doing as a civilian pastor, but it's in a very different setting. I wore the same
uniforms that the soldiers wore. I did PT [physical training] with them in the
mornings, and I went through all kinds of combat training with them. I was
honored to do that. I liked being chaplain to those soldiers.

Later, I worked for the Military District of Washington, which was rather an
awesome task actually. I was the senior pastor of the Memorial Chapel, and
when I arrived I was a major. I realized that I was now preaching on Sundays
to the leadership of the army. I had many generals in my congregation. The
secretary of the army and his wife attended regularly, and I had some members of the White House staff and congressional members who attended that
chapel. So it was an awesome responsibility for a young major to preach to that
congregation week after week. That was from '82 until the fall of '86.

I've got all of those sermons. I don't think I would ever want to read those
things again. [He laughs.] I had a very ecumenical, pluralistic ministry there.
In a sermon one Sunday morning, I spoke of the rededication of the Statue of
Liberty, and I made some comment that we wouldn't truly be a free nation
until every group in America was liberated and free and recognized equally
with every other group. I received an anonymous letter from a former military
officer who had been visiting our congregation, and it was just a poison-pen
letter. I remember sitting there with my mouth open, and one of the staff
members walked in and said, "Paul? What's wrong with you?" I just handed
him the letter. He read it and tore it up. He said it was a powerful and prophetic
sermon—a sermon that needed to be preached. There were certainly risks in
trying to be prophetic and relevant, but I gave it my best shot.

For years, I didn't understand my sexuality—not that I even do now. Although I've known ever since I was just a little child that there was something
different about me, I certainly didn't understand what that was. Then, as I

began to develop into an adolescent and realized that my sexual attractions were apparently different from other boys'. I was confused about that, but I truly believed that if I honored my parents, loved God, and was faithful to the church, that these things would work out. I went into my marriage and into the ministry and into the military with that in mind. It wasn't until many years later that I finally began dealing with those issues more honestly and more openly.

Soldiers would come to me and talk with me sometimes about the conflicts they were having with their sexuality. You might recall 1981–82 was when we first began hearing of HIV/AIDS. I remember a soldier who I happened to know was gay and complained about some suspicious symptoms he was having, and I said, "You know, I was reading the other day in a magazine about this new illness that's being diagnosed now. It's a sexually transmitted disease, and you might need to go have yourself checked out." So HIV/AIDS began to really take its toll, not only in the military, but in our nation, and I saw a lot more soldiers who were stricken with that.

It became a big part of my ministry, especially when I got involved later in ministry in medicine and had my first assignment at Walter Reed Army Medical Center. I developed a lot of knowledge about HIV and AIDS, and I wrote my doctoral dissertation about the spiritual components of HIV and AIDS and the military.

There was an interesting thing that happened while I was at Walter Reed. I lived at that time in Centerville, Virginia, and so several days a week I would ride the Metro from Virginia to Walter Reed. I had to change trains at Metro Center in order to make that trip. One day I was getting off of the subway, and just as soon as my foot hit the platform, I thought of David, a chaplain's assistant who used to work for me. I had not seen him in several years.[20] When a name like that from the distant past comes into my mind, my custom is to say a little prayer for them. And so I said, "God, wherever David is today, just bless him and care for his needs." Then I got on the subway and went on to Walter Reed, and didn't think much more about it. On the way home that afternoon, when I made the change at Metro Center, again, as soon as my foot hit the platform, I had David's name in my mind again, and I said the prayer and got on the subway and went home. And that continued for several days, to the point where I was kind of dreading going through the Metro Center, because I kept having this recurring thought.

One morning I got to my office, and I picked up the phone and called the information operator, and said, "Look, I'm Paul Dodd, and if this person lives anywhere in the metro area: in D.C., Maryland, Virginia—I just need to speak with him. I'm a chaplain here at Walter Reed Army Medical Center." She was so helpful. There was no person by that exact name, but there were some similar names and initials, and I started calling them. I got to one whose voice sounded familiar, and I said, "If this is the David who used to work with Paul Dodd please call me." He called me, and it was David.

He was so surprised to hear from me, so we had to reminisce about old times, and I said, "You're gonna think I'm crazy, but I've got to tell you what's been happening to me for weeks now. Every time I go through Metro Center, all I can think about is you, David. And I have been praying for you every time I go through there." There was just silence for a moment. He said, "Paul, I work a block from there, and get off at the subway there every day." We were just stunned. I said, "Could I meet you after work today?" So we met. I got off the train at Metro Center and rode the escalator to the American Café, and met David there. We talked for a couple of hours, and laughed and reminisced over old experiences. And then David told me that he had AIDS. We cried together, and I held his hands right in front of the American Café and God and every-body else, and we prayed together, and hugged one another.

I kept up with David until he died. He made an impression on my life that I just never, ever forgot. After that, it became my mission to continue working with people who had HIV and AIDS, as long as I could.

Understanding that some devoutly religious people view homosexuality as a sin, I asked Paul if he thought a gay pastor could minister to a soldier who felt this way.

Well, I think I did a pretty good job of that for many years, and obviously other chaplains do. I don't think we have to be of the same sexual orientation to minister to one another. Certainly there are heterosexual ministers who even today have a great influence in my life and whom I consider to be my pastors. On the other hand, there are many people who know that I'm a gay minister and a gay pastoral psychotherapist, who come to me for my counsel, so I don't believe that has any bearing at all.

If a soldier came to me and said, "I'm gay," I wouldn't have turned him or her in. Unfortunately, there have been chaplains who turned soldiers in who came in and said that they were gay, looking for counseling and help. I think it's just outrageous that they would do that. I recall having sat in the Council of Colonels—the executive council of the Chief of Army Chaplains—and we were briefed about gays in the military, and the briefer made a comment that some chaplains had actually turned soldiers in because they thought it was in keep-ing with the welfare of the soldiers as well as the well-being of the army. There were probably about twenty people in that room—including the chief and the deputy chief—and I just said that was outrageous that any chaplain would ever consider breaking the confidence of a soldier because of this issue, and if a chaplain like that worked for me I would fire them on the spot. No one challenged that because they knew I was right. There's just no excuse for a chaplain to ever break the confidentiality of a soldier because they disclose their sexual orientation.

"Don't Ask, Don't Tell" codified the regulations. It's law now to ask soldiers to live in secrecy; it's legislated a culture of secrecy, which is harmful not only to the soldier but to the morale, I believe, of the greater forces. You know, this was implemented back in 1994, and I was placed on a committee by the commander at the time. The committee was called something like "The peaceful integration of gays into the military" or "The transition of/to gays in the military."

There's no doubt in my mind that with strong leadership from the top on down through the ranks we could have done that and it would have been successful. The military already has a strong, effective equal opportunity program, and we're trained to obey the orders and do what is expected of us. If the leadership had said, "This is our policy, and we're going to adhere to it," the great majority of soldiers would have honored that. And we were equipped, I believe, to do it. Of course, it became a political football, and you know the rest of the story.

Near the end of the interview, I asked Paul to talk again about how being at Little Rock Central High during the integration crisis affected his life and his ministry.

I think I began to find my voice for social justice at Little Rock Central High School. Sometimes now I find myself speaking out because I can't *not* speak. You know, the scripture says, "If I don't speak, the stones will cry out" [Luke 19:40]. I think the best part of my coming out is that I am now able to have a voice and to be able to speak out on what I believe are important issues in our society: not only for gays and lesbians, but for other minorities as well.

I truly don't believe my sexual orientation affected the quality of my military service one way or the other, and I know in my heart that our soldiers now who happen to be gay or lesbian are serving honorably and courageously even though they are serving sometimes under hostile conditions and hostile regulations. Nevertheless, they are doing it, and I think it's a great act of courage and patriotism and honor.

In his retirement, Paul has become a pastoral psychotherapist and a member of the Metropolitan Community Church in Austin, Texas.

STRAIGHT TALK

An Interview with Vince Patton

Over the course of his thirty-year career in the U.S. Coast Guard, Vince Patton served in almost every capacity from radioman to recruiter, drug enforcement officer to peacekeeper. At every post and every stage of his career, Patton made it his mission to fight discrimination and foster appreciation for diversity. So it was with excitement and enthusiasm that he accepted a position on President Clinton's commission to study lifting the ban on gays in the military. It turned out to be one of his toughest assignments.

My name is Vincent Patton, and I was born in Detroit, Michigan, on November 21, 1954. My father served in the army. He was active duty army assigned to National Guard and Reserve units. When the unit that he was assigned to had to deploy, he would go with them. Sometimes he would be gone for six months, and he went to Vietnam twice. We always stayed in Detroit. My mother was a nurse.

Four days after graduating from high school, I was in the coast guard. I had walked into the recruiting office, and the recruiter gave me the spiel on the coast guard. But as I got up to leave, he pointed to the pictures on the wall. He said, "You see those pictures up there. Those are pictures of me during my time in the coast guard." There was a boat on fire and a guy working to put it out. There were pictures of people doing rescue operations. One of the pictures was of him on a small boat, helping Vietnamese children. They were real exciting pictures. Then he said to me: "You're going to be in one of these pictures in about a year. I'll guarantee that if you join the coast guard." That stuck in my mind.

When I came home, I was reading literature about the coast guard, and my dad was a little concerned. He had a sense that the coast guard didn't have a lot of African Americans. In fact, at the time I joined in '72, less than 4 percent was African American. My dad said, "The coast guard deals with people who have boats. People who have boats live in rich areas that don't have a lot of blacks. I'm not telling you that you can't join. I'm just telling you that you might be in some uncomfortable situations." When he said that, my mother spoke up and said, "You know, probably the right thing for him to do is to join the coast guard, because it'll never change if he doesn't go in just because it doesn't have a lot of blacks." That kind of sealed the deal for me.

For boot camp, we went to Cape May, New Jersey. All of us were thinking that we were going to summer camp. We thought, "This isn't like going into the real military." We pull into the gate, and some marine gets on the bus and starts yelling at us. "Get your asses off the bus right now!" No one moved. This one guy raised his hand, and said, "Excuse me, sir. I think there's a mistake. We're here for the coast guard." [He laughs.] He grabbed that guy by the neck and threw him off the bus. We were all kind of like, "What the hell's going on here?" As it turned out, the drill instructors were marines! [He laughs.]

After radioman's school, I went to a high-endurance cutter called the *Dallas*. It was doing fisheries patrols in the North Atlantic. We're still talking about the 1970s here. It was the Cold War, so you had Russians out there as well as other communist bloc ships. It was not our primary mission, but we were able to spy on these vessels in the name of enforcing the international fisheries treaties. If we saw a fishing trawler, and we made it out to be a Soviet trawler, it was easy for us to get close to it. If a navy ship went into that area, that could be considered an act of war or an aggressive move.

On the *Dallas*, I was kind of withdrawn for a couple of reasons. One was facing a great deal of discrimination and bigotry on the ship. The chief that I worked for was extremely racist. He told me when I boarded his ship that I didn't belong as a radioman because, "first of all, black people are stupid and this is a job that requires smart people." He didn't want to chance having some "ignorant nigger" in his radio room. He told me that the smartest thing that I could do would be to march my black ass down to the galley and learn how to be a cook like the rest of the blacks and Filipinos on the ship. He was a pretty vicious and evil man. I had experienced discrimination earlier in my years, but nothing as blatant as this.

I remember that the first couple of times I actually cried. I would go find me a quiet part of the ship and just go cry my eyes out. I never really told anybody, because I didn't want to be a wimp, but I had nobody to turn to. Correspondence courses were my way of getting away from this. It turned out to be the best thing that ever happened to me. The executive officer on the ship, Commander Vaughn, knew about Chief Wood. Every time I completed a correspondence course, the executive officer would make a big deal about it. He would gather the crew together and start yelling, "Hey, I just got the mail, and Patton got an 'A' in English 101." Chief Wood would freak out. He'd take his hat off and throw it down, and he would curse. I mean this guy was having a fit. That's when it dawned on me that this is what it takes to get to this guy. I can get to this guy simply by showing him how smart I am. I got more involved with education because it pissed Chief Wood off. If I had had a different motivation, I'm not sure I would have done that well.

After that assignment, I asked to go to Detroit. The coast guard had some units there that covered the river and the Great Lakes region. I worked in the communications center and also served as the unit rescue swimmer if it was needed. I usually had to go out when it was really cold. [He chuckles.] Like going out on ice to pick up fishermen who drove their trucks out on the ice. And of course, the ice would break up, and you go out and pull the fishermen in. They say, "What are you going to do about my truck?" And you feel like throwing them back.

I really began to enjoy the coast guard, and one day my chief called me in and says, "Patton, you've got a set of orders to go to recruiting duty." At first, I was a little angry when I saw this. But I reluctantly took the orders for recruiting duty because I had already reenlisted. It goes back to what my mother had said, "Nothing's going to change unless you do it." Well, this made sense. The coast guard will always remain a lily-white organization unless somebody is there to change it. This was right on the heels of the service being opened to women, so there was another challenge in terms of increasing minorities.

Vince became the only African American coast guard recruiter in Chicago, and he earned an M.A. from Loyola University. Ever since boot camp, Vince had told anyone who would listen that he wanted to be master chief of the coast guard. Some took this for arrogance; others thought he was crazy. For Vince, it was simply a dream. He took one step closer to that dream when the commandant of the coast guard asked him to come to Washington to conduct a study of the service's effectiveness. This study eventually became Vince's Ph.D. dissertation at American University. After serving in the field once again, he returned to Washington, D.C., for a new assignment in 1993.

I was asked by the chief of personnel of the coast guard, because of my academic background primarily, if I would like to be one of the coast guard representatives on the committee that was studying the "Don't Ask, Don't Tell" policy. Of course, it wasn't called that. It was the presidential commission for the study of gays in the military. I quickly jumped on that. President Clinton had said he was going to lift the ban, so my perception was that we were going to figure out how the president was really going to make that happen.

The research took me to Executive Order 99801, which was the order that President Truman signed eliminating racial discrimination in the armed forces, so I kind of studied the Truman approach and put together a series of working papers, reading lists, and documents from the National Archives and the Truman Library that led up to Truman's order. My focus was: the President's going to do this, and he's going to have naysayers saying he can't. So

Vince Patton faced racism in the coast guard, but never direct homophobia, because he is not gay. Still, Vince recognized that prejudice against one group is an injustice for all.
Photo courtesy of Vince Patton.

he's got to say, "This isn't without precedent. Not only is this how I'm going to do this, but this is ironclad, and no one in Congress is going to be able to tell me I can't do it."

Well, many of the people on this committee wanted the president to believe that he didn't have the authority to write an executive order. I was so disheartened. These were people that I thought really could have made a difference in making this right, but they looked for a way to hinder it. Thus the creation of "Don't Ask, Don't Tell," which I thought was ridiculous. We came up with a policy that allowed you to lie when every service's core value says, "Don't lie." It just didn't sit well with me.

I kept pushing my analysis, and I was asked to cease and desist. We did a briefing with then-chairman General Powell, and I didn't keep my mouth shut as I was instructed to do. It wasn't a heated exchange. I thought it was a healthy dialogue between myself and General Powell and a couple of other people about the executive order. I felt that the executive order was all that the president needed, and I referred to President Truman doing it. The difference of opinion was that Clinton didn't have that kind of authority today. There were also concerns from both the House and Senate Armed Services Committees and the fear that if an executive order was put together, Congress would get involved and start making decisions for the military. General Powell argued that this was going to be a debate that Congress was going to answer for us. So let's take the high ground and tell the president that you don't want to do that in your infancy as president. Instead, what you want to do is to find the happy medium. And the happy median is to admit that there are gays and lesbians serving. They can continue to serve, but they just can't tell anybody who they are, and if they do, we'll throw them out. I was a little upset about that, and that's when I resigned from the commission.

There was a little flak about my resigning in the sense that I was a little hostile. I knew there were some people in the group that felt the same way I did, but, unfortunately, they were concerned about their careers. I'm not chastising them for that. They were obviously in a position to lose more than I had to lose. But I had to think about that too. I had people tell me, "Well, if you ever thought you were going to be master chief of the coast guard, it ain't going to happen now." But the chief of personnel took a great deal of liking to me because I stood by my principle, and then when he became commandant of the coast guard, he picked me as his master chief. I think part of the reason was that he saw that I was able to stand up for something. In retrospect, I have to say that I was naive to think when I was on this commission that we were all moving in one direction. I think I did the right thing by stepping out of it.

General Powell made it clear that he was walking a very fine political line. He was in his latter days as chairman, and he was going to be replaced. No one really knew what his political aspirations were going to be and what he was going to do. So I think he was sort of dancing on strings to say, "Well, you've got a good point. It makes sense. However, we don't want to turn this into a bigger political issue than it already is. How do we back down and allow the president to save face with a political promise that he'd made, and at the same time maintain good order and discipline within our services?" You know, I'd love to have this conversation with him again to find out where he really was on it. I didn't walk away feeling that he was totally for the "Don't Ask, Don't Tell" policy. It was just a gut feeling, because he didn't seem to take a great deal of ownership of the argument that this was the right thing to do.

Not long after resigning from the committee, Vince was sent on a peacekeeping mission to Haiti in Operation Support Democracy. Then, he returned home and tried to make his mark on the service as master chief of the coast guard.

I became master chief of the coast guard in 1998, and I had learned from my predecessors that it was really about looking after the concerns of people. It's more than just when somebody has a problem you listen to them and ensure that their problem gets handled. It means also understanding how important our people collectively are. The coast guard's core values are honor, respect, and devotion to duty. The respect part is about treating people equally, teaching people to understand one another, and having an acceptance of their culture. And this story that I've told you is to highlight how I had undergone discrimination when I first came in and how ugly it was and how I overcame it. Every piece of that experience led me to an understanding about discrimination as a whole. I felt that there had to be a deep understanding of diversity within the organization. I go back to my mom, and what she said: "It ain't never going to change unless you are part of the process to make it change." I realized that it was never going to change if I didn't help people understand about cultural differences and appreciate those differences instead of creating hate and anger about them. It was a burning issue with me.

My critics were very upset when I launched into this, telling the entire coast guard, "You better get on board with diversity because hate doesn't belong in this organization." It wasn't a half-shoe issue as far as I was concerned. It really meant people. It meant all kinds of people. It was against the grain of directives that said people, because of sexual orientation, couldn't serve. I found that to be wrong in a lot of ways, more so from working alongside people who I later learned of their sexual orientation. I found that their performance was no different than someone who had the same sexual orientation as I had. I think it's wrong to discriminate, and in my time as master chief of the coast guard, that was my platform.

It's nobody's business what people do in their sexual lives. I find it more appalling that many of the heterosexual guys brag of their conquests and how many women they've had. I find that more appalling and disgraceful than the fact that a man is living with a man or a woman is living with a woman. Why would anybody think it's wrong for gay people to serve in an organization and then also make a statement bragging about their sexual conquests? That just doesn't add up to me. One of my biggest military heroes is Leonard Matlovich. I learned about Leonard Matlovich just in passing in reading the brief articles when he came out. It made *Time* and so forth. I was impressed that here was a man who laid his life on the line, earned a Bronze Star, did all kinds of things, and then all of a sudden, after he comes out, he's no good. What about the lives that he saved—the people who now have grandchildren to tell the story? But we didn't want him because of his sexual orientation.

After Vince retired from the coast guard in 2002, he got a degree in theology from the Graduate Theological Union in Berkeley, California. Shortly after this interview, he moved with his wife to Washington, D.C., where he went to work for the Unitarian Church.

OUT RANKS

In December 2003, for the first time in American history, three retired flag officers publicly declared that they were gay. It is difficult to provide historical context for such an unprecedented event. Historians usually leave such topics to their colleagues in journalism or political science. Yet coming out for these men was a chance to reevaluate careers in the military that stretched back several decades and to focus these years of experience on an open and honest discussion of the ban and "Don't Ask, Don't Tell."

"I wanted to come out to make a statement that 'Don't Ask, Don't Tell' after ten years is not working," Brigadier General Keith Kerr (Retired) told the listeners of National Public Radio's *Talk of the Nation*.[1] A forty-year veteran of the army and army reserves, a former professor of business administration, and a card-carrying member of the Log Cabin Republicans, Keith saw the primary argument for repealing the law as the cost involved. The investigation, dismissal, and replacement of talented personnel that the military has already trained were a waste of taxpayer money, he believed. A study conducted by the Government Accountability Office (GAO) in 2005 supports Keith's position. According to the GAO, the discharges of gay and lesbian enlisted personnel alone cost the United States $200 million in the ten years after "Don't Ask, Don't Tell" was passed.[2] Though it was difficult for a private man like Keith Kerr to come out, he felt that he had no choice.

Brigadier General Virgil Richard (Retired) felt the same way. When "Don't Ask, Don't Tell" was initially debated, this intense, soft-spoken Kansas native had only been retired for two years. After more than three decades in the army and two tours in Vietnam, Virgil had fought his battles. It was time for younger men to enter the fray. Retirement in Texas agreed with him, and he had found a partner with whom he could openly share his life. But after ten years of soul searching and discussion of a political compromise that he felt was unfair and unjust, he could no longer remain silent.

Rear Admiral Alan Steinman (Retired) had joined the Public Health Service in 1972 because he wanted to work with the coast guard. His story epitomizes the sacrifices that gay men have made to rise up through the ranks in service to the country that they love. Relationships with men were out of the question for him, and promotion to flag officer required Alan to find a female companion to accompany him to formal Washington functions. Though he opposed "Don't Ask, Don't Tell" at the time of its passage, he was unable to explain to his coast guard colleagues the range of reasons why.

Admiral Steinman, General Richard, and General Kerr enumerated three reasons why they believe that the ban should be lifted (in addition to the cost of enforcement). First, as they themselves are living proof, gays (and lesbians) have had long, distinguished careers. Second, all of our military allies except for Greece and Turkey have lifted the ban on open gay service since the 1970s and report that there have been few problems integrating gay soldiers into the ranks. Finally, we have fought alongside openly gay troops in these allied forces in Afghanistan and Iraq.

These men are not alone among retired flag officers in opposing "Don't Ask, Don't Tell." As an African American veteran of the Korean War, Major General Vance Coleman (Retired) believes that the military should take people on their individual merits, not their race, ethnicity, or sexuality. "Americans long ago desegregated our military," he has said. "The time has come to end another vestige of inequality in our country."[3] Unlike General Coleman, Rear Admiral John Hutson has not always opposed "Don't Ask, Don't Tell." In fact, he was one of its architects. "It's almost embarrassing," he said in 2003, remembering the debates that occurred ten years earlier. "We worried about, gee, if we open the ranks to gays, are the gays going to come flooding in and drive the heterosexuals out?" More important, he worried that lifting the ban would hurt unit cohesion and undermine the fighting effectiveness of the u.s. military. But ten years of observing "Don't Ask, Don't Tell" in action had changed his mind. "American fighting men and women, if we ask them to do it, will live up to the expectations that we set for them. . . . For years, we've asked them to live down to our expectations rather than living up to our expectations."[4]

The three flag officers whose interviews follow had one final reason for coming out as gay men. They wanted to serve as role models for a younger generation of gay veterans and active duty personnel who may not have known that it was possible to rise up through the ranks. It was their hope that their personal stories would inspire these younger men and women to fight both for their country and for their rights. In this, they succeeded. The two veterans of the Iraq War interviewed in the final chapter of this book explained that they came out precisely because of the courageous examples of General Richard, Admiral Steinman, and General Kerr.

THE GENERAL

An Interview with Virgil Richard

Brigadier General Virgil Richard (Retired) is the highest-ranking army officer to come out publicly as a gay man. For Virgil, coming out and openly opposing the ban on gays in the military shattered a silence and secrecy that had shrouded two tours of duty in Vietnam and a decorated army career, spanning more than three decades.

I am Virgil Richard. I was born in 1937, in Anthony, Kansas. My dad was a wheat farmer, cattle farmer. And my mom was a housewife. I spent all my youth on the farm, until I went to college. The farm was in Oklahoma, right across the Kansas line. I spent a lot of time milking cows, slopping the hogs [laughs], gathering eggs, and working out on the wheat fields with the tractors, combines, and trucks and things like that.

I went to a rural school, a one-room schoolhouse. All eight grades were in one class. We had like fifteen kids in those eight grades. I had one other classmate in my grade, a girl. When I went to high school, I had forty-something people in the high school, and there were eleven students in my graduating class. I was very much into piano. I took music lessons from the time I was seven until I was in college and really intended that to be my career path. But I changed my mind in college, and decided that I needed to do something different.

When I graduated from high school, it was '55. I went to Oklahoma State University. I was involved in a lot of organizations on campus that let me develop my leadership skills. That was where I began my military service. Back then, in your first two years, it was mandatory that you go to ROTC [Reserve Officers' Training Corps]. I was fortunate enough to graduate from Oklahoma State in 1959.

You did basic training between your junior and senior year of college, and I did that at Fort Hood, Texas. It was hot as it could be. You were sleeping in open-bay barracks, and you were up every morning very early. You had classes and PT [physical training] every day. Of the eight weeks, we probably spent two or three weeks on firing ranges, firing different weapons, and that's when I hurt my ears and I failed my flight physical to be a pilot. But I just remember one of the experiences that we had during that time was a military stakes. You had to perform certain military tasks under physical and time stress, and make decisions. You had like twenty stations, and it lasted for half a day. I came out very high in that particular competition; that gave me a lot of confidence.

After I graduated from Oklahoma State, I chose finance as my first choice. I chose armored as my second choice, because I liked George Patton. [He laughs.] I guess that that's the image of armored officers. Because I was a DMG (distinguished military graduate), the army gave me both choices and the assignment I asked for, which was Hawaii. When I was in the armored battalion was where I first became aware of the fact that the army was biased and had a prohibition against any homosexual conduct. [He sighs.] There was a soldier in another platoon in my company that somehow became involved with some other soldiers. He was gone in the next twenty-four hours. That was kind of an eye-opener to me.

When I learned that Virgil confronted racism during the civil rights era, I asked him to tell me the story. Though he had not known many African Americans growing up, Virgil had always opposed racial discrimination, because as he explains, "I grew up in a church environment, and that was not what I was to do."

I came back from Hawaii and became the finance and accounting officer at Fort Rucker, Alabama. I had an office of about eighty-five military and civilian people on at that time in '65 and '66. The army was making a major buildup because of Vietnam. I had to hire a lot of people, and most of those additional people were civilians. I had a job opening for an accounting technician. When I got the referral list and I interviewed the candidates, there was a black lady who was in her middle thirties who had a college degree in accounting. She also had experience in a civilian accounting business. She was head and shoulders above the other people in terms of her qualifications, so I chose her.

When it became known I had made the choice, I had a bunch of women show up at my office door demanding to see me. They basically told me that she was not going to use the bathroom that they used and that she was not going to be in their break room. I just told them to get over it. She had every right to use the same facilities that they did; and I stuck with it. We had a very testy three or four days, but after they kind of observed her and saw that she came to work dressed well and was clean, everything kind of disappeared. They wouldn't necessarily go eat with her or things like that, but the animosity finally went away. It all worked out in the long run. But she was the first civil service black employee that came on the rolls at the Army Aviation Center at Fort Rucker, Alabama.

After he told me about his Fort Rucker experience, I asked Virgil to talk about Vietnam.

In 1966 we probably had less than 100,000 troops in Vietnam. All of these lieutenants and rotary wing pilots were going over there. We were not taking heavy casualties at the time, but I was a little bit apprehensive about my next assignment. Also, I had to worry about what was I going to do with my wife and my young son. So I had a lot of questions in my mind about how it was all going to work out. But this was part of my job and my military duty. I was going to do it.

In the first week that I was there, you went to an orientation program. I lived in a civilian hotel out in the middle of nowhere, and I had to find my way to work on a bus. It just so happened that that first week, about the fifth day, I went to work early. Had I gone to work at the normal time, I would've been at the bus stop when a VC [Viet Cong guerrilla] threw a bomb at that bus stop and killed practically everybody that was there. I figured at that point my life was blessed. [He laughs.] From that point, the rest of the Vietnam tour was downhill.

I did get shot at during my first tour in Vietnam on a trip to Chau Duc, one day down in the delta. I was going with my counterpart, a Vietnamese captain, and we were going there to inspect some construction of military facilities that he was paying for out of his budget. So I went with him to help evaluate things. When we got ready to leave, there was a mountain off to one side of the helicopter, maybe 500 yards away. As we were taking off, we started taking fire from that mountain. You could see some of the tracers coming very close to the chopper, and you wondered if you were going to make it. That was the closest I came to getting a bullet in my body.

You never knew who was going to shoot you or who was going to throw a grenade at you or where that might be coming from. You were always aware of your surroundings and who was around you. I was fortunate enough that I got to travel to twenty-eight of the forty-two or -three provinces which were states in Vietnam during that first tour of duty. I got to see a lot of Vietnam. I traveled because my counterpart got to travel to do his work. He would come on my helicopter, and I would take him where he needed to go. Tried to help him out. He was a Vietnamese captain who was very sophisticated. He and his wife went out of the way to make me feel at home. I always expected that after Vietnam fell that someday that he would come knocking on my door looking to have a home, and I kept in touch with him until that point. But, after that, I never heard from him.

Now, the second time I was there, which was in '72 and '73, it was a very different place. The Vietnamese army had begun shouldering most of the burden of keeping the vc and the North Vietnamese at bay. We were primarily support people at that point, and I really thought when the cease-fire and the withdrawal occurred that the South Vietnamese would be able to stand up to the North Vietnamese. But what I didn't count on was in a year or two the Congress cut off all the money for the supplies, equipment, and ammunition that the South Vietnamese didn't make and didn't have the money to buy. When that happened, it was only a matter of months until they had nothing to defend themselves with, so they turned tail and ran. Some people say that we lost Vietnam in the streets of America, but I say we lost it in the halls of Congress, because we had politicians who didn't have the guts to stick with it. I feel very strongly about that.

I was assigned in the Pentagon when I came back the first time. I was on the front steps there and there in the building the day that the protests oc-curred. In those days, most of us were told to wear civilian clothes to work to help keep our profile low. Being an army officer, a major at that time, having to go to work in civilian clothes on military duty was very unusual to me. I never had anybody say anything to me about "Well, you did a good job" or "Thank you for what you did." [He pauses.]

On his second tour of duty, Virgil was a major working in the u.s. Military Assistance Command, Vietnam (MAC-V) headquarters, overseeing appropria-tions and currency exchange with u.s. allies. Some unscrupulous officials tried to bribe him by offering him sex with women. "They didn't know I wasn't inter-ested," he explained.

I guess it wasn't until after I had come back from Vietnam the second time that I finally accepted the fact that I was gay. I knew I was very attracted to men. [He pauses.] I had roommates both times that I was in Vietnam—one time an Australian officer and another time an American officer. It was very difficult living in the same room in a bed right next to them and having to walk a straight and narrow path. I never accepted the fact that I was gay until about the mid-70s. By that time I was a lieutenant colonel. I had like seventeen years of military service under my belt, and in those days there wasn't "Don't Ask Don't Tell." You had Article 125, and as long as you didn't violate that and were doing a good job, you probably could stay and serve out your time.[5] But I was married. I had three kids. I was three years from retirement, and I just decided that I had too much to lose to try to get divorced and be myself. So I stuck with it.

A general officer pulled me aside one day and told me, "Virgil, if you take

Virgil Richard was one of the first retired flag officers to come out
publicly as a gay man and state for the record that military
discrimination against gays and lesbians is wrong.
Photo courtesy of Virgil Richard.

the jobs the army wants you to have and you do well on them, which you're capable of doing," he says, "you will be a general officer before not too many years." That kind of took me aback because I never ever had aspirations of being a general officer. I did have aspirations that I could retire as a colonel, and I expected that. But I didn't expect to go beyond that. That really set me thinking seriously. The difference in the pay scale with a colonel and general is significant and it means for the rest of your life. I made a decision to stick with it. [He laughs.] So I just kept sticking around.

I had finally decided in January of 1991 that I was going to retire, because I had been a general for three years and I had served my time. I knew the army was going to draw down its military strength significantly. It was approved for me to retire, but then that summer they started to build up in the Persian Gulf. And the four-star general that was in charge of AMC [U.S. Army Materiel Command] at the time told me, "Virgil, I can't get a replacement for you. You've got too much experience and knowledge for this job. I need you to stay until this is over with." I said, "Okay I will stay. But I want to be able to retire sixty days after this thing is over." So I did. I think it ended right at the end of February, and I was retired April 1, 1991.

In 2003, on the tenth year anniversary of "Don't Ask, Don't Tell," Virgil Richard coauthored a New York Times *op-ed piece with two other flag officers, Admiral Alan Steinman (Retired) and Brigadier General Keith Kerr (Retired), arguing that it was time to lift the ban on gays and lesbians serving openly in the U.S. military. At the time of this interview, Virgil Richard was enjoying retirement and living in Austin, Texas, with his partner. He remained active in the fight against "Don't Ask, Don't Tell."*

THE ADMIRAL
An Interview with Alan Steinman

Alan Steinman served with the coast guard as a doctor in the U.S. Public Health Service from 1972 to 1997. He proudly wore the coast guard uniform for those twenty-five years, as he rose up through the ranks to become an admiral. Yet when he publicly came out as a gay man opposed to "Don't Ask, Don't Tell" in 2003, coast guard spokespeople were quick to point out that he had been officially employed by the Public Health Service. For someone who had "bled coast guard blue" for his entire adult life, this was painful. But Alan felt that he could no longer hide the truth. He had done that long enough.

I am Retired Admiral Alan M. Steinman. I was born in Newark, Ohio, on February 7, 1945. My father was a chemist, and ultimately had his own chemical plant after he moved to Los Angeles when I was a young boy. My mother was a homemaker. I got a bachelor of science degree from the Massachusetts Institute of Technology in June of 1966 and a doctor of medicine from Stanford University in June of 1971.

I joined the military after my internship year with the Mayo Clinic. At that time most people did one year of internship and then did their residency training in whatever specialty they wanted to go into. I didn't know what specialty I wanted to go into, so joining the Public Health Service was a way of temporizing that decision. The coast guard was one of the many programs that the Public Health Service offered for people who wanted to go on active duty in their medical career, and I thought the coast guard offered a lot of interesting opportunities in the field of general medicine, family practice, and particularly in emergency medicine. That's why I joined.

I had sort of two different careers in the coast guard. One was as a medical officer and a flight surgeon at coast guard air stations or other shore-based units. My duties were taking care of the active duty population and their families. All the clinics I was at in the field, except for Kodiak, were single doc units. So the day-to-day routine was providing health care for patients who came in and fly on emergency medical evacuations. Whenever we would launch a helicopter for a medevac that required a physician's presence, I would fly either by myself or with a corpsman on the helicopter to the case. That oftentimes involved ships at sea—merchant vessels, recreational boats, or fishing boats—with someone ill or injured on the vessel, in which case we would either lower down a basket or a litter to bring the patient up to the helicopter or on occasion I would be lowered down to the vessel to evaluate the situation and provide emergency care. I would prepare the patient for evacuation and then have the patient hoisted into the helicopter. Then they would drop the hoist down for me and pick me up. Being hoisted up and down is always a dangerous proposition particularly in bad weather when the vessel is moving in all kinds of unpredictable directions. The only time I felt my life was in danger while I was in the coast guard was during these hoists or when I was flying medevacs through particularly bad weather.

Then I had a different career in Coast Guard Headquarters. That was more of an administrative career, although I still was providing service in the Coast Guard Headquarters clinic for much of the time I was there, except when I got promoted to captain and admiral. Then my duties were almost entirely administrative. There was also a period of my career when I sort of straddled both of those areas and I did some primary research in hypothermia and sea survival.

Since I was gay, I had to be in the closet, deep in the closet. The tragedy of that was that I was not permitted to have a normal personal life like everyone else. I couldn't have a family. I couldn't share my life with a loved one. I couldn't do all those other things that the straight people in the coast guard take for granted. I had to be very guarded. Since my service in the coast guard was voluntary and I loved it, I made that choice, but, therefore, my whole personal life was nil [laughs] from the sexuality standpoint while I was on active duty. So how did my sexuality affect my life? In a huge way! I had no sexual life.

On occasion I was required to do discharge physical exams for coast guard members being separated by virtue of sexuality. There were maybe three or four of those that I recall. I did the physical exam on the individual, and then he was gone. I never saw that person again. But other than that, I never knew anybody who was gay while I was on active duty, nor did I ever seek out anybody who was. I mean obviously it was completely forbidden, so I separated that part of myself from my professional duties.

Most of the time I was in the military, there was a policy against homosexuals because they were considered unsuitable for military service. I am not a lawyer, but my understanding of the policy before "Don't Ask, Don't Tell" had to do with homosexual conduct, which then as now is a violation of the UCMJ— Uniform Code of Military Justice. I certainly was never guilty of homosexual conduct, so I was never in violation of UCMJ.

With the coast guard, you've got lots and lots of relatively small units all over the country. In all of the air stations I served at, you maybe had a couple hundred active duty people at most, and the officer corps was obviously much smaller than that. So when you are a gay man in a relatively small work unit, people are always trying to fix you up. You are a single guy, and people always want to fix you up, assume you are straight. I always had problems with fix-ups, and you can only turn them down so many times. So that was always troubling. I obviously had to go on dates I didn't particularly want to go on. It was uncomfortable, and I always made excuses one way or another. Also, the air stations would have a party every other week or so, an officers' party that you were expected to go to, particularly if you are the flight surgeon, because you are a key member of the command. When I got to headquarters, things became much easier because headquarters is a huge organization with lots and lots of coast guard officers who live in geographically dispersed areas, so that you didn't have as many parties that you had to go to anymore. Obviously there were parties that went on, but it was easier not to go to them, until I became eligible for Flag.

As a flag officer you have a fairly large number of social obligations, so if I was going to be a flag, how was I going to deal with those things? I was going to need to have someone to go to parties with. [He laughs.] The commandant who appointed me—his name was Bill Kime, good guy—I don't think the thought ever crossed his mind that I could have been gay. He was more interested in what I had done professionally for the coast guard and for him personally in his tenure as commandant. For example, he asked me to give the coast guard a wellness program, and I had done that very well, created a service-wide, nationwide wellness program, so he was very pleased with that. I was one of the leading candidates, and I don't think this other issue ever crossed his mind. There was no reason for it to.

Of course, it crossed my mind. I mean, how many events can you go to stag? What's wrong with you? You don't have a girlfriend, a lady friend, what's the deal? So I went out looking for a lady friend. I put an ad in *Washingtonian* magazine. This is before Internet chat rooms and that kind of thing. It was like '92. So I put an ad in the personal section of this upscale Washington maga-zine. It said: "Gay Senior Executive seeks female companion for meeting social obligations." I got five or six responses. One of them was from a male prisoner in a federal prison in Virginia. He was getting out soon and was interested in hooking up with me or something, I don't know. But one was a beautifully written letter; the author was obviously head and shoulders above everybody else who had responded. So we agreed to meet for dinner at the Ritz Carlton Hotel in Pentagon City. She had an interesting story, and she thought I had an interesting story and she liked me, so we decided to make a deal. Very shortly after that we became very good friends, and she is still one of my best friends, but that was the way I met her. The primary reason to meet her was having someone to go to parties with.

When "Don't Ask, Don't Tell" was being implemented, I was a brand-new admiral. And every Wednesday morning in Coast Guard Headquarters we had basically a board of directors meeting. All the coast guard admirals in head-quarters and their civilian equivalents from the Senior Executive Service would meet in a centralized secure conference room with the commandant, the vice commandant, and the chief of staff to discuss whatever the business of the day was. One day, this issue came up, as the Pentagon was debating the policy, and they actually formed a committee to discuss this.

At the time, I thought that it was all rather silly. Had President Clinton prevailed in his attempt to remove any kind of ban from gays and lesbians serving openly in the military, I think that very few people would have come out of the closet, because most people don't reveal their sexuality unless they feel safe to do so with their friends or close confidants, and oftentimes that's not the case on a vessel, on a navy vessel, a coast guard vessel, or whatever unit you happen to be on. I think most gays and lesbians would have carried on their business, and nobody would have noticed any difference. Maybe a couple of people would have come out, and if that been a disruptive situation, the military is quite adept at dealing with disruptive situations. I don't think it would have been a problem at all.

I was sort of bemused by all of this pandering going on and was fairly insulted by what I was hearing from people like Senator Nunn and unfortunately, even Colin Powell, who was chairman of the Joint Chiefs at the time. When it came time for the coast guard to discuss it, the commandant at the time, who was the man who appointed me to my job, basically said, "The coast guard will be in lockstep with the Defense Department on this issue," end of story. I mean that was the decision by the commandant. There was no discussion. Now, he was right—the coast guard as I told you earlier, has always valued its affiliation with the armed forces, so you can see how the head of the coast guard would like to stay on the same page with the armed forces.

In the back of my mind, it was conceivable the coast guard could have done something different because they were with the Department of Transportation, not the Department of Defense. They were not under the secretary of defense. They were not in the Pentagon. They were under a separate cabinet secretary. So, had the commandant been so inclined, he might have been able to push for the coast guard to get a different status; maybe that would be a trial balloon for the rest of the country to see if it was going to work or not. I doubt whether most people in the coast guard would have liked that, but I mean it's possible that would have happened. That wasn't to be. The coast guard allied itself with the Defense Department at that time. But there was a fairly lively discussion about coast guard civilian employees. Nobody, as I recall, had any problem with openly gay or lesbian civilian employees. The coast guard almost immediately revised its personnel manual to make sexual orientation for civilians a protected class vis-à-vis harassment and discrimination. We were the first agency to do that.

The silver lining of "Don't Ask, Don't Tell" is that the law says that gays and lesbians can serve honorably so long as they are silent and presumably celibate. So we serve. It's no longer illegal. It's no longer incompatible with military service. We are legally able to serve, and that's something that the opponents of gays in the military always forget. It's very amusing when you hear them talking about privacy issues and undermining good order and discipline. All that's based on the assumption that there are so many homophobes in the military that the mere presence of a gay person would cause such anger and disruption that the military would suffer or that straight people are so fragile that they couldn't possibly endure the thought that some gay guy might be looking at them in the shower or locker room. That's why we can't have them there. But we are there. That's what the law says. We have been there for the last ten years. Where's been the problem?

After Admiral Steinman retired in 1997, he served on the president's committee investigating the effects of chemical weapons and Gulf War illness on veterans from the Persian Gulf War. At the time of this interview he was retired and living in Dupont, Washington.

THE RESERVIST
An Interview with Keith Kerr

Not long after I began conducting interviews for this project, I heard on the radio a retired brigadier general who had just come out publicly. He had been in the U.S. Army at the end of the Korean War era and had then served for the next forty years in California National Guard. It turned out that he lived less than twenty minutes from the university where I was teaching. I tracked him down at his beautiful home in the hills above Santa Rosa, California. What follows is the story he told me that day.

I'm Keith Kerr, and I was born on January 14, 1931, in Kentfield, California, just north of San Francisco. My father was an electrical engineer for PG&E, Pacific Gas and Electric Company. My mother was a homemaker. During World War II, she worked as a grocery clerk and as a school bus driver

My parents moved to the San Joaquin Valley when I was about two years old, and I was raised in the San Joaquin Valley in Oakdale and Lodi. It was in the middle of the Depression, and a lot of people were moving from Oklahoma and Texas to California. I attended school with them, and life was rather sparse in those days during the Depression. I graduated from Lodi High School in 1949 and then went on to college. I wasn't very self-confident as a teenager. So I went to a smaller college first and then transferred to the University of California at Berkeley.

My father served in World War II. He was in the army. He went overseas to serve in the United Kingdom. He never saw action on the continent, though, and he came home right after the war. My father's expectations were that one of his sons would be a military officer, and he wanted one of us to go to West Point. My brother didn't go. My brother went to UC-Berkeley on a navy ROTC scholarship. He was commissioned a marine corps officer and served four years on active duty. He left the service at the end of four years; his wife did not care for the military life.

When I arrived in Berkeley, the Korean War was going on. When I transferred to the University of California, I forgot to notify my draft board, and they contacted me and were ready to induct me. I wanted to finish college, so they gave me a deferment, but the deferment only covered four years of school. After that, they wouldn't continue to defer me. So I decided the best thing to do, even though I had a year of college left, was to go ahead and volunteer for the draft and get my service out of the way and then come back and finish college and that's what I did. That was in the fall of 1953.

Basic training was a little bit of a shock to me. I had never been a particularly athletic person, although I enjoyed basic training and I found out that I enjoyed the military. I was at Ford Ord, California. I remember getting up early, 5:30 every morning, going through the chow line. Having your breakfast on a cold metal tray, shaving, showering, and getting ready for formation at 6:30 or 7:00 in the morning and then marching out to the firing ranges. It's been a long time, it's been over fifty years, so I have a hard time remembering all of the details.

Following more training, I was sent to Germany and assigned to an intelligence unit. My parents hadn't supported me in college, and so after some of the stresses of college, I found I really enjoyed Germany. I enjoyed the army, and I enjoyed being assigned to an army intelligence unit. So it was a wonderful period of my life. I got to travel, meet new friends, learn new skills. The installation to which I was assigned frequently would have people who had defected from behind the Iron Curtain, and they would come there and be debriefed. During World War II, the compound had been Stalag 17 for allied fliers, and after World War II it became an army intelligence center. And it was a beautiful setting, probably about fifteen kilometers outside of Frankfurt.

Keith completed his enlistment and then returned to Berkeley to finish school. He joined the reserves in 1956 after moving across the bay to San Francisco. Keith worked in business for a time and ultimately became dean of the Business School at the City College of San Francisco. At this same time, he was rising through the ranks of the reserves and dealing with his sexuality.

My ambition was really based on two things: one, I wanted to prove that I could be an officer, and, secondly, my father's expectation that I should be an officer had always been there and I was anxious to please him. My father discovered an indiscreet letter that I had written when I was in college, and my father was homophobic so we were estranged for a year. But, ultimately, with my career and with my service in the army he came to accept me on an equal basis with my brother, and he and I never discussed the topic again.

I knew that I was attracted to men. And I knew I had very little attraction to the opposite sex. But I really believed my friends and what I read in the newspapers, that eventually I would be attracted to the opposite sex and that this was a passing phase. Well, I kept this illusion of it in my own mind for a long time, and even after I got my commission in the army reserve, I thought I would marry and have children. To please my army friends and my parents, I was engaged to marry a wonderfully attractive woman, and finally, I realized, several years after I had been going with her that I really had been deceiving myself and while I thought a great deal of her and admired her, I was not in love with her and the worst thing that I could possibly do for her and for myself would be to propose marriage simply to please my parents, the army, or any other friends or colleagues. At that point, I decided that I am really a gay man and I need to accept that.

Being gay or lesbian was grounds for dismissal. The arguments used were that the personnel were a security risk and that their presence was inimical to good order and discipline. So there was always apprehension and I knew of people who were discharged or sent home, not necessarily because of misconduct, but simply because they were gay or lesbian. Later in my career, I heard about other stories. I knew several West Point officers who wanted to make the army their career, but they were discharged because they were photographed entering and leaving a gay bar in Tokyo. That became the grounds for their discharge. For me, I thought, "I will just be discreet and finish my twenty years of service for federal retirement purposes." Plus, I continued to love the army, to enjoy the training, and opportunities, and I said, "I will just keep my personal life to myself."

I was quite surprised beginning with Stonewall in New York City that there were a bunch of gay people standing up for their rights.[6] I thought, "Well, that's wonderful." Because prior to that time, gays and lesbians if they went to a gay bar could be arrested simply for congregating in a bar and not doing anything untoward, simply for having social time together. So I thought that was wonderful, although I was not willing to, nor felt compelled to, take any part as an activist. At that time, teaching was just beginning to emerge as a career for me, and it was a situation where you couldn't get hired if you were gay, or if the principal or the dean or president of the college even thought you were gay.

Unfortunately, the antiwar movement pretty much captured the gay liberation movement, and there were gays who did not want to serve in the military because they were opposed to the administration's policy in Southeast Asia; so the two got tied together, and, in addition, gays and lesbians became aware that if their sexuality was discovered, they would be dismissed from service, perhaps with an undesirable discharge. So it was very hard. I was standing on the sidelines, waiting and observing.

With the emergence of figures like Harvey Milk and George Mosconi, gay liberation really moved to the forefront.[7] San Francisco in the twenties and thirties was fairly conservative, and even into the forties and fifties, but then things began to change. I can't really describe the cause of that. I was looking at some statistics the other day, and I think only 14 percent of registered voters in San Francisco are Republican today, and one of the officers with whom I served is secretary of the Log Cabin Republicans, a gay Republican group. I belong to the group primarily because I admire his courage and want to support him.

Anyway, after the gay liberation movement started, it was my impression that the military was not pursuing gays and lesbians so aggressively, and I became aware of this in the seventies and saw what I perceived to be a change in the policy. Some commands where there might be a homophobic officer or a noncommissioned officer would certainly report gays and do their best to get them out of the service, but others just overlooked it. My observations were that it wasn't uniformly consistent throughout the services.

I never had to enforce the ban as an officer. I never had a situation arise where someone came to me and reported a gay service member and recommended I take some action. Still, you developed a whole sense of paranoia that somebody was watching you, looking over your shoulder to see if someone was following you. I developed a recurring dream where there was an investigator who confronted me. He told me he knew that I was gay and that he was going to expose me. We would have harsh words. I would say, "You can't prove it," and he said, "Yes I can!" Then, I would wake up and realize it was a nightmare and everything was fine until the next night. So it does take a toll on you because you have so much at stake especially after you've put in fifteen, eighteen, nineteen years.

When I accepted my sexuality and I decided that I should not marry, I began dating and I suddenly met the person who became my one love in life.

When Keith Kerr joined two other retired flag
officers in coming out publicly as a gay man in
2003, most of the press coverage naturally focused
on his former rank. Few stories acknowledged that
Keith had been a family man. He is pictured
here with his partner of twenty-six years,
Alvin D. Gomer, an ordained Episcopal priest.
Photo courtesy of Keith Kerr.

We had a wonderful life together. When we went to Washington, he met a number of my military colleagues. We took my high school–age nephews on trips. We hiked in the John Muir trail and stayed at the Iwani Hotel. We went first class to Europe on the QE2. We took the Orient Express. We had a wonderful, rich, and fulfilling life together with his family and my family. My father, who had been a homophobic in his early years, came to love Alvin.

Near the end of our interview, I asked Keith to talk about "Don't Ask, Don't Tell" and why he and the other flag officers decided to come out against it publicly.

"Don't Ask, Don't Tell" was certainly an improvement over the previous policy in which simply being gay was grounds for dismissal. I was hopeful that they would lift the ban completely. A lot of people really counted on President Clinton to lift the ban, and there were some famous cases challenging it. There was a soldier from the Presidio of San Francisco. His name was Joe Zuniga. Joe had been chosen soldier of the year of the Presidio and announces he's gay. Well, the next day he's toast, and the army's determined to kick him out based on the policy. Of course, Clinton retreated, and the issue ended up in Congress. Congress enacted the law.

Today, practically all of our military allies have lifted the ban on gays in the military. We have been fighting alongside Britain in the Middle East, and there doesn't seem to be any hostility or problems that have developed between American troops and the Britons because gays can serve in their military. Younger soldiers, sailors, airmen, marines, and coast guard people do not have trouble with gays in the military. It's the older officers and the older noncommissioned officers, and that's been a part of military culture for a long time.

Myself and two other flag officers had been on the honorary board of Servicemembers Legal Defense Network, and we felt that "Don't Ask, Don't Tell" had failed. We think it should be repealed. Ten thousand service members have been dismissed for being gay or lesbian who were otherwise doing their jobs in an exemplary way over the previous ten years. Harassment is still going on. After the murders of Allen Schindler, who was a seaman, and Barry Winchell at Fort Campbell, Kentucky, four years ago, we asked the Defense Department to institute an antiharassment law.[8] There's no reason why antiharassment can't be incorporated into troop training sessions along with racial tolerance, but as far as we know, the antiharassment policy that was promised us is still sitting on the Pentagon shelf gathering dust.

Also, over the last ten years, the Servicemembers Legal Defense Network has received over 5,400 requests for assistance from service members who are being harassed or investigated who need some advice. We think it's time now that the military services come into the twenty-first century. The military is the only place where official discrimination still exists against gays and lesbians. When you think of police departments, fire departments, sheriffs departments, highway patrols, they allow gay people to serve. There's no reason they can't serve in the military. I guess the Pentagon had denied for some years that there were gay officers, and we wanted to make a statement to criticize the policy and show that sexual orientation has no bearing on the ability to do one's job.

The army made me a much better person and gave me a lot more motivation than I would have otherwise had. I learned from talented and gifted superiors, learned leadership traits, how to get along with people, how to inspire people, how to lead people. The army made a tremendous difference in my life. Admiral Steinman, General Richard, and myself all love our services very dearly, and this criticism is not intended as a criticism of the service; it is intended as a criticism of a personnel policy that is destructive and counter-productive to our military readiness.

> *At the time of this interview, Keith Kerr continued to serve on the board of the Servicemembers Legal Defense Network and continued to speak out against "Don't Ask, Don't Tell."*

KOSOVO, AFGHANISTAN, AND IRAQ

In the years since the passage of "Don't Ask, Don't Tell," the United States has been involved in major military conflicts in the Balkans, Afghanistan, and Iraq, as well as smaller operations in Haiti, Somalia, and elsewhere. Gay and lesbian service personnel have been called to serve in every one of these conflicts.[1] The three interviewees in this chapter each served in two of America's most recent wars, seeing more action than most veterans (gay or straight) saw in the twenty years before the passage of "Don't Ask, Don't Tell."

With the Cold War drawing to a close in the late 1980s and early 1990s, new fissures threatened to divide the peaceful world. Conflicts over religious and ethnic differences along with the impact of globalization eclipsed the ideological battle between capitalism and communism that had dominated the Cold War era. In fact, regions like the Balkans that had been held together by the glue of ideology and Cold War statecraft began to splinter under the pressure of religious and nationalistic forces. President George H. W. Bush had hoped that a "new world order" would emerge in the wake of the Cold War. Yet after Bush left office, his successors came to believe that the only way to maintain that new order was through American military intervention.

The end of the Cold War had an especially destabilizing effect on the part of the Balkans that had been tied together as the country of Yugoslavia. Starting in the early 1990s independence movements emerged in various Yugoslavian states—Slovenia, Croatia, Bosnia, and, ultimately, Kosovo. Led by President Slobodan Milosevic, the Serbians that dominated Yugoslavia fought bitterly against the independence movements, supporting campaigns of "ethnic cleansing" by Serbian ethnic minorities in the breakaway states. The United

States and its allies in the North Atlantic Treaty Organization (NATO) supported diplomatic solutions to the conflicts until 1999. In March of that year, NATO began bombing Serbia when Serbian forces refused to withdraw from Kosovo. The air campaign ushered in an uneasy peace, with NATO forces remaining on the ground to ensure that conflict would not erupt again.[2]

Greg Castleberry, a former mortician from New Mexico, was one of the gay airmen who supported the NATO bombing campaign that ultimately ended Slobodan Milosevic's reign of terror in Kosovo. Though he generally found himself opposed to war, Greg came to believe that the NATO bombing was justified to protect Kosovars and other civilians from the ethnic cleansing that had been occurring in the Balkans. Greg supervised the demolition of explosives and other ordnance from the Balkans. It was a dangerous and stressful assignment, but it was his duty. Few of the men and women who served with Greg even suspected that he was gay. He consciously avoided what he saw as stereotypically gay mannerisms, and he focused on doing his job. At six feet five, he also felt that a "butch" build provided him some camouflage. Greg never faced direct discrimination because he was gay. In fact, because he believed that some gay men in the military made it harder on themselves by being flamboyant, Greg was one of the few gay veterans who expressed ambivalence about the "Don't Ask, Don't Tell" policy.

In 1999, the same year that Greg Castleberry was deployed in support of the Kosovo campaign, nineteen-year-old Private Barry Winchell faced a much more dangerous situation at Fort Campbell, Kentucky. That year, Winchell had begun to explore gay life in nearby Nashville, Tennessee, and rumors began to spread about his sexuality. "Pretty much everybody called him derogatory names," Sergeant Michael Kleifgen later told a reporter. "They called him a faggot, I would say, on a daily basis." Kleifgen, a friend of Winchell's, filed a formal complaint about the harassment, but nothing was done. When Winchell also complained, his captain simply told the other soldiers to "knock that shit off."[3] On the Fourth of July, Winchell got into a fight with another private, eighteen-year-old Calvin Glover, at a keg party outside their barracks. On the surface, the fight had nothing to do with Winchell's being gay, but when he knocked Glover down, the taunts began. Ashamed that he had been beaten by "a fucking faggot," Glover decided to get revenge. Later that night, he attacked Winchell with a baseball bat as he slept. Winchell died the next day.

In the wake of Winchell's murder and a subsequent study of antigay harassment in the military, the Department of Defense added "Don't Harass" to its "Don't Ask, Don't Tell" policy. The military also instituted tolerance workshops modeled on programs to address sexual harassment and racial bigotry.[4]

Yet, as the following interviews reveal, enforcement of the "Don't Harass" directive and tolerance training varied widely from post to post and from unit to unit. As the new millennium dawned, gays and lesbians could serve in the military, but they were expected to do so, as they always had, in silence.

For all Americans, and especially for those Americans serving in the military, the attacks on the World Trade Center and the Pentagon on September 11, 2001, were a watershed moment. Military personnel, such as the three veterans interviewed here, understood almost immediately that their lives and their careers had a new purpose. Many had volunteered for the military because it was a good job, an opportunity for training and education, a way to travel and see the world. But, on that September day, men and women in the military also understood that they would be called to defend the United States and to find those responsible for the terrorist attacks.

The invasion of Afghanistan was America's swift response to the attacks. During the Cold War, the United States had supported the fundamentalist Islamic groups in Afghanistan in their fight against the Soviets. But, in the post–Cold War world, these same groups began to view the secularizing forces of globalization and u.s. influence as the new enemy. The fundamentalist Taliban regime that ruled Afghanistan had allowed al-Qaeda to set up training camps for terrorists bent on attacking Western countries and Western nationals in the Muslim world. After the Taliban refused to turn over Osama bin Laden and other al-Qaeda leaders responsible for the 9/11 attacks, the United States launched missiles and air strikes on the country and sent in Special Forces beginning in early October 2001. Anti-Taliban forces within Afghanistan, called the Northern Alliance, did much of the early fighting, taking control of Kabul, the capital city, on November 12, 2001. u.s. ground forces began to arrive in growing numbers at the end of the year, setting up headquarters at Bagram Air Base just outside Kabul. During 2002 and 2003, the majority of u.s. operations in Afghanistan were aimed at seeking out remaining Taliban forces and al-Qaeda operatives in rural Afghanistan and securing a peaceful transition for a new Afghani government.[5]

Brian Hughes was a gay member of the Special Forces sent to Afghanistan immediately after he finished Army Ranger School in the fall of 2002. This California native, who grew up in England, left Yale University during his senior year in 2000 to join the army as an enlisted man. Though Brian could not speak about particular missions in Afghanistan, he talked in general terms about his assignment. "We were conducting mounted and dismounted patrols in search of men, weapons, and equipment," he recalled. "In other words, [we were] looking for terrorists and munitions, which we found." These missions put Brian's Ranger training to the test. His next assignment, during the American invasion of Iraq in 2003, would be a different challenge.

Back in December 2001, General Tommy Franks had begun to update American plans for invading Iraq and toppling Saddam Hussein's regime. President George W. Bush invited Franks to his ranch in Crawford, Texas, to outline the plan. In the days following 9/11, Deputy Defense Secretary Paul Wolfowitz had suggested that there might be a connection between Saddam Hussein and the al-Qaeda attacks. Others in the Bush administration viewed the Iraqi dictator as a threat because of the possibility that he had access to weapons of mass destruction. This view underpinned President Bush's State of the Union address in January 2002 when he dubbed North Korea, Iran, and Iraq an "axis of evil," concluding, "The United States of America will not permit the world's most dangerous regimes to threaten us with the world's most destructive weapons." Though no proof would ever emerge that Saddam Hussein played a role in the 9/11 attacks or that he had access to weapons of mass destruction in 2003, the administration was taking no chances. With the failure of diplomatic overtures in Iraq and in the United Nations, the United States decided on a preemptive strike with a smaller coalition of allies than had supported the first Gulf War or the war in Afghanistan.[6]

By March 2003 there were 130,000 American service personnel in Kuwait preparing for the invasion that began that month. Launched in conjunction with a bombing campaign that was intended to inspire "shock and awe," the ground invasion went more smoothly than either administration officials or their critics expected. Unlike the first Gulf War, the Pentagon allowed embedded reporters to travel with units, resulting in intense and almost immediate coverage.

One of the leading stories to emerge from the invasion was the ambush and capture of members of the u.s. Army's 507th Maintenance Company, including a private from West Virginia named Jessica Lynch. Injured when her Humvee smashed into another vehicle during the ambush, Private Lynch was ultimately taken by her Iraqi captors to Saddam Hussein General Hospital in Nasiriyah. She was a prisoner of war, yet Private Lynch was treated well by the Saddam General doctors, few of whom were supporters of the hospital's namesake. When word leaked out that Lynch was being held at the hospital, American Special Forces were sent on a rescue mission. Brian Hughes was assigned to this mission, though he was not one of the men who rushed into Lynch's hospital room in a dramatic rescue. Instead, Hughes and his Ranger team were given the grim assignment to recover the bodies of Lynch's comrades who had been killed in the ambush. Seven of the bodies were buried in shallow graves not far from Saddam General. Hughes will never forget that mission, but it was only one of many during his time in Iraq.[7]

By mid-April 2003, less than a month after the initial invasion, American forces controlled Baghdad and the Pentagon declared that major combat operations in Iraq had come to an end. In early May President Bush spoke to sailors on the uss *Abraham Lincoln,* commending them and other American service personnel for a job well done. He spoke in front of a banner that read, "Mission Accomplished." Even historians took on a triumphalist tone in writing about the Iraq War. For example, John Keegan, the dean of British military historians, introduced his 2004 study of the Iraq War by saying, "Some wars begin badly. Some end badly. The Iraq War of 2003 was exceptional in both beginning well for the Anglo-American force that waged it and ending victoriously."[8] But it soon became apparent that if the war produced a relatively easy victory, the occupation that followed would prove more challenging. Even after Saddam Hussein was captured, suicide bombings and attacks on American forces and Iraqi officials intensified.

Robert Stout was a member of an engineer platoon that went to Iraq in February 2004. Working with army demolition teams, Robert's platoon was assigned the dangerous task of finding and destroying the improvised explosive devices (IEDs) that were killing hundreds of American soldiers and thousands of Iraqi police and civilians.[9] This was the "front line" of a war that no longer had discernible advances and retreats. In May 2004, Iraqi insurgents ambushed Robert's platoon, wounding him and the other soldiers in his Humvee. After recuperation in Germany, Robert returned to Iraq, was promoted to the rank of sergeant, and led his own men until his enlistment was up in 2005.

Greg Castleberry, Brian Hughes, and Robert Stout decided to come out publicly as gay veterans to protest what they saw as a discriminatory policy against gays and lesbians serving in the armed forces. Hughes and Stout were particularly adamant in expressing their view that "Don't Ask, Don't Tell" was not working. Though it was intended to preserve unit cohesion, the policy was, these two combat veterans argued, more divisive than unifying. In the decade after the policy was enacted in 1993, more than 10,000 servicemen and women were discharged because of their sexuality. Yet discharges dropped when the United States began to fight the wars in Afghanistan and Iraq. After reaching a peak of 1,273 "Don't Ask, Don't Tell" discharges in 2001, the Department of Defense kicked out only 653 in 2004.[10] As in every modern American war, the u.s. military has once again tacitly recognized that it needs courageous soldiers like Greg Castleberry, Brian Hughes, and Robert Stout, regardless of their sexuality.

FROM KOSOVO TO KABUL
An Interview with Greg Castleberry

Greg Castleberry served during military conflicts that may be forgotten to future generations. Just as the conflict in Vietnam eclipsed the Korean War, the war in Iraq may draw the attention of scholars away from the conflicts in the Balkans and in Afghanistan. Still, these conflicts are important because they exemplify the peacekeeping missions that have become a central part of the agenda of the u.s. armed forces and the immediate military response to the attacks that shocked our nation on September 11, 2001. That gay servicemen like Greg served during these conflicts will come as no surprise to readers of this volume.

I was born in Seminole, Texas, on November 10, 1978. But I grew up in Hobbs, New Mexico. I lived there until my parents divorced around 1987. Hobbs is in the Llano Estacado, which is the state's high plains. It's very flat, with a high elevation. After my parents divorced, I moved with my mother to Las Vegas, New Mexico. My mother worked in state government, so she was on the road a lot. I raised myself and matured very quickly.

After high school, I moved to Dallas, Texas. I attended the Dallas Institute of Funeral Service and received my associate's degree of applied science in funeral services. Once I graduated I was certified as a funeral director. Then, I moved back to New Mexico and worked for a small family that owned two funeral homes. It was just a morbid attraction that I had ever since I was a little kid. None of my family was in the funeral business at all. My father was basically the one who supported me through it. My mother thought it was extremely strange. It kind of frightened her when I was a child. When my father died, I could not stay in the funeral business anymore. So I enlisted in the military out of sheer compulsion in 1998. I was actually very antimilitary my whole life, even in high school. I'm a very stubborn person. When I make up my mind up about something it takes an act of God and Congress to change my mind or my views.

My mother thought it was wonderful that I joined the military. I came out to both my parents when I was fifteen, and my mother has always had a problem with the idea of me being a homosexual. Anything that was going to break the stereotype was good, even though I don't really have any identifiable homosexual characteristics anyways. My mother didn't come right out and say all that, but I could tell that was why she was so excited.

I did not have your garden-variety air force recruiter. My recruiter was very up front with me. Basically, everything that she told me that would happen in boot camp happened. She said it is all a head game. You got to learn how to play the game and all of that. Well, I love head games. I live for head games. I basically had my mind already made up that this is what I was going to do.

In boot camp, I would catch myself getting stressed out, and I would just have to sit back and go, "Okay, it's just a game. It's just a game." I would try to calm some of my other comrades down too, because they were getting freaked out over the littlest things. These are kids that have been just picked out of the nest. My drill instructor saw me talking people down, saying, "Just calm down, you know its not the end of the world." And he made me dorm chief. So much for me standing in the back and staying unnoticed. Now I'm responsible for sixty other individuals, and when they mess up it comes back on me. Me and my mouth.

I've never been surrounded by a bunch of guys my age or younger in that type of situation. I found it very odd, the sexual references that straight men make. I've never experienced that before. How they will purposely act like homosexuals, and I'm sure they're doing it just for a laugh or the attention. Oh God! I'm sitting there, going, "Should I laugh at this? I don't want to laugh too hard." You're constantly worried about being found out, especially in that situation. Guys who are comfortable with their sexual orientation are not going to think twice about joking like that, because to them, it's just another guy. All my friends in high school were female. I wasn't exposed to that type of humor. There were times in there that were extremely uncomfortable for me. I really didn't start finding out about other gay recruits until after boot camp, because, honestly, your mind is in so many other places—worried about if you're going to be able to do enough push-ups, if you're going to be able to run. I mean just stupid stuff. There was one kid that approached me and said that he was bisexual, but I think that was because he was looking for a way out. He didn't want to be there anymore. The whole bisexual thing, I don't know, I don't buy that.

Later, I was stationed at an air force base in California not too terribly far from San Francisco. I was extremely frustrated that I never got the chance to go there, because it's kind of like the Mecca. That was when I started my PRP, which is the Personnel Reliability Program. You're monitored for a year to see if you are of adequate character to hold a top secret or better security clearance. You cannot buy over-the-counter medication. Phone calls can be monitored. You can be followed. I mean you basically lose all rights. That's why I did not go to San Francisco on my time off. Someone said, "Hey, we're going to the De Young Museum." They had some sort of Fabergé egg exhibit. I'm like, "Well, I really don't want to go. I got something to do." I would get the invitations and think: "If they take me into San Francisco, man, I would start waving the flag so bad everyone would notice." No thank you. So under PRP, I kept a very, very boring lifestyle. If I were Catholic, I would have made a good monk.

They were needing air force liaisons for the Kosovo campaign, and they saw that some of us who were new to the PRP program had assignments over in Eastern Europe. "Hey, he's on his way over there, we'll go ahead and grab him." So I got to Italy, processed, and I immediately went to Incirlik Air Base in Turkey. We were air force liaisons to the weapons and logistics group. NATO [the North Atlantic Treaty Organization force] was out there collecting all this ordnance, and whenever unexploded ordnance from an enemy is taken into U.S. hands, they bring it onto a base. We had to make sure that the army EOD [explosive ordinance disposal unit] is following air force protocol in the detonation of unexploded ordnance. There were constantly Allied forces that were working with NATO that were getting their legs blown off by frag mines, anti-tank mines, personnel mines, and stuff like that. It wasn't because they were stepping on them; it was because of the careless handling of them. There was quite a bit of stress riding up there.

I thought that Kosovo was a well-operated task force. I'm antiwar to begin with. I'm not to the point that I'm antigovernment, but if there is a way around military action let's do it. That's why I like Clinton. I like the balance that was in the Clinton administration. You had a very middle-of-the-road, liberal Democrat as president, but you had a very conservative Republican secretary of defense, William Cohen. Whenever the secretary of defense wanted to do something, the president would kind of bring him out of the clouds and vice versa. I thought Milosevic needed to be pulled out. There were horrible things going on over there, but we took the proper steps. It was a NATO task force. We had strong allies, and we were in and out—boom, boom. Minimal casualties, it was how an operation should be. I don't think it could have worked any better.

I asked Greg to talk about where he was on September 11, 2001, and to talk about how that affected him and other military personnel.

I was in Guam on September 11, 2001. I was actually on leave. My mother had been planning the trip to come see me in Guam. All of us in Guam had no idea what was going on. We all slept through it because it was the middle of the night for us. So I get this call from a friend, and she said that the Twin Towers had been bombed. And I say, "Bombed, again?" You know, thinking what happened in '93. And she said, "Go turn on the TV." Well, I didn't have one, so I had to go to the base hotel. They had a big screen. I walk in there, and there were about four people standing in front of it. I walk in about thirty minutes after the second Tower had already fallen. They're showing the live footage, and all you can see is dust everywhere. I'm like, "That's a hell of a bomb! You can't even see the Towers." The guy next to me just said, "No, the Towers are gone." And, I said, "What do you mean gone?" He said, "They're gone; they fell."

Needless to say, I was up for about twenty-four hours straight just thinking, "What's going on?" I'm in touch with my first sergeant saying, "Are we gonna be deployed? What's happening here?" My sergeant said, "I don't know, but don't leave the island." All the airports were reopened, and my mother still came to visit. Two days after my mother left, I was in Diego Garcia, building bombs.

Diego Garcia is in the South Indian Ocean, and it is an RAF base—Royal Air Force Base. It's just an atoll. If you draw a line straight south from India, you will see the word Diego Garcia, but you will not see it on the map. That was actually the campaign that the press here in the United States got so upset about, because the Department of Defense did not tell the press we were bombing Afghanistan until two weeks after we had already started. They didn't want to see what happened in the Persian Gulf War, where enemy fighters were surrendering to CNN cameramen. Troops were finding out more from CNN than they were from their company leaders. So there was a big hush-hush that was going on. We were building a smart bomb called a J-DAM— which is joint direct attack munitions, a precision guided bomb that was being dropped by B-1's and B-52's.

I can't give the actual date, but sometime after September 25, 2001, I was sent to Afghanistan. It was beautiful. I had been to Saudi Arabia several times, and I was expecting this great big desert. Afghanistan looked like parts of New Mexico to me: high deserts, huge mountains. You would not believe the mountain ranges in that country, white capped with snow because it was the winter. You're flying over, looking at some of these places, and seeing these homes down there that people still live in, and who knows when these were built. I wish I could have learned more about that area while I was there, rather than help destroy it. We went to set up an air force base outside of Kabul.

Greg was involved in a friendly fire incident. He couldn't talk about the specifics of when and where this incident occurred, but he described it in general terms.

It was during a training exercise, and a marine's sidearm was locked and loaded and discharged. It went through the airman in front of me, completely through his bicep, and lodged in my left shoulder. I didn't know I had been hit. I saw the guy in front of me get hit, because I got splattered in the face. I'm wiping dirt and blood off my face, and I'm like, "Oh my God!" I'm focused on him. We're making a tourniquet and everything for him. Well, I go to take off my BDU [battle dress uniform] blouse, the outer shirt of the camouflage, and the guy standing next to me goes, "Holy shit!" And I said, "What?" My entire left arm and left side of my shirt going down to my belt was completely saturated. I lost a little over a pint-and-a-half of blood, and I was on the verge of passing out. But you have such an adrenalin rush that you could be practically dead. I lay in a hospital, and I mean, I never thought that they were gonna get enough blood back into me. I'm pretty white to begin with, but that was ridiculous. I'm sitting there going, "I joined the air force, man. This is not supposed to be happening."

Officially, I was there as an air force liaison—there with my security clearance manning an operation with other Department of Defense service members, mainly from army and Marine Corps, as they were setting up what is now an air force base outside of Kabul. After the friendly fire incident, they wanted to award me a medal for going above and beyond because I was doing an operation that was not part of my daily tasks in my career field. I turned it down. If I could have seen the officer face to face, I could have told him exactly where he could have stuck that medal too.

As the tone of this last statement indicates, Greg had grown jaded about this incident. Still, thinking back on the beginning of the Afghanistan offensive, he remembers being very gung ho. When he was given the option of serving in the States instead of Afghanistan, he said: "No, why would I want to go home? We're going after the people who tore up our country and our headquarters, the Pentagon." After discussing Afghanistan, I asked Greg to talk about how his sexuality influenced his time in the military.

I was out before the military, but I never paraded it around. I told my parents because they thought I was on drugs, and I was like, "No, no, no!" I had to put their minds at ease and that is why I was forced to come out. But, other than that, I never even told any of my friends—except the lesbian that I went to prom with. How cliché is that? But she and I would leave town when we wanted to go do things. So I never really had a problem being secretive. It's just kind of my nature anyway to not let everybody know everything about me.

When things slowed down after I was done with PRP, I could have a life. I went to Europe on leave, and there's a lot of gay people that travel to Europe. I remember going with a buddy of mine who wasn't gay, and I never mentioned to him that I was. No one ever thinks that when you're in the military overseas, because you have no family. It's not uncommon to see two guys going out to eat together that are in the military, because we're friends. We're not even thinking about it. There would only be certain times where I would be sitting there at Outback Steakhouse in Guam with a friend of mine, thinking, "Woo! I wonder if anyone thinks we're a couple." Other than that, that thought never enters your mind.

So, as I'm touring around Europe, I'm looking at these gay couples discretely, going: "Wow! Look at them enjoying it." I see them looking back at me, and they're thinking the same thing. "Wow! Look at those two GI's. Just, screw the 'Don't Ask, Don't Tell.' They're just doing it anyways." Of course, that wasn't the case. It became very frustrating because I was thinking, "I really wish that I had someone here that I could be more open with, and really share these same experiences." You know, my buddy over here wants to go to Potsdam, Germany, to go look at where Eisenhower signed the—come on! I don't want to look at that; I want to go to Milan, alright! It starts to wear on you emotionally. After a while, you kind of lose your own identity. After being a chameleon for so long, that color sticks.

After the murder of Barry Winchell in the summer of 1999, the Department of Defense implemented policies designed to thwart antigay harassment and hate crimes.

You know what that spawned in the Department of Defense? Homosexual awareness training. That is the stupidest thing I have ever seen in my life. Basically, it's saying that there are gays in the military. If you think someone is gay, here's what to say and what not to say, because this is considered harassment. It was just a bunch of bullshit. Basically, the government is saving their ass, so that they cannot be brought up on a civil lawsuit by a victim's family later on. The training was a reiteration of existing policy: "Don't Ask, Don't Tell, Don't Harass, Don't Pursue." You need to be aware that there are homosexuals in the military. Deal with it. Do not make any types of jokes about this even if you think it is funny. A guy dressing as a woman for Halloween, if that is offensive to someone and someone brings it to your attention that that's offensive, change your outfit. Basically, we don't want these gays to do a big uprising in our military right now. That's how I was reading it. They're here; deal with it. According to—I almost said scripture—according to Department of Defense doctrine, you can serve and be gay.

Trust me, there are some flamers that I have seen in uniform. It's almost frightening. And they're usually in the nonmilitant positions, like chaplain's assistant or in the medical group. I'm looking at them going, "How in the hell did you ever get through boot camp acting like that? That is absolutely, freaking amazing."

Greg's attitude toward the current policy is more ambivalent than that of many of the veterans in this book. On the one hand, he opposes it, but, on the other hand, he doesn't want special protection for gays who are unfit to serve. I asked Greg if he was ever discriminated against because of his sexuality.

Discriminated against? Directly, no. Indirectly, oh yeah. We all suffered from it. People stop talking to you. People are afraid to be seen alone with you, worried about what other people are thinking. I've never really been the subject of any direct discrimination. I guess it's because I come across as being rather intimidating. I mean, I'm six foot five. I am not a small person. I guess that is why I have never been on the receiving end of any discrimination, because I don't fit a lot of stereotypes. I can, at times, when my true self comes out, but like I said, I'm very conscious of my surroundings, and I know how to behave to not draw attention to myself.

We all know what we're going into. I don't think we should have any special protection. This is what makes me a very middle-of-the-road person, when it comes to a lot of my political philosophies. I don't think we deserve any special protection in the military from discrimination, because we know what the military is all about. If you don't think you can control your actions and your sex drive, surrounded by a bunch of people of the same sex, then you have no business in the military. Not because it's gonna be bad for you, but because it's gonna be bad for the people that don't like you. When you have a big homophobe, who is laying in a foxhole next to you and you two have to rely on body heat to survive, that guy is gonna rather freeze to death than spoon with a known gay. That compromises military strategy. That compromises an entire mission.

The military was forced to accept racial integration. People had to adjust their way of thinking. With African Americans, you know they're black by looking at them. You don't know I'm gay by looking at me. And if a homophobic soldier doesn't know that, he doesn't need to know that. If it's gonna affect his performance, I'm not gonna compromise any of our lives. I don't think that a true, gung-ho, kill, kill, kill soldier should be forced to accept that he is fighting alongside a homosexual. That homosexual should know how to keep it under control. If I can do it, anybody can.

Some people do it just for the challenge: "No one is gonna tell me that I can't join." And here goes *Ms. Thing* signing up. No. No. No. You don't need that. We don't need that, because, it totally breaks down what is being drilled into us in the military. Now, I don't get a lot of sympathy from gay activists on this subject, but, damn it, they were never in the military! They have no clue what I'm talking about. If they were in the military, they were not in active combat, so they have no clue what I'm talking about. Of course, it's just my opinion.

There are those of us who served quietly, and it's not because we are forced to serve quietly. We serve quietly because when we describe ourselves, being gay is not the first thing that comes out of our mouths. We were airmen; we were soldiers who happened to be gay.

Greg Castleberry is an assistant general manager at a hotel in Panama City Beach, Florida. He mentors gay servicemen and servicewomen who are stationed overseas via an informal online support network.

THE CALL OF DUTY

An Interview with Brian Hughes

When Brian Hughes dropped out of Yale University during his senior year and volunteered for the army, his friends and family thought he was crazy. They knew he was gay; the army didn't. Brian was training to become a u.s. Army Ranger when the World Trade Center and the Pentagon were attacked in 2001. At that point, he knew that his training would soon be put to the test. Brian ultimately served in both Afghanistan and Iraq. Because of the sensitive nature of his missions and the fact that his service was so recent, he is not able to divulge many details about his military operations. But Brian's unit did face enemy fighters in Afghanistan and he also served with the Special Forces team that rescued Private Jessica Lynch in Iraq. When he returned to the States and left the army in 2004, Brian came out publicly as a gay veteran, and he was interviewed by United Press International, Good Morning America, and several other media outlets. This interview took place after much of the press about him had died down. Brian graduated from Yale one month before our interview.

I was born in San Francisco, California, on the second of June 1978. My father runs a company that operates private hospitals in England—psychiatric clinics and drug rehab. At the age of two, in 1980, we moved to London, and so I grew up there and lived there for sixteen years before coming back to college in the States. I went to Yale because Yale accepted me. [He laughs.] When I visited the campus, that's when I realized that this was really the place I wanted to go. It was a good fit for both of us. My majors were math and philosophy. It was a great time. I got there in '96, the fall of '96.

I guess I first came out the Christmas of '96, back home, in California, and when I came back to the campus I came out to my friends. So I'd been openly gay for over three years before I enlisted in the army. My parents took it very well; they are very open-minded folks. I came out through my sister, and it was really very easy. The whole family is really very accepting.

I dropped out of Yale towards the end of my senior year to enlist. There was a combination of factors. I wasn't ready to graduate in some sense. I felt that I needed some sort of practical experience before I actually went out into the real world. I felt that I needed the mental and physical discipline that I would get in the army, and I knew it would be immediately rewarding. I knew I would be doing something worthwhile. The call of duty was strong in that sense. I felt that military service was one of the duties of citizenship and something I had to do. As to why I chose to do it before graduating rather than afterwards, it was because I wanted to do my time as an enlisted man rather than as an officer, and if I had a degree I felt the temptation would be too strong to go to ocs [Officer Candidate School] and get a commission. I felt the work would be more interesting, better, and more physical as an enlisted man. I sort of needed a break from more intellectual pursuits and wanted to get down and get my hands dirty.

My family and friends were very upset. My family in particular was very upset, probably because we don't really have much of a history of military service in our family; you have to go back to World War II to find folks who served. Partly, also, because I'm gay and they felt that the army was not really a friendly place for gay people. The murder of Barry Winchell was just a year or two before, and still very much a part of the public consciousness. My friends were also surprised, but less so, because I was right there on the scene to be able to explain what I was doing, whereas my parents found out long-distance. But I'd really gone over all of that already in my mind. I knew what I was getting into.

I think the most difficult thing about boot camp was that you weren't allowed to have any printed material; you couldn't read anything. I was not used to being separated from the printed word for a long period of time. They did allow us to have a *Bible*, so I did read that again, which took awhile. [He chuckles.] The *Bible* is a fantastic piece of work. It's a grand piece of literature. But when it's the only thing you read for fifteen weeks, it becomes—I don't know; you need a little variety. I was sort of starving for the very intellectual stimulation I was running away from.

Well, the physical stuff was sort of the focus of boot camp, because I hadn't really done any physical exercise in a serious way for probably six years before I enlisted. So getting into shape was really what it was all about. And I was very good at that. I came in barely able to meet the minimum standards for getting into boot camp, which are very low, and when I left, I left in good enough shape to get into Airborne school, which has a higher standard than most of the army.

I enlisted specifically for the Ranger program. My feeling was I wanted to be an infantryman and that if I was going to do that, then I wanted to do that properly and do it well. I wanted to be part of the best unit I could in the sort of enlistment I had chosen. And the way to do that was by joining one of the Ranger battalions. So that was my goal from the get-go. Before I signed any papers, I knew that's what I wanted. I was able, through luck and hard work, to achieve that.

But I was still on my initial training path. I had basic training, Airborne school, which is a three-week program, and then the Ranger indoctrination program, which is the selection program for enlisted Rangers, and that's a three-week course at Fort Benning, which is essentially a three-week hell to weed out people who don't really want to be there. You get dropped from the course for failing certain performance standards, but most of the attrition is from people dropping out of their own accord. We started with a class of probably 400 people in the summer of '01. We graduated a class of close to eighty people. So it was quite an attrition rate.

So after that three-week selection, if you are selected to be a Ranger, you go to a Ranger battalion. And I was selected to go to First Battalion, which is on Hunter Air Field, right near Savannah, Georgia. I spent six or eight months there as a private, sort of learning the ropes, before I was sent to Ranger school proper. Ranger school proper is a three-month course, starting at Fort Benning, and then you travel to Dahlonega, Georgia, to do three weeks in the mountains, and then to Florida to do three weeks in the swamps. Ranger school is tough; it's a three-month extended slog during which you have less food and less sleep than you would like, and you are expected to perform to a very high standard under close-to-combat positions. Yeah, it's a slog, but at the end of it, you get your Ranger tab, and you are eligible for promotion in the Ranger battalions.

On September 11, 2001, we were in an airplane hanger on our way to a training mission with a foreign nation; we were going to do a joint mission. We stopped over in an air hanger, and our first sergeant gathered us together and said, "Alright guys, terrorists have crashed two planes into the World Trade Center. The buildings have collapsed. We think they were Islamic terrorists." We didn't believe him, of course. We thought, "OK, this is part of the training scenario. Instead of going where we were going, now we're going to go somewhere in the Middle East and train with Israeli forces or something."

[He laughs.] But then we rigged some radios together, and we got the BBC World Service, and we figured out that in fact, yeah, the World Trade Center had been hit. So we were stuck there for a week or so, until they were able to bring us back home. Then, we just carried on training as usual, because we knew that within a short amount of time we would be deploying somewhere. Sure enough, before the end of the year, a contingent of Rangers was in Afghanistan.

Although Rangers started going to Afghanistan in '01 at the beginning of the war, my first tour was just after I graduated from Ranger school in '02. I went September through December/January of '02. I felt very ready to go, because I had just gotten through Ranger School, and I knew exactly what I was and wasn't capable of. I felt very well prepared, and I was going with a great team, with a great platoon, with a great group of soldiers. I wouldn't say I was exactly looking forward to what I was going to do, but I was ready for it.

There's a certain "desertness" to the area of Afghanistan where I was. Water is a scarce resource there, and up in the mountains they have these very complex irrigation systems that they've built to drive their farms. It was surprisingly barren. I thought it would be a little more fertile. Bagram in particular was very depressing. It's a great big plateau, actually quite beautiful, until you realize why it's such a completely empty plateau. It's because most of the land area has not yet been cleared of mines. There are land mines everywhere, and you just can't walk out of designated areas. That made a strong impression on me.

The people there are very hardy. They have a very strong sense of themselves and what they accomplished in the Soviet war. Every little village that we drove through there had, in the town center, a burned-out, rusted-out old Soviet tank that they had dragged in as sort of the monument in every village square. I think that's quite telling.

We did both mounted and unmounted patrols. So we would walk through the mountains, and we would also go on Humvee patrols along sort of major routes, and some minor routes. [He chuckles.] Well, the concept of "road" out there is an interesting one. We were conducting patrols in search of men, weapons, and equipment. In other words, looking for terrorists and munitions. We found both. Our base camp was mortared and shot at with rockets from time to time, and our patrols would also take fire. But it seemed to me that by the winter of 2002 the Taliban had been gone for a long time, for all intents and purposes. There was never any kind of organized attack on any of our units, for what that's worth. They were just sort of harassment attacks.

Brian was promoted to sergeant in 2003. He explained humbly that most Rangers are promoted early simply because they "are ready to be sergeants before their time." The comments on his evaluation read like boilerplate, but they are no less true: "exhibits a high standard of conduct, discipline and ethics; stands firm on his beliefs and convictions; totally dedicated to the goals of the Army; no sacrifice is too great."

My next combat deployment was to Iraq at the beginning of the war. We might have staged in late February 2003, but certainly we were there in March. My first incursion into Iraq was actually the night of April 1st for the Jessica Lynch rescue. It was tremendously quick. The staging, planning, and executing our mission happened within twenty-four hours of my chain of command being alerted. We did what we had to do. I was a member of the team that was detailed to retrieve the other nine American [casualties] from the site. We thought they were in the morgue. It turned out they were in shallow graves just outside the compound. It was an amazing display of teamwork. Everyone pulled together and got the job done in a tremendously short amount of time. We got out on schedule, despite having to dig up the Americans instead of retrieving them from the morgue.

I understand that there were reports [in the media] that we were carrying blank ammunition and that the whole thing was staged. I can't really speak for any of the other units that were involved, but, you know, we were shot at, and when you think of the fact that we were running short of cargo space coming over from the States to supply us with water, it seems very unlikely to me that there were any blank rounds in Iraq at all, let alone blank rounds taken on a combat mission behind enemy lines. So I have serious reservations about those reports. I was carrying live ammunition.

After that, I moved up to Baghdad and conducted patrols out of Baghdad International Airport. Again, these were all mounted patrols, and we were doing a variety of search missions—again, men, weapons and equipment mostly. Again, we found plenty of all of those, and morale was great. We were an elite, Special Operations unit with everything that entails: all the camaraderie, all the high morale, and all the high proficiency. So yeah, it was a great group of guys. Those friendships are gonna last a lifetime. That's the nature of the beast, you know. Shakespeare was not wrong when he talked about a band of brothers, and we're not wrong to keep it in the cliché of the language of today. It's true. The men you fight with under those conditions are your brothers, and nothing can ever change that.

After his tour in Iraq, Brian served a second tour in Afghanistan as a battalion liaison in the regimental command tent. "I got to see the battle from a very different point of view. I was briefing the colonel of the regiment every morning and coordinating battles as they were being fought. It was really a fascinating experience." After returning to the United States and receiving an honorable discharge from the army, Brian decided to come out publicly and explain why he opposes "Don't Ask, Don't Tell."

I was convinced and remain convinced that "Don't Ask, Don't Tell" is positively bad for our national security, as well as being unnecessarily discriminatory. I felt that I was actually in a unique position to help bring that to public consciousness. And I was so advised by a number of other former service members that had come out, by my family and friends, and we decided it was the right thing.

I knew what I was getting into, because I was openly gay when I enlisted. I knew I would have to stay in the closet if I wanted to keep my job, and I found that I did in fact want to keep my job. It was something that I loved doing, and it was something I felt I ought to do and those things didn't change over the four years of my enlistment. So I never really wanted to come out in that sense, because I wanted to keep my job. On the other hand, because of the close friendships that I was forming, I did want to come out to my friends, to my brothers, because ironically enough, the closer we got, the more I felt that was a wedge between us—that there was this large aspect of my life I wasn't sharing with them, and that was preventing me from bonding as fully and as effectively as I could have with them. After a couple of years I started to feel a little isolated by my homosexuality, and by the fact that I couldn't talk about it— that I couldn't share that aspect of my life with these guys. I became more and more withdrawn, more and more antisocial, and that was unfortunate, I think. I would have had a much fuller experience in the army if I had been allowed to serve openly, and as a result I might have even been a more effective soldier. I don't know, but certainly in terms of unit cohesion, I would have experienced more unit cohesion had I come out, not less.

One of the overriding reasons why I came out publicly was because in the winter of 2003 three flag officers came out: General Kerr, General Richard, and Admiral Steinman. These were the first flag officers—they were retired, but the first flag officers to come out. That made a very strong impression on me; it was on the front pages of a variety of papers, and I felt that if I could make some slight impression, as they had made a large impression on me, that I would be doing something worthwhile, so I did it. I received an overwhelmingly positive response as a result. The flag officers warned me actually that I would receive a lot of negative mail, and that hasn't happened at all. And the response has been overwhelmingly positive. I haven't received *any* hate mail.

At the time of this interview, Brian was living in Washington, D.C. He was working as an intern on Capitol Hill, where he joked that he was "saving the world, one cup of coffee at a time."

WE ALL BLEED THE SAME
An Interview with Robert Stout

There's no question that this humble young man from rural Ohio became a leader during his time in the service. After a deployment with NATO forces in Kosovo in 2002, Robert Stout first went to Iraq early in 2004. He was wounded in an ambush not far from the Tigris River. He had a few months to recuperate in Germany, and then he returned to Iraq to finish his enlistment. During that second deployment, Robert was promoted to sergeant, and he publicly came out as a gay man.

I'm Robert Leeding Stout, sergeant in the United States Army. I was born in North Ohio, grew up in Utica. I went to high school there, went to the same high school that my sisters, parents, and even my grandfather went to. My father spent eight years—from '59 to '67—in the air force in Germany and the southern United States. My sister was in the ROTC [Reserve Officers' Training Corps] program at Kent State University. She's at Lakenheath Air Base right now.

I've been asked a lot of times, especially by people in my unit, why I joined the military. I signed up originally in 1999 under the delayed enlistment program. I was a junior in high school. I have a pretty good sense of patriotism, and it seemed a pretty good way to get out, travel, see the world, and give a bit back to the nation. I mean it is the place I live. I want to protect it. I do love America, and I love Ohio. I went into the recruiter's office. They showed me the video of combat engineering, and my heart was set. I saw the guys in their armored personnel carriers, flying over the hill. You see the land mines exploding, the demolitions being used. It was on point, and I loved it. The more I talked to them, the more I liked it. They mentioned bonuses for signing up, life insurance policy, plus the college money when you get out and the VA benefits. I realized that it's a really good chance, one that doesn't really come along that often.

When I first signed up, they had the paper explaining the army's "Don't Ask, Don't Tell" policy. They sit down with you, make you read it, and ask if you have any questions. It seemed very straightforward to me at the time. Then you sign off this paper saying, "Yes, you understand it." When you get into basic training, they have a one-day training on sexual harassment, racial bigotry, and "Don't Ask, Don't Tell." When you get into the active army, it pretty much depends on your chain of command. I've had chains that would actually make us sit down for an hour or two, going over what you can say, what you can't say, what is considered discrimination, and what is considered harassment under the "Don't Ask, Don't Tell" policy. There's been other times when I've had chains of command going, "OK, if you suck dick, you're going to get discharged. The end." Which I thought was unfair for the lesbians. [He laughs.]

I still remember the first time I told one of my team leaders. It was actually at Fort Irwin. I was E-3, private first class, and he was a sergeant. At that time, all my pronouns were changed. "He" became "she," and the guy I dated at the time, I gave him a feminine name. So my team leader was asking me about her/him. We get talking, and it eventually got to the point where I thought, "This is just not worth it." So I'm like, "Hey Sarge, 'she' is a guy." The only thing he said after that was, "I need a cigarette." He got done smoking the cigarette, and he goes, "Damn it! That means my wife was right." And, shoot, after that we never had any trouble.

When I first got to Fort Hood, that first couple of months, I really didn't know anybody. I really didn't know any areas to go. After a while, just fiddling around on the Internet or listening to rumors and gossip, you eventually go, "OK, well he probably is, and she probably is." So you just start talking to them—like a regular human being. After a couple of weeks of just talking, they'll sit there and go, "Oh, I'm gay." I'm like, "Yeah, I know, that's why I've been talking to you." Or you meet people on the Internet, and it's like, "Where are you?" "Oh, I'm at Fort Hood." I'm like "Oh, that's cool, so am I. Let's go out and get drinks or something." Even in Iraq, there were quite a few gay and lesbian people in my battalion. While I was in Iraq, I was actually tasked out to a cavalry task force. My platoon was. The rest of the battalion was at a different post than us, and I would get emails from back in the battalion going, "Oh yeah, we got four or five guys together the other night. We tweezed eyebrows. We did nails." And I'm just sitting there thinking, "Wow! You're a bunch of sissy Marys."

Then, it's like, "I guess there's a bigger group of family than I thought was in here." That's when I really realized that it's really easy to meet them. It's kind of an underground to a point, where we have our own little—I hate to say—"secret society." Except we don't get the cool handshake or anything. We have no decoder rings. But it really is. We have our little places to go. It's just really nice that way and really supportive too. If anybody within your group of friends has a problem, then normally we all try to help out. It really dawns on you that you become a family within the family. Because the military is a family. You're always part of that. I can walk up to anybody now and say, "Oh, you were in the military." And we could have a thirty- or forty-minute conversation.

After 9/11 people did not know what to think. It got to the point where it was just mass paranoia. People were checking ID cards just to get into the barracks. Of course, to the junior enlisted, we're rolling our eyes, like, "Who's going to blow up the engineering barracks?" We just got put on every kind of guard you can imagine. Between guarding the barracks, the motor pools, the Post Exchange, the Shop Ex. But certain things did become lax. One kid I knew in Fort Hood was really open. There was always rumors going around about it. I remember one time, I was standing in the company office, and I heard the first sergeant yell out [in a gruff voice], "Where's my little gay driver? I need to go somewhere." Of course, we all just thought that was the funniest damn thing ever. He wasn't saying it in a mean way. He was just being a smart-ass. We thought that was funny because he knew he was gay, and nobody cared. I noticed that people got away with a lot more openness after that. People became a lot more relaxed, a lot more human, I guess. It finally dawned on people that we might actually be going to war sometime soon. Anybody could save your butt then.

In 2002 Robert was sent to Germany for a month before going to Kosovo with NATO peacekeeping forces for what was thankfully an uneventful deployment. He first went to Iraq in 2004.

In February, we deployed to Kuwait for a month. After Kuwait, we got in a big, long line of vehicles and marched north up into Iraq. I was there from March to May 2004 and then from July to just last February, so February '05. I was about an hour north of Baghdad and an hour east of Samarra. Just stuck way out in the middle of nowhere. It was probably about fifteen minutes from the Tigris River. There was a really beautiful area, right next to the Tigris, that had these date palms, just absolutely gorgeous. You go five minutes away from that, and it's nothing but sand. That's where we were stuck, in the sand. It was an old Iraqi air base. What we didn't bomb, we used.

We were a little engineer platoon. Our whole mission would be to go out and search the sides of roads for what we called improvised explosive devices (IEDs), which is just nothing but 155 millimeter artillery shells, two or three of them in one hole that the Iraqis fused with a timing device or with a remote det device, and they'd attempt to kill us with them. Or if they found a bunch of

Robert Stout signed up for the army to see the world.
He saw Iraq during his deployment there in 2004 and 2005.
Photo courtesy of Robert Stout.

explosives, weapons, or something in one area, they'd always call us out with the explosive ordnance disposal (EOD) team to either blow it up or bring it back. That was mainly our job.

On May 11, we were on a night mission. We got a call that they found a truck. They were not sure if there were explosives in it. This time, I was tasked out to a cavalry task force with my platoon. As the engineer platoon, we were the only people who really knew about demolitions, land mines, stuff of that nature. We were working with the explosive ordinance disposal team. We head out there. We check out the truck—not a damn thing in it. We were pissed.

It was about 11:30 at night. We were heading back. It was right down by the Tigris. There were a lot of tall stone fences and one- to two- to three-story homes that were just made out of mud brick. We were heading along on this little alley, which was just big enough to fit a Humvee. We were in the rear vehicle, and I was manning the M-2 Browning machine gun, sticking out of the middle of it. It was a factory up-armor, so it was a really nice truck.[11] The only thing I really remember is a loud flash off to my left side, pretty much the loudest noise I've ever heard in my life. After that, I was blinded by the explosion, which in the night vision goggles was insane.

I realized I couldn't see and jumped down in the vehicle, managed to grab underneath my chinstrap, flip my Kevlar off, and threw my glasses down. I rubbed my eyes real good and checked and thought, "OK, I could see spots. That's a good sign." It was about fifteen seconds, but it felt like fifteen years to me. Then I could see, and I looked down and my hands were just covered. I'm like, "What the hell?" I'm sitting there checking my face and I really didn't find anything. I found a little scratch on my cheek.

The driver of the Humvee—this is where the army training kicked in for that kid, thank God. We were always told, "When you get attacked like that, just hit the gas and haul ass out of the area. Stop maybe a click or two up the road, kilometer or two up the road. Then make sure everybody is alive. Well, we get up the road, and then everybody jumps out of the truck. I get out of the truck, and I look over. I remember this one kid we had. He came to the unit about a half a year before we deployed, real quiet, real calm, and he's just wandering around with this lost look on his face. I just look over at him and lose it. I just scream out, "Kimball, pull fuckin' guard!!" The kid's like [gets into a ready position]. I was like, "Well, I guess that worked."

Right about then, one of the guys came over and was like, "Hey, how are you doing, Stout?" I'm like, "Oh, I'm good. I'm good. What about the other guys?" "Oh man, you better check your arm out." And then I looked down, and of course I had a long sleeved shirt on, and I noticed that from here [just below the shoulder] down was nothing but blood. I thought, "Oh, that can't be good." I noticed a big chunk of God-knows-what sticking out of my arm. And I was like, "Why doesn't it hurt?" Naturally, five seconds later it kicked in. So we all decided, nobody's going to die this instant; it's faster just to drive back to post than call up the medevac chopper. We really hauled ass.

I should probably tell you what actually happened to the truck, huh? Best we can figure is a guy had jumped up from behind the stone wall with a rocket propelled grenade, fired it, it hit the rear quarter panel—which is about three feet from me—detonated on the smoke grenade launcher and just sent shrapnel through the armor plate of the vehicle past the head of one of my soldiers by about six inches, and just shot straight up past my squad leader's head by about six inches and slammed into the bulletproof glass.

Anyway, we got on post, and they rushed us straight to the aid station. The first thing they did was shoot me up with Demerol. I still remember that everybody tried to crowd into the aid station, because there were five people on that truck, and all five of us were wounded. The guy in the driver's seat actually ended up getting a piece of shrapnel sliced right across his butt and we still have not figured out how that happened. That poor kid never lived it down.

At this time, the Demerol's really kicking in. They're about done fixing up one leg, and I'm like, "Yeah, I remember back in Nam, I had my leg blown off. I had to gnaw the other one off to replace it." Everybody in there looks over at me and busts out laughing. I'm like [slurring his words], "Whassofunny?" Everybody's like, "Nothing, just do your thing." So I just lay there and I'm like, "Fuck y'all." The whole time, I'm just bleeding everywhere.

One of the guys there is like from deep woods Texas, major dipper too, always had his dip in, always had his can of Copenhagen with him. He's walking around the aid station, has his fly unbuttoned, and he can't hear. Both of his eardrums were blown out. He's just yellin' at the top of his lungs [using a Texas accent], "War's mah Copenhagen? Have ya' seen mah Copenhagen?" One of the other guys goes, "Hey, your dork's hangin' out." Of course, he couldn't hear, so the other guy yells louder: "Your dork's hangin' out!!" "Huh, I don't cur. War's mah Copenhagen?" And it's like, "Oh, my God, this is not the movies. You don't see this stuff in *Saving Private Ryan*."

After surgery and a couple of months in Germany, Robert was ready for duty again. He received a Purple Heart and, later, two promotions.

They sent me back down to Iraq in July. "You're good to go. You're obviously not insane that we know of and your arm's healed up pretty good." I didn't go back with the assumption that "I'm getting revenge." I didn't go back with the assumption that "I made it last time. Oh God, I'm going to die this time." I got to the point where I really refused to think about it. I absolutely would not. If somebody would try to bring it up while I was in Iraq, I would just block them out. It was something that I did not want to deal with at the time. After a while, I was able to start talking to my friends. I mean, hell, they were there with me. Who better to talk to?

So I eventually came to grips with it. I realized that I don't want to be there, but I am, and I would much rather be there with my guys, especially after I got promoted to sergeant. I got very possessive of my guys. They're still my soldiers even now. After being wounded, you really get a good sense of priority: "You know what? All of this other crap doesn't matter. Getting my guys home alive, that's the important thing."

A few months before his enlistment was up, while he was still in Iraq, Robert learned that supporters of legislation to repeal "Don't Ask, Don't Tell" were looking for active-duty gay and lesbian soldiers to talk about why this would be beneficial for the military.

I did not stay closeted all that long in the fairest since of that word. I wouldn't have been able to maintain it. I would not have been able to go as far as I did. I certainly wouldn't have been able to comprehend the stuff that happens in Iraq without both my straight friends knowing and my gay friends there to help me. They really are a safety net. Shared pain is lessened. That's always the case in my opinion. It's just so nice to have them there.

One day, a friend of mine came up to me and goes, "There's a guy I know, working with some other people that are trying to pass this bill in the House that repeals 'Don't Ask, Don't Tell.' They're looking for people that'll tell their story and to help out in any way that they can. I sat down with a lot of my straight friends and a lot of my gay friends. We all decided that somebody needs to say something. Somebody needs to stand up. I kind of looked around and was like, "Aw, you guys are all pussies. Fine. I'll do it."

I was already supposed to get out the thirty-first of May, and this was right at the end of March, beginning of April. So I figured, "I achieved my goal in the army. I did everything I wanted to do. I made it through Iraq. I was wounded. My troopers got through alive. There's nothing the army can do to me now that would change the fact that I did not let myself down. I did not let my soldiers down."

When I did come out and the news articles hit, it really was a relief. I had a lot of people come up and go, "Wow! That must have been really hard." To me, it was harder to lie the whole time. It was harder to go, "No, I'm not going out with you tonight, I'm going with uh, uh, JoAnn." After I came out, "JoAnn" could finally become John. I realized that nobody really had any problems with it. There was nobody who came up to me to say, "Oh, I'm never going to do what you say, because you're a faggot." Never had any trouble.

"Don't Ask, Don't Tell" was a really good stepping-stone, but we've moved past that. The generals of the army really need to get off their butts, get out of their uniforms, and go down and talk to the soldiers. If you're a civilian, and you go up to a soldier by himself, and go, "What do you think of 'Don't Ask, Don't Tell'? What do you think about gays in the military?" Most of the time, they'll say, "Fine, good. Let 'em." Especially the guys that have been to Iraq, because they know that gay people, lesbians, bisexuals, transgenders, they all bleed the same. They all can fire a gun. And they damn sure all die the same.

At the time of this interview, Robert Stout was attending an American Veterans for Equal Rights convention in Los Angeles. He planned to return to Ohio and possibly go back to school to get his college degree.

APPENDIX 1

A NOTE ON ORAL HISTORY AND EDITING INTERVIEWS

Oral history is the oldest tool of the historical profession. Before there was written history, there were stories—voices from the past intended to guide the present and future. Written history superseded oral tradition for a number of reasons. In an era before mass literacy, elites could control the writing of history and thus the history that was written. Yet written history was not simply an effort to harness the past to the agenda of present-day elites. The documentation of written history allowed for verification not always attainable with oral tradition. It was still possible to tell tall tales with documentary evidence, but it was not nearly as easy to get away with it.[1]

The advent of sound recordings in the twentieth century lent documentary power to oral tradition, while democratic social movements inspired historians to tell more than just the stories of "great men." The U.S. government launched a massive oral history project during the Great Depression to provide work for unemployed writers and also to record the experiences of ex-slaves who still had memories of their time in bondage. This slave narrative project undertaken by the Works Progress Administration could be seen as a precursor to the Veterans History Project, though (much to my chagrin) the Veterans History Project does not *pay* its interviewers as the WPA once did. Oral history projects gradually emerged at Columbia University, the University of California, and other institutions of higher education, but public support and professional interest in oral history largely languished in the years after World War II. Journalists, who had long relied on interviews for source material, were at the forefront of the oral history revolution in the 1960s and 70s. Studs Terkel and Alex Haley wove masterful interviews into social documents, biographies, and even historical novels.[2] Professional historians also returned to oral history around this same time in an attempt to tell the stories of individuals and groups who left few written records. Since the 1970s, academic contributions to the field of oral history have only multiplied, producing some excellent models not only of how to conduct interviews, but also of how to edit them for publication.[3]

Oral history is as much art as it is social science. This is most apparent in the actual process of the interview and editing for publication. The process of each interview is a dialogue; the questions are as important as the answers. For this project, I tried to ask simple, straightforward, but open-ended questions that let the veterans set the story-telling agenda as much as possible. I did not have a set script for each interview, but a core list of about fifteen to twenty prepared questions with five to ten additional ones unique to each interview. Another ten to fifteen spontaneous, follow-up questions usually emerged during the interviews. The core questions that I asked included variations on the following list:

> When and where were you born?
> What did your parents do for a living?
> Why did you decide to join the military?
> How did your family and friends feel about your joining the military?
> Had any of your relatives served?
> What was basic training like for you?
> What was your first assignment and where were you stationed?
> What was the average day like on base (or shipboard)?
> Did you ever feel that your life was in danger?
> What was your most memorable experience?
> How did your sexuality affect your military service?
> Did you know other service personnel who were gay or lesbian?
> Did you or others that you knew face discrimination because of your sexuality?
> How was the ban on homosexual service personnel enforced when you served?
> What did you think of the passage of "Don't Ask, Don't Tell"?
> Why did you leave the military?
> How did military service affect your life?
> Is there anything that I did not ask that you'd like to talk about?

By editing the questions from the interviews included in this volume, I aimed for a book that read more like a collective autobiography than a series of conversations. I wanted to keep the focus on the interviewees, not on the interviewer. With this in mind, I have included interview questions only when a transition from topic to topic seemed too jarring or difficult to follow without acknowledging the query that inspired it.

Early on in the project, I spoke with a lawyer who worked with the Servicemembers Legal Defense Network. On his advice, I warned interviewees that they might not want to talk about homosexual acts or relationships that they had while they were on active duty, and I avoided asking direct questions about these topics. Some interviewees, especially older veterans or those who had been discharged for being gay, felt free to discuss such topics anyway, but many of the younger veterans were more reticent. As a researcher, I was saddened by this gap in the narratives, but I felt that it was more important to get these men and women to go "on the record" as much as possible without hiding behind the cloak of anonymity or fearing retribution from the Department of Defense. One day, when the ban is finally lifted, this last veil of silence will be lifted as well.[4]

In addition to eliminating most of the questions from these interviews, honing raw transcripts of one- to two-hour interviews into readable narratives required a creative and arduous editing process. My primary goal in editing the interviews was to remain true to the substance and spirit of what was said, while making sure that the final product was a clear, concise, and linear story. With these goals in mind I added brief transition phrases, rearranged the order of certain answers, shortened some, and cut many more. Some sections of the transcripts required a fair amount of editing, because the natural rhythm of conversation does not always follow such a smooth story line, but others required almost no editing at all, as interviewees answered questions with long fluid narratives. Below, I've juxtaposed two sections from the transcript of Lisa Michelle Fowler's phenomenal interview with the edited versions that appear in this book. Comparing sections of the transcript to the published text gives a sense of the editorial choices that I made in compiling this volume.

TRANSCRIPT (SECTION 1)

STEVE ESTES: So after the R&R ended, you went back to the base?

LISA MICHELLE FOWLER: Correct. And I did mostly security duty.

SE: Yeah, now this base you were saying is called "Camp Jill." Is that where you had been the whole time?

LMF: It was not the whole time, but during the war—well, a little bit before the war and then during the war, that's where I mostly stayed at. There was a big huge camp area, bunch of trailers. There were these little trailers. They were probably about, I don't know, let's say 20 feet by—okay, we'll say 30 feet by I wanna say 15 feet wide. And there was three of us in each trailer. They also had shower trailers, where all they were, were trailers with showers in them and that's it. And there was a bunch of those trailers. I bet there was at least 300 of them. That's how big the camp was.

SE: So how many people, if you had to guess, were in Camp Jill?

LMF: Oh gosh, I'd say over a thousand.

SE: All women?

LMF: No. Just different units.

SE: So it's not called "Camp Jill" because it was an all-women camp?

LMF: No, it was just "Camp Jill" because there was a Camp Jack and a Camp Jill.

SE: What were relations like between the people in the other units? They were not all personnel units, right?

LMF: No, there was MPs, medics, it was just all rear units, you know, personnel, MPs, medics, dentists, you know stuff like that. We all got along real good.

SE: Did you know folks in those other units?

LMF: I got to know some people, of course after it was all said and done, I never really bothered to be in touch with anybody, but we had fun while we was there.

SE: Tell me about guard duty.

LMF: [pause] Well, it was guard duty, play solitaire. [laughs] It was just the open and closing of a gate, just stay up all night, because I had the night shift. And they were twelve hours shifts.

SE: And you're armed, I assume.

LMF: Oh, well, not really.

SE: Really?

LMF: They never gave us any real bullets.

SE: How come?

LMF: I never understood that. Never got any bullets.

SE: Not even rubber bullets?

LMF: Nope.

SE: So you just had a gun that was unarmed.

LMF: Exactly.

SE: Was that scary?

LMF: . . . Well, I had to assume that maybe they didn't think we was in that much danger, seeing as I got a gun with no—or a weapon, with no bullets in it. I mean, I was young. So I guess I could just point it at you and scare you to death. [laughs]

PUBLISHED TEXT (SECTION 1)

When Desert Storm started, I did mostly security duty at Camp Jill. There was a big huge camp area, bunch of trailers. There were these little trailers. They were probably about thirty feet by fifteen feet wide. And there was three of us in each trailer. They also had shower trailers. I bet there was at least 300 trailers with over a thousand people, all different units.

On guard duty, I'd just play solitaire. It was just the opening and closing of a gate, just stay up all night, because I had the night shift. And they were twelve-hour shifts. I had a weapon, but they never gave us any real bullets. I never understood that. I had to assume that maybe they didn't think we was in that much danger, seeing as I got a weapon, with no bullets in it. I mean, I was young. So I guess I could just point it at you and scare you to death. [She laughs.]

TRANSCRIPT (SECTION 2)

SE: So you know, one thing you were saying before—I don't mean to jump around a little bit, but I don't want to forget this—you were saying you were in the back area during the Gulf War, but that you were in the area with the Scuds.

LMF: Oh yes.

SE: Could you talk a little bit about that?

LMF: Oh yes. Ahh, let's see. Let's see, I was young, and I was already scared to death anyway. And I remember when the war started I was back on my little cruise ship and I didn't know nothing about Scuds or Patriot Missiles. I've heard about it but didn't know nothing about it, because I'm out here, Texas little secretary. But I remember that I think at the time I was pulling guard duty on days, or maybe I was still working in the office. But I remember being by myself at nighttime, and I remember—because my roommate, in the trailer, was working nights for some reason. And I was by myself, and I was listening to the Army radio station, and I was reading a Sidney Sheldon book. And all of a sudden, I heard these alarms go off. And I—kinda like a Tornado alarm is what it kinda sounded like—and it kind of scared me a little because they told us in training that once you open your chemical suit it only has about six hours of life. . . . So I'm debating, well, if I open it now, and it's a false alarm, then that's time off my chemical suit. So I don't know what to do. You know, I don't know if this is like a false alarm, you know. But it ended up being actually a real Scud. And our first sergeant came up and knocked on everybody's door. And of course I ain't in full MOP gear. I'm thinking that, you know—I don't know what I was thinking. I should have been in mop gear is what I should of been doing. But I was shaking so badly that I couldn't even put my pants on. My first sergeant had to help me put my MOP gear on. So it was pretty scary.

SE: When you say "mop gear" could you just say what that is?

LMF: Chemical wear, your chemical—

SE: It's M-O-P, is that—

LMF: "MOP." Yes, it's, uh, your chemical . . . your chemical—your whole chemical suit. Your boots, your charcoal suit, your mask and your gloves. and "MOP-4" is what we call it, when you're in total MOP gear. So . . .

SE: And did the Scud hit near the base?

LMF: Actually, what happened was it didn't really hit. I didn't know, but there was Patriot Missiles out there. And these Patriot Missiles actually hit the Scuds before they, you know—had them explode up there before they hit down here. So actually the "boom" was the Patriot Missile actually hitting the SCUD. You could smell, like whatever it was that—whatever it is that you smell when you—it wasn't a chemical bomb, thank God. Because it wouldn't have mattered with that kind. But you could actually smell whatever they put in the bomb. You know, like, I don't know what you'd call it: gunpowder? sulfur? I don't know.

SE: Whatever the explosives are.

LMF: Exactly. You could smell that, but never seen it because I was inside.

SE: Was that the only time that that happened while you were there?

LMF: No. It happened so many times that we actually got used to it.

PUBLISHED TEXT (SECTION 2)

I remember when the war started I didn't know nothing about Scuds or Patriot missiles. I'd heard about it, but didn't know nothing, because I'm a little secretary. But I remember that at the time I was pulling guard duty on days, or maybe I was still working in the office. But I remember being by myself at nighttime, because my roommate was working nights for some reason. I was listening to the army radio station, and I was reading a Sidney Sheldon book. All of a sudden, I heard these alarms go off—kinda like a tornado alarm—and it kind of scared me a little because they told us in training that once you open your chemical suit it only has about six hours of life. So I'm debating, "Well, if I open it now, and it's a false alarm, then that's time off my chemical suit." So I don't know what to do. But it ended up being a real Scud. Our first sergeant came up and knocked on everybody's door. Of course I ain't in full MOPP gear. That's your whole chemical suit—your boots, your charcoal suit, your mask, and your gloves. I was shaking so badly that I couldn't even put my pants on. My first sergeant had to help me put my MOPP gear on. It was pretty scary. I didn't know, but there was Patriot missiles out there. And these Patriot missiles actually hit the Scuds before they hit down here. The "boom" was the Patriot missile hitting the Scud. It wasn't a chemical bomb, thank God, but you could actually smell whatever they put in the bomb.

When you put on your chemical mask, you put it on your face. In order to clear it and seal it, you hold your hands on the sides of the thing and you blow out. If there's any chemicals, you're supposed to hold your breath while you put your mask on. So then you blow out to get the chemicals out of your mask and then put your hand in front of your face and suck in to make sure you get a good seal. So it's like [blows out breath] that. We had so many Scuds or so many incidents that we kind of got used to them after a while.

For scholars who would like to read the transcripts of these interviews in their entirety or listen/view the original interview tapes, copies have been deposited in the Veterans History Project collection at the Library of Congress in Washington, D.C., and the Gay, Lesbian, Bisexual, Transgender (GLBT) Historical Society in San Francisco, California.

In the end, I tried to make the interviews as accessible as possible, and although I cut much of the dialogue in the process, I hope that readers get a sense of who these veterans are and how they served their country. I also hope that readers of this book come to see the power of oral history. More than solitary seekers of historical truth, oral historians learn history from the people who made it. Undoubtedly, the people who shared their stories in this volume and with the Library of Congress made history. These were stories that they had long wanted to tell. All we had to do was ask.

APPENDIX 2
INTERVIEWEES

Below is a list of all of the veterans whom I interviewed. The two whose names are marked by an asterisk were interviewed by others for the Veterans History Project at the Library of Congress; they are listed here because I tell their stories in the book. Although not all of the people listed here are present in the text, each interviewee's story contributed in important ways to *Ask and Tell*. Thus all of these veterans deserve to be recognized and acknowledged.

Arnesen, Cliff
Bartron, Harry
Benfield, Tony
Ben-Shalom, Miriam
Boeckels, Stephen
Carpenter, Tom
Castleberry, Greg
Castro, John
Coleman, Charlotte
Crosby, Judith
DeLeo, Maurine McFerrin
Donovan, Jim
Dodd, Paul
Duwel, Patty
Estep, Jim
Fiola, Tom
Fiscus, Allan
Fowler, Lisa Michelle
Gerrits, Burt
Haas, Michael
Hall, Steve Clark
Hardy, Maurice
Harkness, Harry
Helwig, Bill
Hillman, Beth
Hughes, Brian

Job, Michael
Johnston, Chris
Jordan, Paul*
Kerr, Keith
Landes, Mark
Martin, Ken
Mendoza-Gleason, Ric*
Mooneyham, Greg
Moreno, Tony
Oscar, David
Patton, Vince
Peters, David
Petrie, Jeff
Puckett, Greer
Pruitt, Dusty
Richard, Virgil
Robbins, Bud
Samora, Ted
Shaddix, Elizabeth (Barry Gladstein)
Steinman, Alan
Stout, Robert
Taylor, Barbara
Taylor, Bill
Turner, Vince
Walker, Kary
Welch, John

Westrick, Edward
Winn, William
Wood, Perry
Voland, Howard
Vosbein, Brenda
Yeargan, Bob

NOTES

INTRODUCTION

1. For political and legal analysis of "Don't Ask, Don't Tell," see Aaron Belkin and Geoffrey Bateman, *Don't Ask, Don't Tell: Debating the Gay Ban in the Military* (Boulder, Colo.: Lynne Reinner Publishers, 2003); Janet E. Halley, *Don't: A Reader's Guide to the Military Anti-Gay Policy* (Durham, N.C.: Duke University Press, 1999); Gary L. Lehring, *Officially Gay: The Political Construction of Sexuality in the U.S. Military* (Philadelphia: Temple University Press, 2003); and Melissa Wells-Petry, *Exclusion: Homosexuals and the Right to Serve* (Washington, D.C.: Regnery Gateway, 1993).

2. For more on the regulation of speech and silence inherent in "Don't Ask, Don't Tell," see Judith Butler, *Excitable Speech: The Politics of the Performative* (London: Routledge Press, 1997), 103–26. Tobias Barrington Wolff, "Compelled Affirmations, Free Speech, and the U.S. Military's Don't Ask, Don't Tell Policy" *Brooklyn Law Review* 63 (1997): 1141–1211; and Wolff, "Political Representation and Accountability under Don't Ask, Don't Tell" *Iowa Law Review* 89 (2003–4): 1633–1716 (quote from 1638).

3. Public Law 106–380 created the Veterans History Project in 2000. For more information on the project, see <http://www.loc.gov/vets/> (August 2, 2006). WPA interviews with former slaves were published by George P. Rawick in *The American Slave: A Composite Autobiography* (Westport, Conn.: Greenwood, 1977). Tom Wiener, *Voices of War: Stories of Service from the Home Front and the Front Lines* (Washington, D.C.: National Geographic and the Library of Congress, 2004).

4. One of the first publications to emerge from this project was C. Dixon Osbourne, Cheryl Jacques, and A. J. Rogue, *Documenting Courage: Gay, Lesbian, Bisexual, and Transgender Veterans Speak Out* (Washington, D.C.: Human Rights Campaign, 2004).

5. Gary J. Gates, *Gay Men and Lesbians in the U.S. Military: Estimates from the Census 2000* (Washington: Urban Institute, 2004), iii–iv.

6. Allan Bérubé, *Coming Out under Fire* (New York: Free Press, 1990); Randy Shilts, *Conduct Unbecoming: Lesbians and Gays in the U.S. Military, Vietnam to the Persian Gulf* (New York: St. Martin's Press, 1993); Mary Ann Humphrey, *My Country, My Right to Serve: Experiences of Gay Men and Women in the Military, World War II to the Present* (New York: HarperCollins, 1990); Steven Zeeland, *Barrack Buddies and Soldier Lovers: Dialogues with Gay Young Men in the U.S. Military* (New York: Haworth Press, 1993); Zeeland, *Sailors and Sexual Identity: Crossing the Line between 'Straight' and 'Gay' in the U.S. Navy* (New York: Harrington Press, 1995); Zeeland, *The Masculine Marine: Homoeroticism in the U.S. Marine Corps* (New York: Har-

rington Press, 1996); Zsa Zsa Gershick, *Secret Service: Untold Stories of Lesbians in the Military* (Los Angeles: Alyson Books, 2005); and Belkin and Bateman, *Don't Ask, Don't Tell.*

CHAPTER ONE

1. For recent popular histories of World War II, see Stephen E. Ambrose, *Band of Brothers: E Company, 506th Regiment, 101st Airborne from Normandy to Hitler's Nest* (New York: Simon and Schuster, 2001); Ambrose, *Citizen Soldiers: The U.S. Army from the Normandy Beaches to the Bulge to the Surrender of Germany, June 7, 1944– May 7, 1945* (New York: Simon and Schuster, 1998); and Tom Brokaw, *The Greatest Generation* (New York: Random House, 1998). For a more critical account based on oral history, see Studs Terkel, *"The Good War": An Oral History of World War II* (New York: Pantheon, 1984).

2. Allan Bérubé, *Coming Out under Fire: The History of Gay Men and Women in World War Two* (New York: Free Press, 1990), 23. Another gay veteran of World War II, Ted Allenby, expressed it even more succinctly: "Like every other American, I was superpatriotic." Quoted in Terkel, *"The Good War,"* 179.

3. Discussion of the Pearl Harbor veteran in Tim Bergling, "Coming Out of World War II," *Advocate*, June 8, 2004, 32–35. Role of psychiatric screening, draft numbers, and estimates of gay men who served are from Bérubé, *Coming Out under Fire*, 3, 8–10, 14–20.

4. Bérubé, *Coming Out under Fire*, 6–7, 113–14, 125–26.

5. For an analysis of the WAC image, see Leisa D. Meyer, *Creating GI Jane: Sexuality and Power in the Women's Army Corps during World War II* (New York: Columbia University Press, 1996), 6–8. Pat Bond quote from *Word Is Out* transcript, p. 6, file 5, box 3, Pat Bond Papers, San Francisco Public Library.

6. Meyer, *Creating GI Jane*, 9–10, 177.

7. Malcolm F. Willoughby, *The Coast Guard in World War II* (New York: Arno Press, 1980), 18–20; Robert T. Nelson, *Women in the Coast Guard Study* (Washington, D.C.: Department of Transportation, 1990), II-1–II-5.

8. Bérubé, *Coming Out under Fire*, 138–40.

9. Bergling, "Coming Out of World War II," 32.

10. Ed Armstrong, chairman of the board of the Maine Aviation Historical Society, conducted this interview with Paul Jordan for the Veterans History Project, Library of Congress, in 2003.

11. Three days after the initial D-Day invasion.

12. Burt Gerrits's story in this chapter is a composite of two interviews, one with the author and one with Allan Bérubé. Both interviews are housed in the Veterans History Project collections at the Library of Congress and in the Gay, Lesbian, Bisexual, Transgender Historical Society in San Francisco.

13. During the war, Charlotte Coleman was married and went by the name of Russell. She did not talk about her husband in our interview.

14. Here, Coleman refers to the historical practice, dating back to the Revolutionary War era, of "drumming out" soldiers for dishonorable acts.

CHAPTER TWO

1. The discharge figures are from Randy Shilts, *Conduct Unbecoming: Lesbians and Gays in the U.S., Military Vietnam to the Persian Gulf* (New York: St. Martin's Press, 1993), 70.
2. John D'Emilio, "The Homosexual Menace: The Politics of Sexuality in Cold War America," in D'Emilio, *Making Trouble: Essays on Gay History, Politics, and the University* (New York: Routledge Press, 1992), 61–62. Using overall figures for the U.S. armed forces, D'Emilio argues that gay discharges were actually on the rise in the late 1940s and early 1950s.
3. Ibid., 58–60. See also John D'Emilio, *Sexual Politics, Sexual Communities: The Making of a Homosexual Minority in the United States*, 2nd ed. (Chicago: University of Chicago Press, 1998), 40–53; Allan Bérubé, *Coming Out under Fire: The History of Gay Men and Women in World War Two* (New York: Free Press, 1990), 268–69; and David K. Johnson, *The Lavender Scare: The Cold War Persecution of Gays and Lesbians in the Federal Government* (Chicago: University of Chicago, 2004). Monica Kehoe was one of the unfortunate individuals caught up in the lavender scare. She lost her job at the United Nations when she was arrested for "necking" with a woman in New York City in 1950. Since the UN did not explain why they fired her, Kehoe immediately got another job working for the U.S. government as a Korean language specialist in Tokyo. Monica Kehoe interviewed by Peg Cruikshank and Allan Bérubé (1981); transcript at the Gay, Lesbian, Bisexual, Transgender Historical Society, San Francisco.
4. Bérubé, *Coming Out under Fire*, 268; and Johnson, *The Lavender Scare*, 9–10.
5. Gary L. Lehring, *Officially Gay: The Political Construction of Sexuality by the U.S. Military* (Philadelphia: Temple University Press, 2003), 75–80. See also Elizabeth Lutes Hillman, *Defending America: Military Culture and the Cold War Court-Martial* (Princeton: Princeton University Press, 2005).
6. D'Emilio, "Homosexual Menace," 61.
7. D'Emilio, *Sexual Politics, Sexual Communities*, 23–39. See also Alfred Kinsey, *Sexual Behavior in the Human Male* (Philadelphia: W. B. Saunders, 1948); and Kinsey, *Sexual Behavior in the Human Female* (Philadelphia: W. B. Saunders, 1953).
8. Cory was actually Edward Sagarin, who would later become a professor at the City University of New York. Quoted in Martin Duberman, "The 'Father' of the Homophile Movement," in Duberman, *Left Out: The Politics of Exclusion, Essays, 1964–1999* (New York: Basic Books, 1999), 69–70.
9. For more on the subversive nature of gay themes in the literature of the Cold War era, see Robert J. Corber, *Homosexuality in Cold War America: Resistance and the Crisis of Masculinity* (Durham, N.C.: Duke University Press, 1997). For more on the Mattachine Society and the Daughters of Bilitis, see D'Emilio, *Sexual Politics, Sexual Communities*.

10. D'Emilio, *Sexual Politics, Sexual Communities*, 150–55. See also an interview with Frank Kameny in the Veterans History Project, Library of Congress.

11. "Report of the Board Appointed to Prepare and Submit Recommendations to the Secretary of the Navy for the Revision of Policies, Procedures and Directives Dealing with Homosexuals" (1957), reprinted in *Homosexuality and the Military: A Sourcebook of Official, Uncensored Documents* (Upland, Pa.: Diane Publishing, 1993), 5, 7–8. The report was kept secret by the U.S. Navy until a court ordered its release in 1977. For more on this, see Bérubé, *Coming Out under Fire*, 277–78.

12. Katia Boré-Falecker, Lara Ballard, and Lee Lampos of American Veterans for Equal Rights conducted this interview of Ric Mendoza-Gleason for the Veterans History Project, Library of Congress, in 2003.

CHAPTER THREE

1. Though historians debate what actually occurred during the Gulf of Tonkin incident in the summer of 1964, there is no question that President Lyndon Johnson used the incident to garner support for a long-planned American military intervention. For draft figures, see "Induction Statistics," Selective Service System, <http://www.sss.gov/induct.htm> (July 28, 2005).

2. "Hoaxosexual" advice quoted in Randy Shilts, *Conduct Unbecoming: Lesbians and Gays in the U.S. Military, Vietnam to the Persian Gulf* (New York: St. Martin's Press, 1993), 67–68. In fact, Shilts reported that only 1 percent of the 5 million young men judged unfit for service during the Vietnam War era draft after the physical exam were exempted because of a "moral defect," including homosexuality. Pete Zavala interviewed by Amelia Zavala (2005), 4; transcript in author's possession. For more on draft resistance, see Michael S. Foley, *Confronting the War Machine: Draft Resistance during the Vietnam War* (Chapel Hill: University of North Carolina Press, 2003).

3. For more on Watkins, see Shilts, *Conduct Unbecoming*, 60–65, 155–56, 395–98, and 729–30.

4. The Society for Individual Rights quotation is from Shilts, *Conduct Unbecoming*, 67.

5. Ian Lekus, "Queer and Present Dangers: Homosexuality and American Antiwar Activism during the Vietnam Era" (Ph.D. diss., Duke University, 2003). In his introduction, Lekus offers a detailed analysis of this quote (1–39).

6. Ibid., v–vi, 43.

7. Ibid., 4.

8. For a brief overview of the emergence of GLF and its connections to the antiwar movement, see John D'Emilio, *Sexual Politics, Sexual Communities: The Making of a Homosexual Minority in the United States, 1940–1970*, 2nd ed. (Chicago: University of Chicago Press, 1999), 231–39. A 1966 Armed Forces Day demonstration in San Francisco was advertised with a flier that read: "The draft dodges homosexuals— homosexuals don't dodge the draft!" The flier is reprinted in Allan Bérubé, *Coming Out under Fire: The History of Gay Men and Women in World War Two* (New York:

Free Press, 1990), 209, 274. The short-lived Committee to Fight Exclusion of Homosexuals from the Armed Forces was founded in Los Angeles in 1968, but its goals quickly shifted to opposition to the war and gay service in it. Shilts, *Conduct Unbecoming*, 66.

9. FMLN refers to Farabundo Martí para la Liberación Nacional, a leftist resistance movement in El Salvador.

CHAPTER FOUR

1. David Lipsky, *Absolutely American: Four Years at West Point* (New York: Houghton Mifflin, 2003), 6.

2. Ibid., 7, 19. As Tom Carpenter's interview reveals, this joke has been picked up by other academy alumni.

3. John Lovell, *Neither Athens nor Sparta? The American Service Academies in Transition* (Bloomington: Indiana University Press, 1979), 9–10, 16–17, 38, 179, 207, 215. Helen Rogan, *Mixed Company: Women in the Modern Army* (New York: G. P. Putnam's Sons, 1981), 188.

4. Lipsky, *Absolutely American*, 175–76.

5. Ibid., 50. Linda Francke Bird, *Ground Zero: The Gender Wars in the Military* (New York: Simon and Schuster, 1997), 23, 216.

6. Allen B. Bishop, "Gays in the Military: It's a Question of Liberty," *Army Times*, March 14, 2005.

7. The lyrics for "The Queen Berets" (1993) by Pinkert and Bowden begin with the following stanza: "Falling fairies from the sky. / I broke a nail, Oh I could cry. / Don't you like how my tushy sways? / We are the fags of the Queen Berets." Later verses blame Clinton for the queering of the military. The tune is based on the "Ballad of the Green Berets" by Sergeant Barry Sadler (1965).

8. For more on the 1999 beating of Barry Winchell, see the introduction to chapter 9.

CHAPTER FIVE

1. Noncommissioned officer quoted in Melissa S. Herbert, *Camouflage Isn't Only for Combat: Gender, Sexuality, and Women in the Military* (New York: New York University Press, 1998), 2, 55.

2. Most primary and secondary accounts of women in the military from World War II to the Gulf War reference the false dichotomy of the "dyke or whore" and analyze the relationship between gender and sexuality in the military. See Helen Rogan, *Mixed Company: Women in the Army* (New York: G. P. Putnam's Sons, 1981), 96; Leisa D. Meyer, *Creating GI Jane: Sexuality and Power in the Women's Army Corps* (New York: Columbia University Press, 1996); Meyer, "The Myth of Lesbian (In)-Visibility: World War II and the Current 'Gays in the Military' Debate" in *Modern American Queer History*, ed. Allida M. Black, (Philadelphia: Temple University Press, 2001), 271–81; Linda Bird Francke, *Ground Zero: Gender Wars in the Military* (New York: Simon and Schuster, 1997), 166–67, 177; Joshua S. Goldstein, *War and*

Gender: How Gender Shapes the War System and Vice Versa (Cambridge: Cambridge University Press, 2002), 96, 379; and Zsa Zsa Gershick, *Secret Service: Untold Stories of Lesbians in the Military* (Los Angeles: Alyson Books, 2005), 11, 93, 95, 205. As Ziva Mataric, a lesbian who served in the air force from 1986 to 1997, said to Gershick, "Basically I was told that I had to sleep with someone on the team to prove that I wasn't a lesbian" (205).

3. Rogan, *Mixed Company*, 156.

4. Vosbein quoted in Gershick, *Secret Service*, 284.

5. See the chronology of milestones in Dorothy Schneider and Carl J. Schneider, *Sound Off! American Military Women Speak Out* (New York: Paragon House, 1992), 293–96. The journalist Helen Rogan interviewed many of the women involved in the integrated basic training experiment; several of these women were lesbians. Rogan, *Mixed Company*, 96–97. The army ended the experimental integration of basic training because they feared an increase in fraternization and a lowering of physical standards for male recruits. Herbert, *Camouflage Isn't Only for Combat*, 15. Goldstein offers a brief overview of shifting women's roles in the military during the 1970s and early 80s, but he cautions that the numbers of women in the service advanced much faster than their roles in the service. Goldstein, *War and Gender*, 41–42.

6. In fact, even though the proportions of women in the armed services gradually grew to 10 percent during the 1980s, two-thirds of military women continued to work in jobs traditionally tied to their gender, including clerical/administrative positions, health care, communications, and service/supply positions. Goldstein, *War and Gender*, 103.

7. As late as the Gulf War, marine training for women included "instruction in hair care, techniques of make-up application, guidance on poise, and etiquette." Francke, *Ground Zero*, 156.

8. Randy Shilts, *Conduct Unbecoming: Lesbians and Gays in the U.S. Military, Vietnam to the Persian Gulf* (New York: St. Martin's Press, 1993), 414–20.

9. Shilts argues that even though lesbians were probably a higher percentage of their gender in the military than was true of gay men, their disproportionately high discharge rate bespeaks a level of discomfort with women in the military in general. Ibid., 419; Gershick, *Secret Service*, 95.

10. Herbert, *Camouflage Isn't Only for Combat*, 86, 94.

11. According to a General Accounting Office (GAO) report, women's discharge rates for homosexuality were two to three times as high as their proportion in the armed services during the 1980s. Government Accounting Office, *Defense Force Management: Statistics Related to DoD's Policy on Homosexuality* (Washington, D.C.: GAO/NSIAD-92-98S, 1992), 21, 63–64. For figures from the 1990s, see Audrey Denson and Judy Rolfe, *10 Year Timeline of "Don't Ask, Don't Tell,"* (Washington, D.C.: Servicemembers Legal Defense Network, 2004).

12. Herbert, *Camouflage Isn't Only for Combat*, 128.

13. Brenda related a slightly different version of this story to me. The dialogue here is from an interview she did with Zsa Zsa Gershick, published in the latter's book, *Secret Service*, 283.

CHAPTER SIX

1. Randy Shilts, *Conduct Unbecoming: Lesbians and Gays in the U.S. Military, Vietnam to the Persian Gulf* (New York: St. Martin's Press, 1993), 356, 378, 387, 426; Gary Lehring, *Officially Gay: The Political Construction of Sexuality in the U.S. Military* (Philadelphia: Temple University Press, 2003), 131–32; and Wilbur Scott and Sandra Carson Stanley, eds., *Gays and Lesbians in the Military: Issues Concerns, and Contrasts* (New York: Aldine de Gruyter, 1994), xiii.

2. Steven M. Gillon, *The American Paradox: A History of the United States since 1945* (New York: Houghton Mifflin, 2003), 350.

3. Steve Zeeland, *Barrack Buddies and Soldier Lovers: Dialogues with Gay Young Men in the U.S. Military* (New York: Harrington Park Press, 1993), 75, 101–3.

4. Steve Yetiv, *The Persian Gulf Crisis* (Westport, Conn.: Greenwood, 1997), 5–10.

5. For more on the comparison between Hussein and Hitler, see the August 1990 article by William Safire titled "The Hitler Analogy," reprinted in *The Gulf War Reader: History, Documents, Opinions*, ed. Micah L. Sifry and Christopher Cerf (New York: Times Books, 1991), 210. For the debate in Congress, see the *Congressional Record*, 102nd Congress, 1st sess., January 10–12, 1991.

6. Jean Edward Smith, *George Bush's War* (New York: Henry Holt, 1992), 9; Thomas Kearny and Eliot A. Cohen, *Gulf War Air Power Survey: Summary Report* (Washington, D.C.: Office of the Secretary of the Air Force, 1993), 5–7. For more on the units that Landes served with, see Richard Swain, *Lucky War: Third Army in Desert Storm* (Fort Leavenworth, Kans.: U.S. Army Command and General Staff College Press, 1997).

7. The 1982 report is quoted in Joshua Goldstein, *War and Gender: How Gender Shapes the War System and Vice Versa* (Cambridge: Cambridge University Press, 2001), 93.

8. Hedrick Smith, ed., *The Media and the Gulf War* (Washington, D.C.: Seven Locks Press, 1992), 4–12, 45–47; W. Lance Bennet and David L. Paletz, eds., *The Media, Public Opinion, and U.S. Foreign Policy in the Gulf War* (Chicago: University of Chicago Press, 1994), 8, 149–63; Hamid Mowlana, George Gerbner, and Herbert I. Schiller, eds., *Triumph of the Image: The Media's War in the Persian Gulf, a Global Perspective* (Boulder, Colo.: Westview Press, 1992).

9. For a discussion of stop-loss, see Gary Lehring, *Officially Gay*, 1–4. Lehring implies that stop-loss officially included a halt in gay discharges, but this was not official policy.

10. SANDY is the air force call sign for rescue escort pilots trained to locate pilots and planes that have crashed or have been shot down.

11. Mission Oriented Protective Posture (MOPP) is the term used for chemical protection suits.

CHAPTER SEVEN

1. Matlovich interview in Mary Ann Humphrey, *My Country, My Right to Serve: Experiences of Gay Men and Women in the Military, World War II to the Present* (New York: HarperCollins, 1990), 151. Leonard Matlovich Birth Certificate Folder 75, box 2; Recommendation for AF Commendation Medal (February 1966) Folder 6, box 3; Leonard Matlovich Papers owned by the Gay Lesbian Bisexual Transgender (GLBT) Historical Society, temporarily housed at the San Francisco Public Library.

2. Sergeant Performance Report (June 14, 1973 to June 13, 1974), box 2, Matlovich Papers.

3. Andrew Kokind, "The Boys in the Barracks," *New Times*, August 8, 1975, 19–27; "Gays on the March" *Time*, September, 8, 1975, 33–43; and Lesley Oelsner, "Homosexual Is Fighting Military Ouster," *New York Times*, May 25, 1975, 1, 24.

4. U.S. District Court Opinion of the Honorable Gerhard A. Gesell, July 16, 1976, file 58, box 2; Appellant Brief by David F. Addlestone, May 17, 1979, file 56, box 2; and Gregory Gordon, UPI Wire Story on Matlovich, November 24, 1980, file 64, box 2, Matlovich Papers.

5. Wilbur J. Scott and Sandra Carson Stanley, eds., *Gays and Lesbians in the Military: Issues, Concerns, and Contrasts* (New York: Aldine de Gruyter, 1994): David Burrelli, "An Overview of the Debate on Homosexuals in the U.S. Military," 19; Garry L. Rolison and Thomas K. Nakayama, "Defensive Discourses: Blacks and Gays in the U.S. Military," 123; Lawrence Korb, "Evolving Perspectives on the Military's Policy on Homosexuals: A Personal Note," 221. Department of Defense Directive 1332.14, *Federal Register*, vol. 46, no. 19 (July 29, 1981), 9571–78. For more on the limitations of the comparison between the discourse surrounding the ban on gays and the racial segregation of the armed forces, see Alycee J. Lane, "Black Bodies/Gay Bodies: The Politics of Race in the Gay/Military Debate," *Callaloo* 17, no. 4 (1994): 1074–88.

6. Frederick W. Hagan (Chaplain, USA, Assistant) letter to Chaplain Charles O. Dutton (Fort Bliss, Texas) August 17, 1943; and William R. Arnold (Chaplain, Major General) to Chaplain William P. Byrnes (Fort McDowell, California), January 11, 1945, file 10, box 13, World War II Project Papers, GLBT Historical Society.

7. When Paul Dodd came out as a gay man, he was no longer welcome in the Southern Baptist fold. In 1993 the Southern Baptist Convention promised to eject congregations and pastors who "endorse homosexual behavior." See Don Lattin, "Southern Baptists Take Drastic Action on Gays," *San Francisco Chronicle*, June 16, 1993.

8. Susan Yoachum, "Clinton for the Record," *San Francisco Chronicle*, July 20, 1993.

9. Clinton gives the estimated cost of the ban and his personal take on this meeting in his memoirs. Bill Clinton, *My Life* (New York: Knopf, 2004), 482–87. See also Eric Schmitt, "Clinton Aides Seek Indirect Solution to Gay-Rights Rift," *New York Times*, January 13, 1993; and Schmitt, "Joint Chiefs Fighting Clinton Plan to Allow Homosexuals in Military," *New York Times*, January 23, 1993.

10. Sharon Cohen, "Marines Arrested in Gay Attack," *San Francisco Sentinel*, February 4, 1993. See also Larry Rohter, "Open Hostility to Homosexuals outside Navy Base," *New York Times*, January 31, 1993.

11. "Gay Sailor Tells of a 'Living Hell,'" *New York Times*, March 8, 1993; "Gay Sailor's Killer Had 'No Regrets,'" *San Francisco Chronicle*, May 26, 1993; and "Gay Sailor's Killer Given Life Sentence," *San Francisco Chronicle*, May 27, 1993. The second assailant was granted immunity for testifying against Terry Helvey, and Helvey did apologize to Allen Schindler's mother at the sentencing hearing.

12. For analysis of the Senate hearings aboard the *Montpelier*, see Gary L. Lehring, *Officially Gay: The Political Construction of Sexuality by the U.S. Military* (Philadelphia: Temple University Press, 2003), 126–28.

13. For more on Nunn's views of the ban, see "Excerpts from the News Conference by Clinton and Nunn," *New York Times*, January 30, 1993. Kate Dyer, a congressional staffer in 1993, believed that part of Nunn's motivation was competition with Clinton. Both Nunn and Clinton were moderate southern politicians with presidential aspirations, Dyer points out, speculating that Nunn wanted to teach the idealistic president a lesson about the legislative process. Kate Dyer interview by Lee Jenkins (1994), GLBT Historical Society.

14. Carolyn Lochhead, "Gays Denounced and Defended at Dellums' Lively Hearing," *San Francisco Chronicle*, May 5, 1993; and "Rep. Dellums Assails New Gay GI Policy," *San Francisco Chronicle*, July 22, 1993. For a full transcript of the House hearings, see "Policy Implications of Lifting the Ban on Homosexuals in the Military: Hearings before the Committee on Armed Services, House of Representatives," *Congressional Record*, 103rd Congress, 1st sess., May 4–5, 1993.

15. The scholar in question, Roger Wilkins, was quoted in Alycee J. Lane, "Black Bodies/Gay Bodies: The Politics of Race in the Gay/Military Debate," *Callaloo* 17, no. 4 (1994): 1086. Lane is primarily critical of the comparison between black and gay rights in the "Don't Ask, Don't Tell" debate.

16. Powell quote cited in Charles Moskos Jr., "From Citizens' Army to Social Laboratory," in Scott and Stanley, *Gays and Lesbians in the Military*, 63. For more on Powell's position, see Eric Schmitt, "Clinton Aides Seek Indirect Solution to Gay-Rights Rift," *New York Times*, January 13, 1993; Scmitt "Joint Chiefs Fighting Clinton Plan to Allow Homosexuals in Military," *New York Times*, January 23, 1993; and Anthony Lewis, "The Powell Factor on Gays in the Military," *San Francisco Chronicle*, June 16, 1993. For more on the comparison between race and sexuality in the military, see Garry L. Rolison and Thomas K. Nakayama, "Defensive Discourses: Blacks and Gays in the U.S. Military," in Scott and Stanley, *Gays and Lesbians in the Military*, 121–33.

17. Polling data reported in Eric Schmitt, "Pentagon Chief Warns Clinton on Gay Policy," *New York Times*, January 25, 1993; "Public Views of Gays in the Military," *San Francisco Chronicle*, January 28, 1993. Ten years later, in 2003, a Gallup Poll reported that 79 percent of Americans supported gays and lesbians serving openly

in the U.S. armed forces. Servicemembers Legal Defense Network, *10th Annual Report on "Don't Ask, Don't Tell"* (Washington, D.C., 2003). Clinton acknowledged his reliance on these polls. See Clinton, *My Life*, 485.

18. Susan Yoachum, "Clinton for the Record," *San Francisco Chronicle*, July 20, 1993; Clinton, *My Life*, 514. For much more detail on the "Don't Ask, Don't Tell" controversy and legislation, see Lehring, *Officially Gay*; Aaron Belkin and Geoffrey Bateman, *Don't Ask, Don't Tell: Debating the Gay Ban in the Military* (Boulder, Colo.: Lynne Reinner Publishers, 2003); Janet E. Halley, *Don't: A Reader's Guide to the Military Anti-Gay Policy* (Durham: Duke University Press, 1999); and Melissa Wells-Petry, *Exclusion: Homosexuals and the Right to Serve* (Washington, D.C.: Regnery Gateway, 1993).

19. After Paul visited Little Rock Central High School in 2001, the principal invited him to walk with the graduating seniors at the end of the school year. At the school's graduation ceremony in May 2002, he was the first person to receive a diploma.

20. "David" is a pseudonym for the chaplain's assistant whom Paul knew.

CHAPTER EIGHT

1. *Talk of the Nation*, National Public Radio, transcript of December 17, 2003, program, 2.

2. John Files, "Rules on Gays Exact a Cost in Recruiting, a Study Finds," *New York Times*, February 24, 2005.

3. Quoted in C. Dixon Osbourne, Cheryl Jacques, and A. J. Rogue, "Documenting Courage: Gay, Lesbian, Bisexual, and Transgender Veterans Speak Out" (Washington, DC: Human Rights Campaign, 2004), 3. See also the "Gays in the Military" episode on the *Newshour with Jim Lehrer*, Public Broadcasting System, January 6, 2000.

4. *Talk of the Nation*, National Public Radio, transcript of December 17, 2003, program, 21, 22. Other flag officers who oppose "Don't Ask, Don't Tell" include Lieutenant General Claudia Kennedy (U.S. Army, Retired), Brigadier General Evelyn "Pat" Foote (U.S. Army, Retired), and Major General Charles "Bud" Starr Jr., (U.S. Army Reserves, Retired).

5. Created in 1950 and implemented in 1951, the Uniform Code of Military Justice (UCMJ) established a legal framework for enforcement of military rules and regulations. Article 125 of the UCMJ makes "unnatural carnal copulation with another person of the same or opposite sex" a crime punishable by court-martial.

6. In 1969, when police raided the Stonewall Inn, a gay bar in New York City, the bar's patrons decided to fight back. The incident is often cited as the spark of the modern gay liberation movement.

7. When he won a position as San Francisco city supervisor in 1977, Harvey Milk, a Korean War veteran, became the first openly gay politician to win elected office in the United States. George Mosconi, a liberal friend and ally of Milk, was the mayor at the time. Both were gunned down in a tragic shooting in 1978.

8. Allen Schindler's death at the hands of his fellow sailors in 1992 and Barry Winchell's death at the hands of other soldiers in 1999 are both widely viewed as hate crimes. After Winchell's death, the Department of Defense added "Don't Harass" to the "Don't Ask, Don't Tell" policy.

CHAPTER NINE

1. C.Dixon Osbourne, Cheryl Jacques, and A. J. Rogue, *Documenting Courage: Gay, Lesbian, Bisexual, and Transgender Veterans Speak Out* (Washington, D.C.: Human Rights Campaign, 2004).
2. Robert D. Kaplan, *Balkan Ghosts: A Journey through History* (New York: Vintage, 1994).
3. Thomas Hackett, "The Execution of Private Barry Winchell: The Real Story behind the 'Don't Ask, Don't Tell' Murder," *Rolling Stone*, March 2, 2002, 80–88, 108.
4. Gary L. Lehring, *Officially Gay: The Political Construction of Sexuality in the U.S. Military* (Philadelphia: Temple University Press, 2003), 117–18.
5. Anthony H. Cordesman, *The Lessons of Afghanistan: War Fighting, Intelligence, and Force Transformation* (Washington, D.C.: Center for Strategic and International Studies, 2002).
6. John Keegan, *The Iraq War* (New York: Knopf, 2004), 234. Todd S. Purdum, *A Time of Our Choosing: America's War in Iraq* (New York: Henry Holt, 2003), 9, 21–22.
7. Purdum, *Time of Our Choosing*, 132–43, 165–73; and Rick Bragg, *I Am a Soldier Too: The Jessica Lynch Story* (New York: Knopf, 2003).
8. Keegan, *Iraq War*, 1.
9. The homemade bombs or IEDs were becoming the weapons of choice for Iraqi insurgents during 2004 and 2005. In 2004 there were 5,607 insurgent attacks with homemade bombs, and the following year there were 10,593 such attacks. In 2005 nearly half of the Americans killed in action were victims of IEDs (407 out of 846). Eric Schmitt, "Pentagon Widens Program to Foil Bombings in Iraq," *New York Times*, February 6, 2006.
10. Discharge statistics available in Servicemembers Legal Defense Network, *Annual Report* (Washington, D.C., 2005).
11. According to GlobalSecurity.org, an "up-armored" Humvee "includes 200-pound steel-plated doors, steel plating under the cab and several layers of bonded, ballistic-resistant glass to replace zip-up plastic windows" (http://www.globalsecurity.org/military/systems/ground/hmmwvua.htm, accessed October 24, 2006).

APPENDIX ONE

1. For more on the history, historiography, and methodology of oral history, see Michael Frisch, *A Shared Authority: Essays on the Craft and Meaning of Oral History* (Albany: State University of New York Press, 1990); Robert Perks and Alistair Thomson, *The Oral History Reader* (London: Routledge Press, 1998); and Donald Ritchie, *Doing Oral History: A Practical Guide* (Oxford: Oxford University Press, 2003).

2. Studs Terkel, *Hard Times: An Oral History of the Great Depression* (New York: Pantheon, 1970); Terkel, *"The Good War": An Oral History of World War II* (New York: Pantheon, 1984); Alex Haley (with Malcolm X), *Autobiography of Malcolm X* (New York: Grove Press, 1965); and Alex Haley, *Roots* (Garden City, N.Y.: Doubleday, 1976). For a critical reading of this type of popular oral history by academic historians, see Michael Frisch, "Oral History and *Hard Times*" in *A Shared Authority*, 5–14.

3. Two of the best recent examples of oral histories edited for publication by scholars are Kathryn Nasstrom, *Everybody's Grandmother and Nobody's Fool: Frances Freeborn Pauley and the Struggle for Social Justice* (Ithaca: Cornell University Press, 2000); and Christian G. Appy, *Patriots: The Vietnam War Remembered from All Sides* (New York: Penguin Books, 2003).

4. Many of these interviewees had had long-term partners over the years or were in long-term relationships at the time of the interview. The 2000 Census includes information about such "unmarried partners" and "wives/husbands" for same-sex couples, providing raw data to analyze the service rates for coupled gay men and lesbians. According to a study by Gary Gates for the Urban Institute, "Coupled gay men are less likely to report military service than other men, while coupled lesbians are more likely than other women to serve." In fact, Gates found that "military service rates for coupled lesbians far exceed rates for other women in every military era of the twentieth century" and coupled lesbians reported serving for longer enlistments than other women. Though coupled gay men were less likely to report being veterans than other men, the percentages reporting military service were still significant (11.11 percent of coupled gay men were veterans as opposed to 16.52 percent of other men). Gary J. Gates, "Gay Men and Lesbians in the U.S. Military: Estimates from the Census 2000 (Washington: Urban Institute, 2004), iii–iv, 10.

INDEX